1 MONTH OF
FREE
READING

at

www.ForgottenBooks.com

By purchasing this book you are
eligible for one month membership to
ForgottenBooks.com, giving you
unlimited access to our entire
collection of over 1,000,000 titles via
our web site and mobile apps.

To claim your free month visit:
www.forgottenbooks.com/free929205

ISBN 978-0-260-12151-6
PIBN 10929205

Return this book on or before the
Latest Date stamped below.

The White Apron

A COMPILATION OF THE

History of Occidental Lodge,

No. 40, A. F. & A. M.,

OTTAWA, ILLINOIS,

With a Complete List of Members from the Date of Dispensation, 1845, to
October 10, 1906, and a Summary of her Daughter,

HUMBOLDT LODGE, No. 555,
A. F. & A. M.,

Together with a History of

OTTAWA LODGE, No. 114,
A. F. & A. M.,

Working under the Jurisdiction of the Grand Lodge of Kentucky, 1839 to 1845.

·Also a Resume of her Daughter,

ST. JOHN'S LODGE, No. 13,
A. F. & A. M.,

Located at Vermillionville in 1841, and transferred to Peru, Illinois,.1843.

Also a Synopsis of the

Introduction of Freemasonry Into America

And the First Lodges in Illinois.

BY

W. L. MILLIGAN, 33°

Past Master Occidental Lodge, No. 40, A. F. &·A. M.
Past High Priest Shabbona Chapter, No. 37, R. A. M.
Past Thrice Ill. Master Oriental Council, No. 63, R. & S. M.
Past Commander Ottawa Commandery, No 10, K. T.
Past Grand High Priest Grand Chapter, R. A. M., of Illinois.
Past Grand Master Grand Council, R. & S. M., of Illinois.

Anno Lucis 5907.

REPUBLICAN-TIMES,
PRINTERS,
OTTAWA, ILL.

WILLIAM LEE ROY MILLIGAN

Worshipful Master 1884, 1885 and 1886

W. L. MILLIGAN, Ottawa, Illinois.

Dear Sir and Brother:

It gives me great pleasure to know that you have completed by many years of labor the compilation of the history of Occidental Lodge, No. 40, A. F. & A. M., containing a list of the members from the date of the dispensation in 1845 to and including October 10, A. D. 1906, a period of sixty years. This volume preserves to Occidental Lodge the most interesting portion of her history, and, as the old records of the Lodge were destroyed by fire, it will be invaluable for future reference. The volume certainly should be, and I sincerely hope will be, in the possession of every member.

Yours fraternally,

RICHARD D. MILLS,

W. M. of Occidental Lodge.

JOHN FISK NASH

Worshipful Master 1863 and 1864.   The oldest living Past Master.

THIS WORK

IS MOST RESPECTFULLY DEDICATED

TO

THE GOOD MAN AND TRUE MASON,

JOHN FISK NASH,

Past Master Occidental Lodge, No. 40, A. F. & A. M.
Past High Priest Shabbona Chapter, No. 37, R. A. M.
Past Commander Ottawa Commandery, No. 10, K. T.
Past Grand Commander of the Grand Commandery K. T. of Illinois.

———————

" Type of a generation dropping fast,
 Pillar of faultless worth and dignity,
This record of the unreturning past
 Is dedicated with loving heart to thee."

History, in every age, is only popular among a few thoughtful men. It was scarcely known or understood in the early ages of the world, but the place of history was everywhere supplied by myths and legends. —DE GROOT.

MASONIC CALENDAR.

Ancient Craft Masons commence their era with the creation of the world, calling it *Anno Lucis* (A. L.), "in the year of light."

Scottish Rite same as Ancient Craft, except the Jewish chronology is used, *Anno Mundi* (A. M.), "in the year of the world."

Royal Arch Masons date from the year the second temple was commenced by Zerrubbabel, *Anno Inventionis* (A. Inv.), "in the year of the discovery."

Royal and Select Masters date from the year in which the temple of Solomon was completed, *Anno Depositionis* (A. Dep.), "in the year of the deposit."

Knights Templar commence their era with the organization of their Order, *Anno Ordinis* (A. O.), "in the year of the Order."

---

*Not claimed to be coeval with the creation, but has symbolic reference to the Light of Masonry.

RULES FOR MASONIC DATES.

1. Ancient Craft—add 4000 to the common time. Thus 1907 and 4000 equal 5907.

2. Scottish Rite—add 3760 to the common era. Thus 1907 and 3760 equal 5667. After September add another year.

3. Royal Arch—add 530 years to the vulgar year. Thus 1907 and 530 equal 2437.

4. Royal and Select Masters—add 1000 to the common time. Thus 1907 and 1000 equal 2907.

5. Knights Templar—from the Christian era take 1118. Thus 1118 from 1907 equals 789.

THE PRESENT.

Year of the Lord, A. D. 1907—Christian Era.

Year of Light, A. L. 5907—Ancient Craft.

Year of the World, A. M. 5667—Scottish Rite.

Year of the Discovery, A. Inv. 2437—Royal Arch.

Year of the Deposit, A. Dep. 2907—Royal and Select Masters.

Year of the Order, A. O. 789—Knights Templar.

THE VALLEY OF THE ILLINOIS

From the South Bluff, one-half mile east of Ottawa

PREFACE.

The introduction of Freemasonry in Ottawa, Illinois, is coeval with the transformation of the wild prairies of the Valley of the "Illini" to wheat fields and corn fields; of the wigwam of the red man to the beautiful homes of the white man.

Where, not more than a century ago, the Indian was the sole possessor of the prairies and forests of this beautiful valley, and the buffalo, elk and deer were his herds, and the Indian wigwams were pitched in the shady groves, fragrant with blossoms of the wild plum and wild apple, along the banks of rippling streams of pure and crystal-like waters, from which the Indian maiden angled the most delicious of black bass and pickerel for the evening meal of the Indian warrior on his return from the chase, is now the center of the most highly civilized nation on the face of the earth.

Only three-quarters of a century ago the first white settler dared the western wilds and located in the Valley of the Illinois. In a few years, others began to arrive, and among them were members of the craft who brought some knowledge of Freemasonry from the East to the West. Many came from Massachusetts, Connecticut, Pennsylvania, Virginia and Kentucky. And when they would gather around the back-log fires in their log-cabin homes during the long, cold winter nights, far from the influences of schools and churches and former homes, their minds wandered back to their old Masonic homes and fraternal circles at labor and refreshment.

Is it any wonder, then, that when Henry D. Gorbett, Benjamin Thurston, Andrew J. Kirkpatrick and Dr. James

G. Armstrong suggested the establishment of a Masonic
Lodge at Ottawa in 1838, it was hailed with joy, and that
Colonel Daniel Fletcher Hitt, in the bigness of his heart,
opened his purse and gave the price to obtain a charter from
the Grand Lodge of Kentucky, and that Captain Henry J.
Reid, who until recent years lived on the road between Ottawa and Dayton, rode on horseback across the wild prairies of Illinois, and through the trackless forests of Indiana,
to attend the annual communication of the Grand Lodge
of Kentucky, held in Louisville in the month of August,
1840, and brought to Ottawa the charter for Ottawa Lodge,
No. 114, under the jurisdiction of the Grand Lodge of Kentucky?

Such elongations of the cable-tow were rarely witnessed in the search for "Light" as that exemplified in the
organization of the first Masonic Lodge in Ottawa, and I
am proud to have the honor of having my name enrolled as
a member of a fraternity of Freemasons organized in the
Valley of the "Illini," when the atmosphere was sweet and
pure with the fragrance of the wild rose of the prairie and
the aroma from the blossoms of the wild plum and the wild
apple.

In compiling a history of Occidental Lodge, No. 40,
A. F. & A. M., it has been a source of private pleasure to me,
a labor of love, notwithstanding it has been attended with
a considerable amount of time and labor, to search among
the dusty records and brush the mould from the time-worn
pages of the history of our fraternity, and trace the genealogy of Occidental Lodge far down the vista of time, a
direct descendent of the mother Grand Lodge of England.

In compiling this work, I found myself surrounded by
sacred memories and historic associations.

The gavel of Occidental Lodge has been sounded by

strong right hands that wielded the victor's sword on the battlefields of our country.

The voice of authority has been uttered in Occidental Lodge by lips of men that plead the cause of justice in our courts and swayed the minds of men in the halls of the Congress of our Nation.

The Masters and brothers of Occidental Lodge have come from every walk in life—the mechanic, the artisan, the merchant. the banker, the editor and the farmer. and many have held positions of trust, not only in private enterprises, but in public capacities.

. Many of our members have gone forth to found other Masonic homes and shed lustre upon the name of Occidental Lodge, in which they first saw the Light of Masonry.

In compiling the roll of members of Occidental Lodge from date of organization, we are most forcibly reminded of the "inevitable destiny of man."

Many voices that have been heard in song at our communications are silenced forever.

Lives useful and honored have been ended.

Hands whose brotherly grasp we have felt have mouldered to dust.

Eyes that flashed upon us the light of intelligence and love are closed.

"And many rest in sleep by dreams unbroken,
    By winds unswept, by storms unseen;
  Never to speak again as they have spoken
    Or know lost joys that might have been.
  When slow departing summer day yet lingers
    Behind the purpling western bars,
  When winds sound faint, as if some far off singers
  Were touching harps with tired trembling fingers,
    We see lost eyes smile in the stars."

The labor expended upon this volume will best be estimated when it is realized that the early records of both Occidental Lodge and the Grand Lodge of Illinois were destroyed by fire, and that, without a predecessor in a history of Occidental Lodge, I have been twenty years in compiling this work, and that for every statement of facts and names of members recorded, an amount of research has been expended amounting to real extravagance in point of time and labor. Every detail, in comparing conflicting statements and reconciling discrepancies, out of which this work has been compiled, partakes, therefore, almost of the nature of a discovery.

I trust that it will meet the requirements for not only a correct history of Occidental Lodge, but a ready reference from which to gather data otherwise unobtainable, and that it may be the province of some brother more competent than I to continue to compile the future history of Occidental Lodge when I am "at rest" in that beautiful city of silence and repose on the banks of the peaceful Illinois.

Fraternally,

W. L. MILLIGAN.

Tell us then no more that our Lodges are the receptacles of sacriligious and revolutionary miscreants,—I see them frequented by men of unaffected piety, and undaunted patriotism. Tell us no more that our brethern of the order are traitors, or indifferent to the welfare of their country,— I see them in the form of heroes, at the head of our fleets and our armies; and the day will arrive when a Freemason shall sway the sceptre of these kingdoms and fill with honor and with dignity the British throne.

—SIR DAVID BREWSTER.

King Edward VII. is a Freemason and Past Grand Master of the Grand Lodge of England.

Theodore Roosevelt is a Freemason and the President of the United States of America.

THE LEVEL AND THE SQUARE.

We meet upon the level and we part upon the square,
What words of precious meaning these words Masonic are!
Come, let us contemplate them! They are worthy of a thought,
With the highest and the lowest, and the rarest they are fraught.

We meet upon the level, though from every station come—
The King from out his palace and the poor man from his home,
For the one must leave his diadem without the Mason's door,
And the other finds his true respect upon the checkered floor.

We part upon the square, for the world must have its due;
We mingle with its multitude, a cold, unfriendly crew;
But the influence of our gatherings in memory is green,
And we long upon the level, to renew the happy scene.

There's a world where all is equal—we are hurrying toward it fast.
We shall meet upon the level there when the gates of death are past;
We shall stand before the Orient, and our Master will be there,
To try the block we offer by His own unerring square.

We shall meet upon the level there, but never thence depart;
There's a Mansion—'tis all ready for each zealous, faithful heart;
There's a Mansion and a welcome, and a multitude is there,
Who have met upon the level and been tried upon the square.

Let us meet upon the level, then, while laboring patient here,
Let us meet and let us labor, tho' the labor seem severe,
Already in the western sky the signs bid us prepare
To gather up our working tools and part upon the square!

Hands round, ye faithful Ghiblelmites, the bright, fraternal chain;
We part upon the square below to meet in Heaven again,
O what words of precious meaning these words Masonic are—
We meet upon the level, and we part upon the square.

—ROB. MORRIS.

The above is the original form in which this poem was written. Its history, as often told, is simple enough, and has none of the elements of romance.

In August, 1854, as the author was walking home from a neighbor's, through the sultry afternoon, he sat upon a fallen tree, and upon the back of a letter dashed off, under a momentary impulse, and in stenographic characters, the lines upon this page.

Brother George Oliver, D. D., eminent above all others in English Masonry, and the Masonic historian for all time, said of the poem: "Brother Morris has compassed many fervent, eloquent and highly poetic compositions, songs that will not die, but in 'The Level and the Square' he breathed out a depth of feeling, fervency and pathos, with brilliancy and vigor of language, and expressed due faith in the immortal life beyond the grave."

WE, T G R H E L, I G R H E L, ESQUIRE, Right Worshipful Grand Master of Masons in and for the Commonwealth of Pennsylvania and Masonic Jurisdiction thereunto belonging.

To all Free and Accepted Masons wheresoever dispersed.

G R E E T I N G.

Reposing the greatest Confidence in the Zeal, Fervor and Constancy in the Craft of Our dear and beloved Brother James Colgar, a Past Master Ancient York Mason, residing at Kaskaskia in the Indiana Territory in the United States. We do by Virtue of the Powers and Authorities Vested in Us, We do hereby Authorize Empower and by Warrant to call to his Assistance a sufficient Number of known and approved Master Masons to open a Lodge at the Town of Kaskaskia aforesaid and there Instruct, Try and Raise Free Masons according to the most Ancient and Honourable Customs of the Craft in all Ages and Nations throughout the known World and not contrary unto rights made Prior to Us herein disposed of their proceedings. This Dispensation to remain in force for One Month from the Date hereof and no longer,

Given under Our Hand and the Seal of Our Grand Lodge at the City of Philadelphia this Twenty-fourth Day of September in the Year of Our LORD 1805 and in the Year of Masonry 5805.

Attest
e. S. Baker

Israel Israel
G. M.

CHAPTER I.

INTRODUCTION OF FREEMASONRY IN AMERICA.

The real history of Freemasonry in America may be said to have its commencement in 1730, when on June 5, 1730, Daniel Cox, the Duke of Norfolk, was appointed Provincial Grand Master of New York, New Jersey and Pennsylvania, by the Grand Lodge of England, to whom application was made by Bro. Henry Bell and others, who on frequent occasions had been meeting at Tun Tavern, Water street, Philadelphia, and opening a Lodge of Masons, for a charter, which was granted in 1730. The above evidence rests on the authority of the Library Committee of the Grand Lodge of Pennsylvania.

Benjamin Franklin, who was made a Mason in February, 1731, printed a notice of this Lodge in the *Pennsylvania Gazette,* then published by him, December 8, 1730.

Benjamin Franklin was Provincial Grand Master in 1734.

Franklin was succeeded as Grand Master by James Hamilton, and he in turn by Thomas Hopkinson. James Hamilton afterwards became Governor of Pennsylvania, and Thomas Hopkinson at the time of his election was Admirality Judge in the province of Pennsylvania.

The first Masonic hall in America was erected in Philadelphia in 1754.

In 1758 Pennsylvania was invaded by the "Ancients," and from that time the lodges under the old sanction declined, and the last printed notice of any of them occurred in 1760, and the last official act of the first Lodge occurred

B   17

in 1782, and about eleven years later all the lodges in Philadelphia under the original Grand Lodge of England ceased to exist, and September 26, 1786, the present Grand Lodge was originated.

MASSACHUSETTS.

Viscount Montague, Grand Master of the Grand Lodge of England, appointed Henry Price Provincial Grand Master of New England in 1733, and the Earl of Crawford appointed him Provincial Grand Master over all America in 1734. July 30, 1733, Price opened a Provincial Grand Lodge in Boston, which was known on the rolls of the Grand Lodge of England (list 1756) as Royal Exchange, No. 65.

The second Lodge in Boston was constituted February 15, 1750. Only two degrees were conferred in the first Lodge, the third not being given until 1794. A separate set of minutes was kept of the "Lodge of Masters." Independent records of the third degree were frequently kept in England also.

December 27, 1769, St. Andrews Lodge, with the assistance of three British Army Lodges, organized the Grand Lodge of Massachusetts, and elected Joseph Warren Grand Master. The two Grand Lodges united and formed the present Grand Lodge in 1792, and elected John Cutler Grand Master.

VIRGINIA.

Among the list of lodges in America on the roll of the Grand Lodge of England we find—

No. 236, Royal Exchange, Norfolk, Virginia, 1753.

No. 205, Swan, Yorktown, Virginia, 1755.

No. 457, Williamsburg Lodge, Virginia, 1773.

No. 458, Botetourl Lodge, Virginia, 1773.

And the following Lodges obtained their charters from the British Isles, other than the Grand Lodge of England:

No. 82, Blandford, Va., Scotland, 1756.

No. —, Fredericksburg, Va., Scotland, 1758.

No. —, Tappahannock, Va., Killarney, 1758.

No. 117, St. John, Norfolk, Va., Scotland, 1763.

No. —, Falmouth, Va., Killarney, 1775.

And one from the Grand Orient of France, No. —, Sagessee, Portsmouth, Virginia, 1785.

One Lodge received a charter from Boston, and the jurisdiction of Ireland is also supposed to have been represented in the state. The Provincial Grand Lodge of Pennsylvania (Ancients) established a Lodge at Winchester, 1768; Alexandria, 1783; and Portsmouth, 1784.

The Grand Lodge of Virginia was organized October 13, 1778, by Lodges working under the Grand Lodge of England. John Blair, of Williamsburg, was unanimously elected Grand Master, and was installed October 30th, ensuing.

THE FIRST LODGE IN ILLINOIS.

The first Lodge of Ancient, Free and Accepted Masons organized within the present limits of the state of Illinois, was at Kaskaskia, in the year 1805, by virtue of a dispensation from the Grand Lodge of Pennsylvania, one of the oldest Grand Lodges on the American continent, and whose first Grand Master was Benjamin Franklin.

On the 9th day of March, 1805, the following letter was addressed to the Right Worshipful Grand Lodge of Pennsylvania:

"To the Right Worshipful Lodge of Pennsylvania—Greeting:

"The subscribers, and many others of our brethren in the counties of St. Clair and Randolph, beg leave to ap-

proach your worshipful body, and state to you, that they
are far removed from those social enjoyments which they
once as Masons have experienced; that from the growth
of population many worthy and respectable brethren have
settled, and many more will soon come to this country; and
that your suppliants, from a sense of duty incumbered on
them as Masons and as men, to promote their mutual happiness, the happiness of their neighbors, and as far as in
their power lies humanize society; and furthermore, to im-
press on their memory what has long been written on their
hearts; wherefore, your suppliants thus presume to approach your worshipful body and request that, if in your
councils you think it expedient, your worshipful body will
grant to your suppliants a warrant, or, if that can't be obtain
ed, a dispensation, authorizing them to hold a regular Lodge
in the town of Kaskaskia, appointing such of your suppliants
to preside therein as may seem proper to your worshipful
body, sending with your said warrant your constitution, all
other necessary instructions and the amount of expenses
attending the same, which will be duly remitted by your
suppliants, etc., etc.

(Signed)   "Robert McMahan,
                  Stanton, No. 13.

"Wm. Arundel,
St. Andrews Lodge, No. 2, Quebec.

"James Edgar,
Lodge No. 9, Philadelphia.

"Michael Jones,
          No. 45, Pittsburg.

"James Galbreath,
          No. 79, Chambersburg.

"Rufus Easton,
Roman Lodge, No. 82, Chambersburg.

"Robert Robinson,
                  Stanton, No. 13.

"Indiana Territory, Kaskaskia, March 9, 1805."

To this letter, or petition, the following answer was
made:

"We, Israel Israel, Esquire, R. W. Grand Master of Masons in and for the Commonwealth of Pennsylvania and Masonic jurisdiction thereunto belonging, to all Free and Accepted Masons, wheresoever dispersed—Greeting:

"Reposing the greatest confidence in the zeal, favor and constancy in the craft of our worthy and beloved brother James Edgar, a past Master Ancient York Mason, residing at Kaskaskia, in the Indiana Territory, in the United States, and by virtue of the powers and authority vested in us, we do hereby authorize and empower and request him to call to his assistance a sufficient number of known and approved Master Masons to open a Lodge at the town of Kaskaskia aforesaid, and then and there *Initiate, Pass* and *Raise Freemasons,* according to the most ancient and honorable custom of the craft in all ages and nations throughout the *known world,* and not contrarywise, and to make report to us hereon endorsed of their proceedings. This dispensation to remain in full force *six months* from the date hereof, and no longer.

"Given under our hand and the Seal of the [SEAL.] Grand Lodge at the city of Philadelphia, this 24th day of September, in the year of our Lord 1805, and in the year of Masonry, 5805.

(Signed) ISRAEL ISRAEL, Grand Master.
"Attest: (Signed) GEORGE A. BAKER, Grand Sec'y."

This dispensation was received, the Lodge regularly organized, and the corner stone of our Masonic edifice laid for the first time on the soil of Illinois at Kaskaskia, Randolph county, Indiana Territory, on Saturday, the 14th of December, 1805, A. L. 5805.

At the end of six months the dispensation was returned to the Grand Lodge of Pennsylvania, and a charter granted, dated the 18th day of June, 1806, A. L. 5806, and signed by James Minor, Grand Master, and attested by George A. Baker, Grand Secretary.

On Saturday, the 13th day of September, 1806, A. L.

5806, the Lodge was duly constituted as "Western Star Lodge, No. 107," by Robert Robinson.

At this time all business was transacted in the Entered Apprentice degree, except the conferring of the second and third degrees, installation of officers, and trial of charges against members.

The first petitions ever received for the degrees of Masonry in Illinois were those of Andrew Henry, Walter Fenwick and George Bullett, of Ste. Genevieve, Louisana Territory, now state of Missouri.

On the 3d day of February, 1806, Charles Query, the first to receive the "Light" of our mystic circle in Illinois, was initiated.

The first demit was granted on June 5, 1811, to Wm. Arundel, and signed by P. Fonke, Master, Wm. C. Greenup, S. W., James Edgar, J. W., and Michael Jones, Sec'y P. G.

The first diploma was granted to Brother Philip Rocheblave on March 2, 1816, and because of its novelty we take space herewith to insert it:

"To all Free and Accepted Masons—Union, Health and Happiness:

"We, the Master and Wardens of Western Star Lodge, No. 107, held at Kaskaskia, in the county of Randolph, under the Grand Warrant of Pennsylvania, assembled in due form, adorned with all our honors, do hereby declare and attest to all men enlightened on the face of the earth, that our beloved brother, Philip Rocheblave, who hath signed his name in the margin, hath been received as an Entered Apprentice, passed as a Fellow Craft, and after having sustained with firmness, strength and courage the most painful works and wonderful trials, we have given to him as a recompense due to his zeal, diligence and capacity the sublime degree of Master, and have admitted and initiated him as such into our mysteries and secret works, in which he has helped us with his talents, skill and knowledge.

In testimony whereof, we have granted to him this present certificate, signed by our Master and Wardens, and attested by our Secretary, with the private seal of the said Lodge, the twenty-fifth day of April, in the year of Masonry 5816, and of salvation 1816.

"S. BOND, W. M.
"P. FONKE, S. W.
"SAMUEL WALKER, J. W.
"Attest: D. S. SWEARINGEN, Secretary."

On the 23d day of January, 1816, the Worshipful Master announced to the brethren the melancholy death of their worthy brother, Thomas Todd, who departed this life on Monday evening about 9 o'clock, the 15th inst. The Treasurer was directed to procure crepe and blue ribbon for the members, the crepe to be worn on their hats and the ribbon at the third buttonhole of the vest, to be worn thirty days.

SECOND LODGE, 1815.

From 1805 until the year 1815, Western Star was the only Lodge of Masons in the state. In 1815, the second Lodge of Free and Accepted Masons was organized in Illinois, to be holden at Shawneetown, and known as Lawrence Lodge, No. 34, by authority of a dispensation issued by the Grand Lodge of Kentucky. Date of dispensation, September, 1815. Charter, August, 1816.

THIRD LODGE, 1819.

The third Lodge was organized at Edwardsville in 1819, under dispensation of the Grand Lodge of Tennessee, and issued to sundry brethren to open a lodge at Edwardsville, to be called Libanus Lodge, No. 29.

FOURTH LODGE, 1820.

The fourth Lodge was organized at Belleville, under dispensation dated June 28, 1820, from the Grand Lodge of Tennessee, to David Blackwell and others, to be called Temple Lodge, No. 35. This Lodge surrendered its dispensation in 1821.

FIFTH LODGE, 1821.

On October 30, 1821, on recommendation of Libanus Lodge, No. 29, the Grand Lodge of Missouri granted a dispensation to the requisite number of brethren residing at, or near, Alton, Illinois, constituting them into a regular Lodge of Free and Accepted Masons, to be opened in the town of Alton, by the name of Olive Branch Lodge, No. 5.

SIXTH LODGE, 1822.

The sixth Lodge was organized at Albion, Illinois, as Albion Lodge, under dispensation from the Grand Lodge of Indiana, dated March 12, 1822.

SEVENTH LODGE, 1822.

The seventh Lodge was organized in February, 1822, at Vandalia, as Vandalia Lodge, No. 8, under dispensation from the Grand Lodge of Missouri, on recommendation of Libanus Lodge, No. 29.

EIGHTH LODGE, 1822.

The eighth Lodge, known as Sangamon Lodge, No. 9, was organized at Springfield, Sangamon county, under dispensation from the Grand Lodge of Missouri, dated April 5, 1822. A charter was granted Oct. 25th, following.

NINTH LODGE, 1822.

The ninth Lodge was organized at Jonesboro, under dispensation from the Grand Lodge of Missouri, dated May 4, 1822. This Lodge was duly organized as Union Lodge, No. 10, on the 22d of June, 1822.

TENTH LODGE, 1822.

The tenth Lodge was organized at Covington, as Eden Lodge, No. 11, under dispensation from the

James Milton GRAND MASTER.

Jos. H. Wolbert DEPUTY GRAND MASTER.

Robert Lewis — SENIOR GRAND WARDEN. *Robert Poalk* JUNIOR

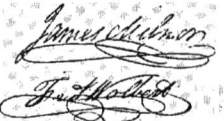

To all whom it may Concern.

THE GRAND LODGE OF PENNSYLVANIA AND MASONIC JURISDICTION THEREUNTO BELONGING is.
Philadelphia, in the Commonwealth of Pennsylvania.

WISDOM!!!   STRENGTH!!!   FRATERNITY!

Know Ye, That WE The said Grand Lodge of the most Ancient and Honorable Fraternity of Free and Accepted Masons (a
tions, revived by his Royal Highness Prince Edwin, at York, in the Kingdom of England, in the Year of the Christian Æra Nine Hundred Tw
Year of Masonry Four Thousand Nine Hundred Twenty and Six) by Virtue of the Powers and Authorities vested in US, DO hereby constitute
well-beloved Brethren James Edgars ____ Master, Michael Jones ____ Senior Warden, and
____ Junior Warden of a Lodge, to be called "The Western Star Lodge" ____ Number One Hu
to be held at Kaskaskia in the Indiana Territory in the United States ____
or within Five Miles of the same. AND WE DO FURTHER authorize and impower our said trusty and well-beloved Brethren Jam
Jones and James Galbraith ____ to admit and make Free Masons according to the most Ancient and Hono
Craft in all Ages and Nations throughout the known World, and not contrarywise. AND WE DO FURTHER impower and appoint the sai
Jones and James Galbraith ____ and their Successors to hear and determine all and singular matters and things
the Jurisdiction of the said Lodge, with the assistance of the Members of the said Lodge. And lastly, WE DO hereby authorize and impower our
Brethren James Edgar, Michael Jones and James Galbraith ____ to install their Successors, being first duly elected and chosen, to whom
rant, and to invest them with all the Powers and Dignities to their Offices respectively belonging, and such Successors shall in like manner, from time to
&c. &c. &c. Such Installation to be upon or near St. JOHN THE EVANGELIST's Day, during the continuance of this Lodge for
That the said above-named Brethren, and their Successors, pay due respect to this Right Worshipful Grand Lodge and the Ordinances thereof, o
of no Force, or Effect.

GIVEN in open Grand Lodge, under the Hands of our Right Worshipful Grand Officers and the
at Philadelphia, this Second Day of ____ A. C. One Thousand Eight Hundred an
Masonry Five Thousand Eight Hundred and Six.

Attest.
George A. Baker GRAND SECRETARY.

Thos Armstrong G

CHARTER OF WESTERN STAR LODGE 1806
The First Masonic Lodge in Illinois

Grand Lodge of Missouri, dated June 13, 1822. This was the last Lodge organized in Illinois prior to the organization of the first Grand Lodge in 1822.

THE FIRST GRAND LODGE.

Thus we have borne you along over the trackless prairies of Illinois from the year 1805, when the first Lodge was organized in our state, until the year 1822, when the first Grand Lodge of A. F. & A. M. was organized in Illinois. During that period of seventeen long years but ten Lodges were organized in the state—

1st. Western Star, No. 107, at Kaskaskia in 1805.

2d. Lawrence Lodge, No. 34, at Shawneetown in 1815.

3d. Libanus, No. 29, at Edwardsville in 1819.

4th. Temple, No. 35, at Belleville in 1820.

5th. Olive Branch, No. 5, at Alton in 1821.

6th. Albion, No. 5, at Albion in 1822.

7th. Vandalia, No. 8, at Vandalia in 1822.

8th. Sangamon, No. 9, at Sangamon in 1822.

9th. Union, No. 10, at Jonesboro in 1822.

10th. Eden, No. 11, at Covington in 1822.

Pursuant to a circular letter addressed to the several Lodges heretofore named by Vandalia Lodge, No. 8, the following brethren having produced their certificates, and being recognized as delegates, met in convention at Vandalia, Ill., (then the state capital) Dec. 9, 1822, and proceeded to organize a Grand Lodge of Masons in Illinois:

Western Star Lodge, No. 107. Thomas Reynolds and Shadrach Bond.

Lawrence Lodge, No. 34. Thomas C. Brown and James Hall.

Libanus Lodge, No. 29. Richard J. Kinney, Dennis Rockwell, John Y. Sawyer, Nathaniel Buckmaster, William H. Hopkins and David Pricket.

Olive Branch Lodge, No. 5, James W. Whitney, Charles Gear and Charles W. Hunter.

Albion Lodge. Benjamin J. Mills and Gilbert T. Pell.

Vandalia Lodge, No. 8. William H. Brown, James M. Duncan, John S. Duncan, Russell Botsford, E. C. Berry, John Warnock.

Union Lodge, No. 10. Abner Field and Charles Dunn.

Eden Lodge, No. 11. James Turney.

Brother Thomas C. Brown was appointed chairman, and Brother William H. Brown, secretary.

On December 10th, a constitution was adopted, and on December 11th, the following grand officers were elected:

Shadrach Bond, Grand Master.

John G. Sawyer, Grand Senior Warden.

William M. Alexander, Grand Junior Warden.

Richard T. McKinney, Grand Secretary.

James O. Wattles, Grand Treasurer.

And the first Grand Lodge of Ancient Free and Accepted Masons was organized in Illinois.

The last known of this, the first Grand Lodge, was April 10, 1829, from which time until 1835 Masonry was a blank in Illinois. Western Star, the first Lodge organized within the present limits of Illinois, was the last to surrender its gavel.

Kaskaskia Lodge, No. 107, was absolved from allegiance to the Grand Lodge of Pennsylvania by the Grand Master, November 30, 1826, as by the following letter:

"In pursuance of the power vested in us, by virtue of a resolution of the R. W. Grand Lodge of Pennsylvania, adopted on the 21st day of November, A. D. 1825, A. L. 5825, we do hereby authorize and empower the W. M. and brethren of Lodge No. 107 to surrender the warrant thereof to us and to apply to the R. W. Grand Lodge of Illinois to hold a Lodge under warrant from that Grand Lodge.

"Given under our hand and seal the 30th day of November, A. D. 1826, A. L. 5826.

[Seal]   "H. KITTERA,
Grand Master."

The Lodges which at this time were under the jurisdiction of the Grand Lodge of Illinois were:

Western Star, No. 1, Kaskaskia, Ill.

Lawrence, No. 2, Shawneetown, Ill.

Libanus, No. 3, Edwardsville, Ill.

Olive Branch, No. 4, Upper Alton, Ill.

Vandalia, No. 5, Vandalia, Ill.

Union, No. 6, Jonesboro, Ill.

Eden, No. 7, Covington, Ill.

Hiram, No. 8.

Albion, No. 9, Albion, Ill.

Palestine, No. 10.

Green, No. 11, Carrolton, Ill.

Illion, No. 12.

Frontier, No. 13, Lewistown, Ill.

Lafayette, No. 14.

Sangamon, No. 15, Springfield, Ill.

None of them survived and entered into the organization of the present, or second, Grand Lodge of Illinois.

THE SECOND, OR PRESENT, GRAND LODGE.

Having the Grand Lodge of Virginia, a direct descendant from the mother Grand Lodge of England, we will now proceed to follow the lineage down to the Grand Lodges of Kentucky and Missouri, from whence (Kentucky) Ottawa Lodge, No. 114, obtained its charter, and the Lodges entering into the foundation of the present Grand Lodge in 1840, from whose authority Occidental Lodge is now working.

KENTUCKY.

Five Lodges were established in Kentucky under warrants from the Grand Lodge of Virginia, the earliest of which, in 1788, was the first Lodge instituted west of the Alleghany mountains. These Lodges met in convention October 16, 1800, and organized the Grand Lodge of Kentucky, the first Grand Lodge west of the Alleghany mountains, by which warrants were issued to Lodges in Tennessee, Indiana and Missouri, which entered into the formation of Grand Lodges in their respective states.

MISSOURI.

Lodges were constituted in Missouri by the Grand Lodges of Pennsylvania in 1807 and 1808, Tennessee in 1816 and 1819, and Indiana in 1820. Three of these Lodges met in convention April 23, 1821, and organized the Grand Lodge of Missouri.

OTTAWA LODGE, No. 114, A. F. & A. M.

The first Lodge of A. F. & A. M. organized in Ottawa, Illinois, was under dispensation from the Grand Lodge of Kentucky, dated December 19, 1839. It was issued to Henry D. Gorbett, Master, Benjamin Thurston, Senior Warden, and Andrew Kirkpatrick, Junior Warden. The Lodge was to be called Ottawa Lodge, and the dispensation was issued by M. W. George Breckenridge, Grand Master. Bro. Henry J. Reid, stepfather of our late townsman, George Hayward, who lived on the Dayton road, about two miles from Ottawa, and was known as Captain Reid, rode on horseback from Ottawa, Illinois, to Louisville, Ky., and represented Ottawa Lodge, U. D., at the annual communication of the Grand Lodge of Kentucky, held at Louisville, Ky., in the month of August, 1840, and returned to Ottawa with the charter for Ottawa Lodge, as No. 114, dated September 1, 1840.

The following is a copy of the returns of Ottawa Lodge,

U. D., for the year 1840; stated meetings on the Thursday preceding the full moon.

OFFICERS.

Henry D. Gorbett ....Worshipful Master.
Benjamin Thurston ....Senior Warden.
Andrew Kirkpatrick ....Junior Warden.
James G. Armstrong ....Secretary.
David Wells ....Treasurer.
Lucius Woodruff ....Senior Deacon.
Henry J. Reid ....Junior Deacon.
William K. Brown ....Steward and Tyler.

Past Masters: Henry D. Gorbett, Benjamin Thurston

Master Masons: Luther Woodward, Jabez Fitch, C. G. Miller, J. Hall, Asa Holdridge, Champlain R. Potter, William L. Dunavan, T. Bole, Thomas Russell, Seth B. Farwell, J. Stadden, G. F. Weaver, W. F. Walker, Benjamin Thompson, R. Miller, Gilbert L. Thompson, William Stadden, J. Cooper (undoubtedly Jesse Cooper, formerly Sec'y Western Star Lodge, at Kaskaskia, Ill.), Alson Woodruff, James Clark, James Armour, A. R. Dodge.

Fellow Crafts: Aaron Daniels, Walter Lamb.

Entered Apprentices: J. J. Hill, L. W. Liske, Dr. Hennessee.

Returns from Ottawa Lodge, No. 114, to Grand Lodge of Kentucy, 1841:

OFFICERS.

George H. Norris ....Worshipful Master.
Lorenzo P. Sanger ....Senior Warden.
James Armour ....Junior Warden.
Geo. F. Weaver ....Secretary.
Marshall Miller ....Treasurer.
James W. Roberts ....Senior Deacon.

Gilbert L. Thompson ....Junior Deacon.
Thos. A. Henry, Benj. Thompson.............Stewards.
Joseph Avery ....Tyler.

Past Masters: Benj. Thurston, George H. Norris, Benj. Thompson, Henry D. Gorbett.

Master Masons: P. M. Kilduff, Z. H. Baxter, Samuel Rodecker, Abram R. Dodge, William L. Dunavan, Thos. Russell, Seth B. Farwell, Walter Lamb, Alson Woodruff, Adam Lamb, Herman Whitehead, C. H. Charles.

Entered Apprentices: William Chumasero, John H. McFarren, John J. Hill.

Died: Lucius Woodruff, M. M., Aug. 27, 1840; Christian H. Charles, M. M., July 20, 1840; James G. Armstrong, M. M., Dec. 3, 1840.

Rejected: Josiah Fairchild, about 40, Mormon preacher, residence Dayton, Illinois, Feb. 1, 1841.

Suspended: W. F. Walker, H. J. Reid and Jabez Fitch, all unmasonic conduct, Aug. 1, 1841.

At the annual communication of the Grand Lodge of Kentucky, September 1, 1841, the committee on returns made this report about Ottawa Lodge:

"Your committee have also examined the return of Ottawa Lodge, No. 114, and find their work correct and dues paid; and your committee would further recommend that the prayer of said Lodge petitioning for a dissolution of their allegiance to this Grand Lodge, and a recommendation by this Grand Lodge to the M. W. Grand Lodge of Illinois be granted. Your committee would therefore recommend the adoption of the following resolution:

"*Resolved,* That this Grand Lodge do absolve Ottawa Lodge, No. 114, from all allegiance to this Grand Lodge, and with pleasure recommend said Lodge to the favorable care and protection of the M. W. Grand Lodge of Illinois; said Ottawa Lodge having conformed to all the regulations of this Grand Lodge while under its jurisdiction."

During the time intervening between the last known of the first Grand Lodge, April 10, 1829, and the organization of the second, or present, Grand Lodge in Illinois, April 6, 1840, the following Lodges were organized in Illinois, under dispensation, as follows:

Bodley Lodge, Quincy, Ill., by dispensation from the Grand Lodge of Kentucky, dated Aug. 31, 1835.

Franklin Lodge, Alton, Ill., by dispensation from the Grand Lodge of Missouri, dated Dec. 9, 1836. (This Lodge balloted for a candidate for the third degree in a lodge of E. A., the candidate being present at the time.)

Equality Lodge, Equality, Ill., by dispensation from the Grand Lodge of Kentucky, A. D. 1836. (The first meeting was held April 7, 1837.)

Temperance Lodge, Vandalia, Ill., by dispensation from the Grand Lodge of Missouri, dated June 30, 1838.

Harmony Lodge, Jacksonville, Ill., by dispensation from the Grand Lodge of Missouri. Constituted Nov. 30, 1838.

Springfield Lodge, Springfield, Ill., by dispensation from the Grand Lodge of Missouri, dated February 25, 1839.

Columbus Lodge, Columbus, Ill., by dispensation from the Grand Lodge of Missouri, dated June 3, 1839.

Far West Lodge, Galena, Ill., by dispensation from the Grand Lodge of Missouri, 1838. Chartered by the Grand Lodge of Missouri, Oct. 12, 1839, as No. 29.

Mount Moriah Lodge, Hillsboro, Ill., by dispensation from the Grand Lodge of Missouri, dated August 17, 1839.

Ottawa Lodge, Ottawa, Ill., by dispensation from the Grand Lodge of Kentucky, dated Dec. 19, 1839. Charter issued September 1, 1840, as No. 114.

Far West Lodge, No. 29, Galena, Grand Lodge of Missouri, and Ottawa Lodge, No. 114, Ottawa, Grand Lodge of Kentucky, were the first two Lodges organized in Northern Illinois.

ORGANIZATION OF THE PRESENT GRAND LODGE OF ILLINOIS.

On the 20th day of January, A. D. 1840, A. L. 5840, at a convocation of Masons, composed of delegates from several of the subordinate Lodges in Illinois, held in the Masonic Hall, in the town of Jacksonville, it was unanimously

Resolved, That it is expedient and proper that a Grand Lodge for the State of Illinois be established upon principles consistent with, and subordinate to, the general regulations and ancient Constitutions of Free Masonry; and that brothers W. B. Warren and V. S. Vance, of Jacksonville, and J. Adams and M. Helm, of Springfield, be a committee to correspond with the several Lodges in the state, and ask their co-operation and assistance, and request their attendance by representative or proxy at a convocation to be holden at Jacksonville, on the 6th day of April, A. D. 1840, A. L. 5840, for the purpose of discussing the propriety of establishing a Grand Lodge for the State of Illinois, and determining the best place for locating same.

Accordingly, on the 6th day of April, A. D. 1840, A. L. 5840, a convocation was held at Mason's Hall, in the town of Jacksonville. Present:

J. T. Jones .... Worshipful Master.
W. B. Warren .... Senior Warden.
A. Dunlap .... Junior Warden.
A. V. Putnam .... Secretary.
S. W. Lucas .... Treasurer.
W. S. Vance .... Senior Deacon.
J. M. Lucas .... Junior Deacon.
A. C. Dixon .... Steward and Tyler.

And the following representatives:
Bro. James Adams, Springfield Lodge, No. 26.

SHADRACH BOND

The first Territorial Governor 1808.   The first Grand Master of the First Grand Lodge 1822

Bro. H. Rodgers and H. Dills, Bodley Lodge, No. 97.

Bro. W. D. McCann, Columbus Lodge, No. 20.

Bro. J. T. Jones, proxy, Equality Lodge, No. 102.

Bro. D. Rockwell, proxy, Far West Lodge, No. 29.

Bro. W. B. Warren and A. Dunlap, Harmony Lodge, No. 24.

The object of the convocation held here fully considered, the following was adopted:

"*Resolved,* That the several subordinate Lodges of Ancient Free Masonry in the state of Illinois here assembled, represented by delegates and proxies, properly authorized, as a matter of right and as conducive to the general benefit of Masonry, that a Grand Lodge be established in the state of Illinois, and that they now proceed to establish, organize and locate the same accordingly, to be known and designated by the name of the Grand Lodge of Illinois."

A constitution and by-laws for the government of the Grand Lodge was adopted, and the following grand officers elected:

M. W. Abraham Jonas ....Grand Master.

R. W. James Adams ....Deputy Grand Master.

W. W. S. Vance ....Grand Senior Warden.

H. Rodgers ....Grand Junior Warden.

W. B. Warren ....Grand Secretary.

A. Dunlap ....Grand Treasurer.

The Lodges entering into the formation of the present Grand Lodge were working under the jurisdiction of the following Grand Lodges:

Springfield, No. 26, Grand Lodge of Missouri.

Equality, No. 102, Grand Lodge of Kentucky.

Bodley, No. 97, Grand Lodge of Kentucky.

Columbus, No. 20, Grand Lodge of Missouri.

Far West, No. 29, Grand Lodge of Missouri.

Harmony, No. 24, Grand Lodge of Missouri.

C

On September 2, 1841, the present Grand Lodge being organized and recognized by the Grand Lodge of Kentucky, Ottawa Lodge, No. 114, was dismissed from the jurisdiction of the Grand Lodge of Kentucky and recommended to the Grand Lodge of Illinois.

Ottawa Lodge took no part in the formation of the Grand Lodge of Illinois, nor had it a representative there until 1846, when it was represented by Rev. Charles V. Kelley, proxy for the Worshipful Master. Rev. Charles V. Kelley was elected Grand Chaplain of the Grand Lodge October 7, 1845.

What Ottawa Lodge was from the time the Grand Lodge of Kentucky surrendered control over the same until its formal recognition by the Grand Lodge of Illinois we cannot say, further than that the committee on work and returns of Lodges reported in 1843 and 1844 that no returns had been received from Ottawa Lodge, U. D.

This Lodge held its communications in a room set apart for its use in the old Mansion house, corner Court and Main streets, which was at that time the fashionable hotel of Ottawa, and tradition has handed down to us the fact that a certain prominent citizen of Ottawa at that period of its history, having a favorable opinion of the institution of Free Masonry, and being desirous of becoming a member thereof, conceived the idea of secreting himself in the lodge room to learn if possible what trials and hardships he would have to endure to become a full fledged Mason. On being discovered by the brethren, he soon learned, by being pitched into the middle of the street, that his action was severely rebuked by the brethren. He always claimed that he had received two degrees in Masonry by being pitched down two flights of stairs, and that he would have received the third, had there been another flight of stairs.

October 14, 1845, Most Worshipful Brother W. F.

Walker, Grand Master of the Grand Lodge of Illinois, revoked and annulled the dispensation of Ottawa Lodge, for
having justly forfeited its being by non-use of its powers
and a non-fulfillment of its duties, and at the same time
granted a dispensation to brothers Geo. H. Norris, Maurice
Murphy, Alson Woodruff and the requisite additional brethren, to form and open a Lodge at Ottawa, to be called Occidental Lodge, designating and appointing brothers Geo. H.
Norris, Worshipful Master, Maurice Murphy, Senior Warden, and Alson Woodruff, Junior Warden. No fees were
required for the dispensation.

John Dean Caton and Milton H. Swift were raised December 11, 1845, Worshipful Brother John Barney, Grand
Lecturer, presiding, as he also did November 29, 1845,
when the above brethren and Brother Lorenzo Leland were
passed. A peculiar state of things having followed affecting
the interest of the Lodge, a dispensation was subsequently
granted for holding an election, and the first officers were
changed.

Lorenzo Leland was raised January 2, 1846, Theophilus
Lyle Dickey and Jos. O. Glover January 17th, Burton C.
Cook February 24th, Wm. Osman June 13th, Shelby Doo-
little, Wm. Reddick, Nov. 30th.

On February 6th brothers C. V. Kelley, John D. Caton,
T. Lyle Dickey and M. H. Swift were appointed a committee on the resolutions of Harmony Lodge, No. 3, Jacksonville, Illinois, which Lodge had complained to the Grand
Lodge, and forwarded resolutions to the various subordinate Lodges under the jurisdiction of the Grand Lodge of
Illinois, complaining and objecting to a certain lodge in
Cook county allowing negro Masons to sit in their Lodge,
and also to having received petitions from negroes for the
degrees, etc., which resolution of Harmony Lodge, No. 3,

caused the following resolution to be unanimously adopted by the Grand Lodge of Illinois in 1846:

"*Resolved,* That this Grand Lodge is unqualifiedly opposed to the admission of negroes or mulattoes into Lodges under her jurisdiction."

February 24th Worshipful Brother John Barney presided in Occidental Lodge, at which time brother Burton C. Cook was raised. Wm. Osman was passed June 12th and raised June 13th, the records stating that the reason for the apparent haste was the fact that Brother Osman intended leaving the country for Mexico.

On the 23d of June, the following officers were elected:

John D. Caton .... Worshipful Master.
G. L. Thompson .... Senior Warden.
Joseph Avery .... Junior Warden.
L. Leland .... Treasurer.
J. O. Glover .... Secretary.
B. C. Cook .... Senior Deacon.
Marshall Miller .... Junior Deacon.

August 21st James Lafferty was appointed Tyler.

CONSTITUTION AND CHARTER.

On Wednesday morning, October 7, 1846, A. L. 5846, at the seventh annual communication of the Grand Lodge of Illinois, held in the city of Peoria, the committee on Lodges U. D., consisting of brothers H. Dills, W. W. Happy and A. R. Robinson, examined the by-laws, returns and work of Occidental Lodge, U. D., and found them correct, and a charter prayed for by brothers J. D. Caton, G. L. Thompson, Joseph Avery and the requisite number of brethren, and the committee recommended the adoption of the following resolution:

Resolved, That a charter issue to said Lodge as Occidental Lodge, No. 40, and that brother Chas. V. Kelley be invited to take a seat as proxy for the Worshipful Master of said Lodge.

(Signed) H. Dills,
W. W. Happy,
A. R. Robinson,
Committee.

On motion the report was accepted, and the resolution was adopted, and on the same date a charter was issued, and on October 10, 1846, Occidental Lodge was duly constituted as No. 40, and brother John D. Caton installed as Master.

The returns of Occidental Lodge, No. 40, to the Grand Lodge in 1846 showed that the Lodge then met on the first and third Fridays of each month, and that the officers were as follows:

George H. Norris ....Worshipful Master.
Rev. Chas. V. Kelley ......Senior Warden and Chaplain.
Alson Woodruff ....Junior Warden.
Gilbert L. Thompson ....Treasurer.
Milton H. Swift ....Secretary.
Burton C. Cook ....Senior Deacon.
Marshall Miller ....Junior Deacon.
James Lafferty ....Tyler.

Past Masters: Jacob B. Rich, Thomas Tracey, John D. Caton.

Master Masons: Lorenzo Leland, Matthew Diamond, Daniel Newton, William K. Brown, David Walker, John Palmer, William Osman, Theophilus L. Dickey, Joseph Avery, William H. L. Wallace, Daniel Lyons, Shelby Doolittle, Edward Bacon, J. Otis Glover.

Entered Apprentices: William Reddick, Madison E. Hollister, William Palmer.

Initiated: Milton H. Swift, William Osman, J. Otis Glover, John D. Caton, Shelby Doolittle, William H. L. Wallace, Madison E. Hollister, Burton C. Cook, Lorenzo Leland, William Reddick.

Passed: Milton H. Swift, Shelby Doolittle, Lorenzo Le- land, John D. Caton, Burton C. Cook, William H. L. Wal- lace, William Osman, Theophilus L. Dickey, J. Otis Glover,

Raised: Milton H. Swift, William H. L. Wallace, Lo- renzo Leland, John D. Caton, William Osman, Shelby Doo- little, Theophilus L. Dickey, Burton C. Cook, J. Otis Glover.

Admitted: Marshall Miller, Matthew Diamond, Ed- ward Bacon, Thomas Tracy, Daniel Newton, Joseph Avery, William K. Brown, James Lafferty, David Walker.

One petition was rejected.

Occidental Lodge had at this time a membership of 25, and paid $6.25 Grand Lodge dues, and $6.25 to the Grand Charity fund. They also paid the Grand Lodge $2.00 for a seal for the Lodge.

1847.

June 18, 1847, the following officers were elected in Oc- cidental Lodge:

Gilbert L. Thompson . . . . Worshipful Master.
David Walker . . . . Senior Warden.
Burton C. Cook . . . . Junior Warden.
Lorenzo Leland . . . . Treasurer.
Madison E. Hollister . . . . Secretary.
H. W. Hopkins . . . . Senior Deacon.
James Lafferty . . . . Junior Deacon.

Past Masters: George H. Norris, John Dean Caton.

Raised: William Reddick, M. E. Hollister, William Palmer, George W. Hyde, H. W. Hopkins, John Dillon.

Affiliated: A. Keefer, William Baldwin, William Rich- ardson.

The election of officers was for some cause suspended on June 18th and resumed on June 24th, when M. E. Hol- lister was elected Secretary and H. W. Hopkins and James Lafferty, Deacons.

On August 20th it was resolved that every brother absent from the Lodge at regular meetings, unless excused, should be fined 6¼ cents; if an officer, 12½ cents.

In 1845 the Grand Lodge adopted a resolution requiring all Lodges under her jurisdiction to transact all their business in a Lodge of Master Masons, except conferring the first and second degrees. Prior to 1845, as previously stated, the business of the Lodges, except conferring the second and third degrees, was transacted in the lodges of Entered Apprentices.

On Monday afternoon, October 6, 1845, at the fifth annual communication of the Grand Lodge, Rev. Bro. W. F. Walker offered the·following resolution, which was laid on the table until the following day, when it was adopted:

Resolved, That the Lodges under the jurisdiction of this Grand Lodge be, and are hereby, instructed to require of every candidate initiated, that he perfect himself in the lecture appertaining to the first degree before being passed to the second, and in that of the second before being raised to the third; and in that of the third degree within one year from the time of his being raised; and that he satisfy the brethren, by examination in open Lodge, of his being so perfected; and that the Worshipful Master of each Lodge is expected to provide for such instruction being given in each case as is contemplated by this resolution.

1848.

August 21, 1848, the following officers were elected:

William H. L. Wallace .... Worshipful Master.
Burton C. Cook .... Senior Warden.
H. W. Hopkins .... Junior Warden.
L. Leland .... Treasurer.
William Osman .... Secretary.
John D. Caton .... Senior Deacon.
William Reddick .... Junior Deacon.
Rev. C. V. Kelley .... Chaplain.
William K. Brown .... Tyler.

These officers were not installed until February, 1849.

On the 17th of January, 1848, the death of Bro. Shelby Doolittle was announced to the Lodge as having occurred on the 9th inst., at Princeton, Ill. This was the first death among the brothers of Occidental Lodge.

Brother B. B. Fellows was raised August 7, 1848, and was the only work done by Occidental Lodge in 1848.

W. L. Dunavan, formerly a member of Ottawa Lodge, A. Delano and F. Mendelbaum, affiliated.

1849.

On October 1, 1849, the following officers were elected:

William H. L. Wallace .... Worshipful Master.
David Walker ......:............... Senior Warden.
F. Mandelbaum .... Junior Warden.
M. E. Hollister .... Treasurer.
William Osman .... Secretary.
George H. Norris .... Senior Deacon.
James Lafferty .... Junior Deacon.
W. K. Brown .... Tyler.

Two brothers were raised in 1849, Nelson Knickerbocker, April 2d, and John M. Quimby, October 15th.

N. P. Heath and Henry Beach affiliated.

Bro. J. B. Rich died at sunrise this morning, Dec. 23d (record), and Occidental Lodge performed the funeral services and deposited the sprig of acacia in the grave of Bro. Rich Dec. 24, 1849. This was the first Masonic funeral by Occidental Lodge, No. 40, A. F. & A. M.

General W. H. L. Wallace represented Occidental Lodge, No. 40, at the Grand Lodge in April, 1850, and the name of Thomas J. Wade appears as representing Mount Joliet Lodge, No. 42, at the same communication of the Grand Lodge.

It appears that the Grand Lodge did not meet in 1849,

ABRAM JONAS

The first Grand Master of the present Grand Lodge, 1840

but met, as above stated, in April, 1850, and again in October, 1850.

W. H.'L. Wallace was Grand Sword Bearer of the Grand Lodge in 1849.

1850.

The officers of Occidental Lodge for 1850 were:

John D. Caton ....Worshipful Master.
George H. Norris ....Senior Warden.
F. Mandelbaum ....Junior Warden.
William Reddick ....Treasurer.
H. Beach ....Secretary.
N. P. Heath ....Senior Deacon.
G. L. Thompson ....Junior Deacon.
J. M. Quimby ....Tyler.

But one brother, Philo Lindley, was raised in 1850, on Dec. 23d.

James Lafferty and Joseph Avery demitted, and William K. Brown died August 16, 1850, and was buried in Ottawa Avenue cemetery.

Thomas L. Boughton, E. A., died May 31, 1850, and is buried in the Ottawa Avenue cemetery.

W. H. L. Wallace represented Occidental Lodge at the communication of the Grand Lodge in April, 1850.

1851.

The officers of Occidental Lodge in 1851 were:

John Dean Caton ....Worshipful Master.
Arthur Lockwood ....Senior Warden.
Wm. L. Gibson ....Junior Warden.
Rev. C. V. Kelly ....Chaplain.
Wm. Palmer ....Treasurer.
Philo Lindley ....Secretary.
E. C. Henshaw ....Senior Deacon.
H. W. Hopkins ....Junior Deacon.
John M. Quimby ....Tyler.

Initiated: George S. Fisher (no further record).

Raised: Arthur Lockwood, Edward C. Henshaw, William L. Gibson, William I. Moore and John Fiske Nash.

Affiliated: C. G. Miller, A. N. Tuttle and H. M. Kellogg.

Demitted: G. W. Hyde and Henry Beach.

Suspended N. P. D.: A. Keefer, A. Delano and Wm. Richardson.

It seems Occidental Lodge had no regular time for holding elections in the early days, as any time from April to October seemed to suit.

1852.

No returns were made to the Grand Lodge by Occidental Lodge in 1852.

Brother Philo Lindley was Worshipful Master. Brother John D. Caton represented Occidental Lodge at the Grand Lodge, and was a member of the Jurisprudence Committee.

The following brethren were raised: Daniel D. Thompson, Lipman Raugh, R. Eaton Goodell, Wm. P. Thomas (or Thompson), A. Vogle, J. J. Finley, D. McIntosh.

P. V. N. Smith and Ira Patton affiliated.

E. C. Henshaw and Frank Mandelbaum demitted.

John Palmer died July 22d.

1853.

John M. Quimby ....Worshipful Master.
Alexander Magill ....Senior Warden.
Marshall Miller ....Junior Warden.
William Palmer ....Treasurer.
Isaac V. Waterman ....Secretary.
Rev. Chas. V. Kelly ....Chaplain.
John F. Nash ....Senior Deacon.
Bradford C. Mitchell ....Junior Deacon.
John Dean Caton ....Steward.

Theophilus Lyle Dickey ....Steward.
Madison E. Hollister ....Steward.
William Masters ....Tyler

Raised: Alexander Magill, Bradford C. Mitchell, Jared B. Ford, Isaac V. Waterman, Joshua Whitmore and George Churchill.

Affiliated: Isaac Reed, Henry Moore and Wm. Masters.

Demitted: Wm. I. Moore and Thomas Tracy.

It will be noticed that the offices of stewards were filled by three of the most distinguished members of the lodge—two of whom were in later years judges of the Supreme Court of Illinois, and the other judge of the Circuit Court and, later, Supreme Judge Supreme Court of Idaho.

1854.

The officers of Occidental Lodge in 1854 were:

Oliver Cromwell Gray ....Worshipful Master.
Alexander Magill ....Senior Warden.
Joshua Whitmore ....Junior Warden.
Philo Lindley (P. M.) ....Treasurer.
William L. Gibson ....Secretary.
Rev. Chas. V. Kelly ....Chaplain.
John F. Nash ....Senior Deacon.
William P. Thomas (or Thompson) ......Junior Deacon.
John M. Quimby (P. M.)....................Steward.
William Palmer ....Steward.
David Robbins Gregg ....Tyler.

Raised: David Robbins Gregg, W. W. Cavarly, Theodore Hay, Silas W. Cheever, Robert Hickling, Wm. C. Smith, Avon Pearson, Azro C. Putnam, Reuben Sherman, Wesley B. Hall, John Morrill, Moses R. Brown, Henry P. Brunker, Wm. Fry, Rev. S. F. Denning and Francis C. Warner.

The records show one Eli Plumb as having been initiated only, and no further record can be found.

Affiliated: Oliver Cromwell Gray, John Stout, Thomas Jefferson Wade, Daniel C. Stone, Richard Stadden, Chauncey U. Wade, Frank C. Flora, John D. Morgan and Daniel Fletcher Hitt.

1855.

The officers of Occidental Lodge were:

Thos. J. Wade ....Worshipful Master.
Oliver C. Gray ....Senior Warden.
Daniel D. Thompson ....Junior Warden.
Philo Lindley (P. M.).....................Treasurer.
Lipman Raugh ....Secretary.
Rev. S. F. Denning ....Chaplain.
John F. Nash ....Senior Deacon.
John Morrill ....Junior Deacon.
John M. Quimby (P. M.)...................Steward.
William Palmer ....Steward.
David R. Gregg ....Tyler.

Raised: Charles Turk, Aaron Daniels, R. W. Batcheller, William P. Gregg, Edward L. Herrick, James Hatheway, Henry G. Cotton, Joseph Ware.

Affiliated: Octavius R. Hanbury, Charles Phillips, F. S. McNamara and William Breg.

Demitted: R. Eaton Goodell, Henry W. Hopkins, Theophilus L. Dickey, Aaron Daniels, A. N. Tuttle, D. C. Stone, David McIntosh and Charles Phillips.

Initiated: Richard Thorne and Casper Meyer. No record of their having taken any other steps in Masonry.

Died: W. W. Cavarly and Wm. P. Thomas (or Thompson).

1856.

The officers of Occidental Lodge were:

Philo Lindley ....Worshipful Master.
Daniel D. Thompson ....Senior Warden.

John F. Nash ....Junior Warden.
Edward L. Herrick ....Treasurer.
Lipman Raugh ....Secretary.
John Morrill ....Senior Deacon.
Wm. C. Smith ....Junior Deacon.
John M. Quimby (P. M.)....................Steward.
William Palmer ....Steward.
David R. Gregg ....Tyler

Raised: Levi Mason, Theodore Cunningham Gibson, William C. Fash, George M. Dunavan, George W. Fuchs.

Affiliated: Edward M. Wade, Henry D. Gorbett, William L. Dunavan and Quincy D. Whitman.

Fellow Craft: Orville L. Moore.

Initiated only: R. F. Taylor, W. L. F. Jones and Warren R. Brundage.

Demitted: R. W. Batcheller, Henry Moore and Joseph Ware.

Died: Henry G. Cotton, Sr., and Alson Woodruff.

1857.

Officers of Occidental Lodge were:

Thos. J. Wade ....Worshipful Master.
John F. Nash ....Senior Warden.
John Morrill ....Junior Warden.
Edward L. Herrick ....Treasurer.
Avon Pearson ....Secretary.
Wesley B. Hall ....Senior Deacon.
Levi Mason ....Junior Deacon.
W. P. Gregg ....Tyler.

Raised: Joseph Ford, John M. Earl, Moses D. Calkins, Jeremiah Abbey, Erasmus N. Jenks, William K. Stewart, Joseph Cushman Hatheway and Charles H. Froese, F. C. only.

Affiliated: Adolph Hoffman, Samuel Eyster, Coleman Olmstead and Daniel C. Stone.

Demitted: D. F. Hitt, James Hatheway, S. F. Denning and R. Stadden.

Thomas J. Wade was appointed Grand Lecturer of the Grand Lodge this year.

1858.

The officers for 1858 were:

Burton C. Cook ....Worshipful Master.
John Morrill ....Senior Warden.
Levi Mason ....Junior Warden.
Bradford C. Mitchell ....Treasurer.
Avon Pearson ....Secretary.
Rev. Chas. P. Clark ....Chaplain.
Wesley B. Hall ....Senior Deacon.
John M. Earl ....Junior Deacon.
Quincy D. Whitman ....Senior Steward.
Frank Warner ....Junior Steward.
Wm. P. Gregg ....Tyler.

Raised: Hosea B. Williams, Simon Zimmerman, Solomon Degen, Nelson Conrad, Julius C. Avery, Holmes Slade, Samuel A. W. Jewett and Samuel C. Walker.

Affiliated: Theron Johnson, James Russ Murphy, Daniel H. Ashton and H. F. Clark.

Franklin D. Sweetser received the E. A. Degree and never went any further.

Demitted: Robert Hickling.

Thos. J. Wade was again appointed Grand Lecturer for Illinois by the Grand Master.

There is no record that Rev. Chas. P. Clark was a member of Occidental Lodge. It was customary at times in early days to appoint the Chaplain from among the ministry, if they were Masons, regardless of their affiliation.

1859.

OFFICERS.

Thomas J. Wade .... Worshipful Master.
Levi Mason .... Senior Warden.
Wesley B. Hall .... Junior Warden.
Philo Lindley (P. M.) .... Treasurer.
Henry F. Clark .... Secretary.
Rev. Samuel A. W. Jewett .... Chaplain.
Julius Avery .... Senior Deacon.
John M. Earl .... Junior Deacon.
Daniel D. Thompson .... Senior Steward.
Azro C. Putnam .... Junior Steward.
William K. Stewart .... Tyler.

Raised: W. G. Earl, James Keeler, John F. Lamb, Samuel D. Cole, Isaac R. Hill, W. A. McCullom, S. O. Wade, Henry Gondolf, Calvin Wilson, Samuel Thanhauser, R. P. Vorce, Frank J. Crawford and George H. Walker.

Admitted: Herman Alschuler, Robert H. Pierce, Wells Wait, J. W. Fay and George J. Burgess.

Demitted: George H. Norris, Henry D. Gorbett, John M. Quimby, Dan. C. Stone, N. P. Heath, Daniel F. Newton, J. J. Finley and P. V. N. Smith.

During the year death claimed as her reward Bradford C. Mitchell, father of Bro. Marshall B. Mitchell, James Russ Murphy and Orville C. Moore, Fellowcraft. Bro. Bradford C. Mitchell died Sept. 18, 1858, and was buried with Masonic honors, and the writer, at that time, a small boy, remembers this as the first Masonic funeral and procession of the brethren witnessed by him. Brother Mitchell was Treasurer of Occidental Lodge when he died.

Brother Orville L. Moore, Fellow Craft, lies buried in Ottawa Avenue cemetery, and his monument was erected by the members of the Illinois and Mississippi telegraph operators, whose instrument factory was at that time located in

Ottawa. Bro. Moore was the first telegraph operator to receive messages by sound.

Henry D. Gorbett demitted in 1859, and was elected Chaplain of Cement Lodge, at Utica, Ill., which was organized in 1859.

1860.

OFFICERS.

Levi Mason .... Worshipful Master.
D. D. Thompson .... Senior Warden.
W. L. Gibson .... Junior Warden.
P. Lindley .... Treasurer.
Q. D. Whitman .... Secretary.
C. G. Miller .... Senior Deacon.
S. Thanhauser .... Junior Deacon.
J. C. Hatheway .... Senior Steward.
C. Wilson .... Junior Steward.
C. S. C. Crane .... Tyler.

Raised: George B. Schneider, Cornelius Claggett, J. B. Rice, Joel Pierce, Geo. W. Adams and O. P. Stumph.

Admitted: C. S. C. Crane.

Demitted: Joshua Whitmore, William Smith, James Keeler, Holmes Slade and Nelson Conrad.

Initiated: C. A. Mathewson and Samuel R. Lewis.

Suspended N. P. D.: Francis McNamara, Theron Johnson, William C. Fash, Adolph Hoffman.

Died: Theodore Hay, Sept. 26, 1860.

1861.

OFFICERS.

D. D. Thompson .... Worshipful Master.
W. L. Gibson .... Senior Warden.
H. F. Clark .... Junior Warden.
Geo. W. Adams .... Treasurer.
J. W. Fay .... Secretary.

CHARTER OF OCCIDENTAL LODGE

S. Thanhauser ....Senior Deacon.
T. C. Gibson ....Junior Deacon.
C. S. C. Crane ....Tyler.

Raised: John Powe, E. C. Hatheway, N. A. Heinsfereter, A. H. Strobel, T. H. Clark, W. S. Easton, A. Wolford, D. Hapeman, E. J. Campbell, Charles Stout, D. M. Clarke, George Cloud, C. Huston, S. B. Griswold, E. G. Halbert and H. C. Nash.

Admitted: S. B. Olmstead, E. S. Hobert and J. Colwell.

Demitted: William Breg, John M. Earl and R. P. Vorce.

1862.

OFFICERS.

D. D. Thompson ....Worshipful Master.
E. L. Herrick ....Senior Warden.
J. B. Rice ....Junior Warden.
C. Stout ....Treasurer.
J. W. Fay ....Secretary.
G. W. Adams ....Senior Deacon.
E. S. Hobert ....Junior Deacon.
C. S. C. Crane ....Tyler.

Raised: J. R. Cameron, J. O. Harris, D. P. Jones, E. L. Armstrong, G. Koch, M. Osman, P. S. McKay, G. B. Morgan, F. F. Maybury, F. F. Brower, Geo. S. Stebbins, Geo. B. Mitchell, A. B. Moore, W. H. Williams, C. Irion and John A. Carton.

Admitted: S. Harvey, D. H. Porter.

Demitted: George H. Walker, George Cloud, P. S. McKay, C. W. Adams, C. Wilson, S. Harvey and S. O. Wade.

General W. H. L. Wallace killed in the battle of Shiloh.

1863.

OFFICERS.

John F. Nash ....Worshipful Master.

D

T. C. Gibson ....Senior Warden.
John Stout ....Junior Warden.
J. R. Cameron ....Treasurer.
W. S. Easton ....Secretary.
Chas. Stout ....Senior Deacon.
C. Claggett ....Junior Deacon.
H. Alschuler ....Senior Steward.
Samuel D. Cole ....Junior Steward.
George J. Burgess ....Tyler.

Raised: S. H. Hill, S. Poundstone, Chas. Houghtaling, W. W. Gardner, T. Y. Mickle, George Beatty, R. W. King, R. M. McArthur, George Woelfel, Joseph Gondolf, J. C. Warner and Justus Harris.

Demitted: I. V. Waterman, N. A. Heinsfereter and John F. Lamb.

Died: Jared B. Ford, C. U. Wade, F. C. Flora and Chas. Turk.

Initiated only: James Spencer.

1864.

OFFICERS.

J. F. Nash ....Worshipful Master.
W. S. Easton ....Senior Warden.
Chas. Stout ....Junior Warden.
J. R. Cameron ....Treasurer.
J. W. Fay ....Secretary.
Henry Gondolf ....Senior Deacon.
W. K. Stewart ....Junior Deacon.
Geo. Beatty ....Senior Steward.
Chas. Huston ....Junior Steward.
George J. Burgess ....Tyler.

Raised: T. C. Fullerton, Thos I. Conger, F. G. King, S. I. Haney, S. M. Pettingill, C. G. Lutz, H. Warlick, J. F. Marriner, Edward C. Mills, Henry Bilharz, L. N. Kennedy, Samuel Degen and Washington Bushnell.

Admitted: Oscar H. Mann, A. E. Gibbs and W. E. Bell.

Initiated: C. P. Stimpson and J. B. Smith, who died the same month. James Way received E. A. (and second, and third in No. 417, Marseilles, Ill.).

Demitted: T. Johnson, W. H. Williams, ~~John Stout~~ and Geo. Woelfel.

Philo Lindley was killed in battle at Altoona June 25, 1864, and his remains were brought to Ottawa and lay in state in the court house, from thence they were conveyed to the Ottawa Avenue cemetery, and deposited in their last resting place by Occidental Lodge. S. I. Haney and Thos. I. Conger were also killed in battle.

No officers reported in proceedings of 1865, 1866, 1867, 1868, 1869 and 1870, except the Masters.

1865.

W. S. Easton .... Worshipful Master.

Raised: Sidney C. Bates, Henry M. Godfrey, Jacob Hess, W. H. Carey, Mathew B. Lamb, Thomas Ryburn, Simon Alschuler, Champlain P. Chester, John F. Gibson, Francis L. Fiske, Frank B. Chapman, Warren V. Cooley, Randall Lyman, A. P. Barnes, Jacob Schmid and John L. Morrison.

Affiliated: M. F. Goodspeed, F. P. Childs and J. M. Crosby. .

Demitted: E. J. Campbell, J. W. Fay, Levi Mason, Wm. A. McCullom, S. B. Olmstead, R. H. Pierce, David Walker, R. W. Batcheller, E. G. Halbert, G. B. Morgan, Avon Pearson, A. C. Putnam and O. P. Stumph.

Died: S. M. Pettingill.

Initiated: H. D. Williams (Passed and Raised in Polar Star Lodge, No. 113, Iowa).

1866.

W. S. Easton .... Worshipful Master.

Raised: Ozell Trask, Peleg A. Hall, Robert Henning, William H. Cushman, Francis B. Metcalf, A. E. Grow, Robert G. Murphy and Henry Koch.

Affiliated: Wm. C. Smith, Leman A. Rising, Wm. S. Jackson and Edward H. Smith.

Initiated: Wm. N. Richardson and Jesse B. Charles.

Demitted: Albert Wolford, Gustav Koch, Moses Osman, James C. Warner, Thomas C. Fullerton, A. P. Barnes, Samuel A. W. Jewett, Moses R. Brown, Erasmus N. Jenks and F. F. Maybury.

1867.

W. S. Easton .... Worshipful Master.

Raised: George W. Cummings, Charles Henry Nattinger, Gilbert Goff, William H. Long, Benjamin Padgett, Joseph W. Dow, Alexander Hanna, John A. Gray, Frederick F. Crane, A. D. Simon, Andrew J. Sawyer, John H. Druitt, F. P. Duplain, Ebenezer E. Lewis, N. C. Walker, S. Thorsen and D. Batcheller.

Initiated: W. J. Pigott, Abram Cummings and Harvey J. Logan.

Demitted: Wm. H. Cushman, J. R. Hill, C. G. Miller, C. Claggett, L. Raugh, Henry Bilharz, Wells Wait, John A. Carton, Chas. Houghtaling, Jacob Schmid, Henry Koch, Jacob Hess, Herman Warlick, C. G. Lutz, Henry Gondolf, Joseph Gondolf, Christian Irion, A. H. Strobel and Herman Alschuler.

Admitted: Ross Denny, James Rhoads, Robert E. Riale, Frank B. Stearns, Wm. Cullen, Wm. E. Bowman, George W. Francis, Avon Pearson.

Suspended: Daniel H. Ashton, Reuben Sherman and S. B. Griswold.

Expelled: Marshall Miller, for disobedience of summons to pay dues.

Died: Alexander W. Magill and Geo. S. Stebbins, both of whom were buried with Masonic honors.

On March 14, 1867, permission was given Polar Star Lodge, No. 113, Iowa, to confer the Fellow Craft and Master Mason degrees on H. D. Williams, who was initiated in Occidental Lodge October 16, 1865.

A general Masonic celebration of St. John's day was held in Ottawa June 24, 1867, and was one of the greatest Masonic events ever held in Ottawa. Masonic Lodges and Commanderies of Knights Templar from surrounding towns participated, and the Masonic procession, under escort of Commanderies of Knights Templar, was the most imposing ever witnessed in Ottawa. A festival and speaking was the program in Washington park, and a Masonic ball was the social feature in the evening in Washington hall.

A charter was granted to Humboldt Lodge, No. 555, October 1, 1867, and the following severed their membership with Occidental Lodge, No. 40, November 18, 1867, and became charter members of Humboldt Lodge, No. 555:

H. Alschuler, Geo. W. Fuchs, A. H. Strobel, Christian Irion, Joseph Gondolf, H. Warlick, C. G. Lutz, Jacob Schmid, Henry Koch and Henry Gondolf.

1868.

W. S. Easton .... Worshipful Master.

Raised: John F. MacKinlay, Fred March, Edwin Coan, Francis M. Rose, Walter Todd, Austin C. Cregar, John W. Collins, James N. Colwell, William Stadden, Fernando C. Prescott, Wm. A. Brundage and John H. Shepherd.

Affiliated: Daniel J. Holmes, George J. Randell and Isaac N. Beem.

Demitted: Chas. Huston, Lewis N. Kennedy, Oscar H. Mann, Andrew J. Sawyer, Daniel C. Stone, Randall Lynne and George W. Cummings.

Suspended for N. P. D.: Ira Potter and M. E. Hollister. M. E. Hollister was reinstated in 1874.

June 4, 1868, W. S. Easton, Julius Avery and Samuel C. Walker, as trustees of Occidental Lodge, purchased the property on which the old Masonic temple and opera house now stands.

W. S. Easton was appointed District Deputy Grand Master, Seventh Masonic District.

1869.

Geo. J. Burgess .... Worshipful Master.

Raised: James R. Cross, Chas. M. Catlin, Samuel W. Porter, Obadiah Jennings, James O'Donnell and John Bohlander.

Affiliated: William W. Estabook and Phillip R. Martin.

Demitted: Edwin Coan, George Churchill, Ross Denny, Francis M. Rose, Jeremiah Abbey, S. Thanhauser, Wm. K. Stewart, W. S. Jackson, David H. Porter and Walter Todd.

Died: Samuel Walker, Oct. 23, 1869.

Expelled: J. F. Marriner.

An act to incorporate the Masonic Association of Ottawa was approved March 26, 1869.

Occidental Lodge, assisted by Humboldt Lodge, under escort of Ottawa Commandery, No. 10, Knights Templar, participated in the laying of the corner stone of the soldiers' monument, October 14, 1869. There was a large attendance of Masons and Knights Templar from sister bodies.

La Salle county was changed to the Sixth Masonic District in 1869.

1870.

W. S. Easton .... Worshipful Master.

Raised: Edward K. Walbridge, Geo. G. Wentz, Henry A. Howland, Wm. K. Cash, Henry Stead, Amasa C. Childs.

Affiliated: Benjamin S. Porter, Dwight W. Fuller.

Fellow Craft: Elisha Smith (received M. M. Degree Rockton Lodge, No. 516, Kent, Ohio).

Demitted: John W. Collins, S. H. Hill, Fred'k March and Geo. J. Rundell.

Died: Samuel C. Walker, Julius C. Avery and Frank F. Brower (all prominent members of the La Salle county bar; were buried with Masonic honors), and Charles H. Nattinger.

Thos. J. Wade, District Deputy Grand Master, the Eighth Masonic District.

1871.

OFFICERS.

Robert Henning .... Worshipful Master.
Wm. W. Estabrook .... Senior Warden.
James C. Warner .... Junior Warden.
Henry C. Nash .... Treasurer.
Wm. S. Easton .... Secretary.
Geo. J. Burgess .... Senior Deacon.
Frederick F. Crane .... Junior Deacon.
James N. Colwell .... Senior Steward.
Benjamin S. Porter .... Junior Steward.
David R. Gregg .... Tyler.

Raised: Albert J. Pool, Thomas, Thomeley, James J. Kellogg, Charles W. Cook.

Affiliated: Michael Huthmaker.

Demitted: Phillip R. Martin, William Reddick, Joseph

W. Dow, E. M. Wade, Geo. W. Francis, Wm. H. Long, Charles Stout, Colemen Olmstead, Dorr M. Clark, Frank B. Chapman, Seward Thorson, Warren V. Cooley, Wm. W. Estabrook.

Suspended N. P. D.: Edward C. Mills.

Died: Champlain P. Chester and O. C. Gray. O. C. Gray was one of the most prominent members at the La Salle county bar. (See obituary.)

Bro. Thos. J. Wade was chairman of the committee to examine visiting brethren at the annual communication of the Grand Lodge in 1871.

Thos. J. Wade, District Deputy Grand Master, Eighth Masonic District.

1872.

OFFICERS.

Robert Henning .... Worshipful Master.
James C. Warner .... Senior Warden.
Benjamin S. Porter .... Junior Warden.
Henry C. Nash .... Treasurer.
Edward L. Herrick .... Secretary.
Francis P. Duplain .... Senior Deacon.
James N. Colwell .... Junior Deacon.
Charles W. Cook. .... Senior Steward.
Samuel Degen .... Junior Steward.
Justus Harris .... Tyler.

Raised: George V. Hull, Alexander Richards, Reuben F. Dyer, Sidney V. Wise.

Affiliated: Jesse C. Allen, Wm. K. Stewart.

Demitted: Mathew F. Goodspeed, Quincy D. Whitman, John H. Druitt, Thomas H. Clark.

Died: H. P. Brunker, Geo. H. Schneider, John H. Shepherd. The returns of Occidental Lodge reports the death of Dr. John Paul September 25, 1872. We can find no record of his being a member of Occidental Lodge.

NOTICE TO W. H. L. WALLACE

At a stated communication of Occidental Lodge, May 5, 1872, on motion of Bro. John F. Nash, it was unanimously resolved that the Masons of Ottawa and vicinity desired the erection the coming season of a Masonic building, and that we make the attempt to raise the money for the same. This was the beginning, or first move, toward the erection of the Masonic hall and opera house block, which is more fully treated of under the head of Masonic Hall and Opera House Block in this work.

La Salle county changed to the Ninth Masonic District in 1872. W. S. Easton appointed District Deputy Grand Master.

1873.

OFFICERS.

Robert Henning ....Worshipful Master.
Benjamin S. Porter ....Senior Warden.
David Batcheller ....Junior Warden.
Henry C. Nash ....Treasurer.
Edward L. Herrick ....Secretary.
Francis P. Duplain ....Senior Deacon.
Sidney V. Wise ....Junior Deacon.
Charles W. Cook ....Senior Steward.
Samuel Degen ....Junior Steward.
Justus Harris ....Tyler.

Raised: Patrick Ryan, John L. Steele, Enoch S. Yentzer, David Krouse, Charles Snow and George N. Cash.

Affiliated: Hubert A. McCaleb and George L. Austin.

Demitted: John Bohlander, James J. Kellogg, Burton C. Cook, George M. Dunavan, Ebenezer E. Lewis, Frank B. Stearns.

Died: Simon Alschuler, in Denver, Colorado, and was buried there with Masonic honors.

Thomas J. Wade was a member of the committee to examine visiting brethren at the annual communication of the Grand Lodge, October, 1873.

Occidental Lodge moved from the Lynch building, on Main street, to their new hall in the opera house block and Masonic temple this year. (See history of Masonic Building Association.)

The corner stone of the Masonic hall was laid in 1873. Occidental Lodge, assisted by Humboldt and neighboring Lodges, under escort of Ottawa Commandery, No. 10, K. T., and sister Commanderies, formed the escort.

William S. Easton, District Deputy Grand Master.

1874.

OFFICERS.

John F. Nash .... Worshipful Master.
David Batcheller .... Senior Warden.
James O'Donnell .... Junior Warden.
Rev. John L. Steele .... Chaplain.
Henry C. Nash .... Treasurer.
Charles M. Catlin .... Secretary.
Edwin S. Hobert .... Senior Deacon.
Fred F. Crane .... Junior Deacon.
William K. Cash .... Senior Steward.
David Krouse .... Junior Steward.
Justus Harris .... Tyler.

Raised: Henry G. Cotton, Daniel C. Mills, Henry Mayo, John H. Widmer, James E. Rathburn, William Thomas, William Stormont, John L. Piergue, Frederick W. Mattocks, Allen Jordan, Jr., Roswell W. Holmes, H. A. Shuler, Frank A. Kendall, C. C. Glover, Geo. A. Mills, W. B. Titus and Jesse B. Ruger.

Affiliated: E. Follett Bull, James A. Comstock, S. R. Helmick, August Haeberlin and Charles Blanchard.

Demitted: George G. Wentz, Jesse C. Allen, Thomas Thomeley, John Stout.

Died: Fernando C. Prescott and Amasa C. Childs.

The Grand Master rendered a decision, which was approved by the Grand Lodge in 1874, that before the Worshipful Master elect can be installed, he must have been invested with the secrets of the chair in a convocation of actual Past Masters, notwithstanding such a brother may be in possession of the degree of virtual or chapter Past Master, and that none but actual Past Masters should be present during the ceremony of investing the Master elect with the secrets of the chair.

It was formerly the law in symbolic Lodges that the Masters elect should be invested with the secrets of the chair. It is not now in force.

W. S. Easton, District Deputy Grand Master.

1875.

OFFICERS.

Henry F. Clark ....Worshipful Master.
Charles M. Catlin ....Senior Warden.
Frederick F. Crane ....Junior Warden.
Henry C. Nash ....Treasurer.
Roswell W. Holmes ....Secretary.
Walter B. Titus ....Senior Deacon.
Alexander Hanna ....Junior Deacon.
Patrick Ryan ....Senior Steward.
Clarence C. Glover ....Junior Steward.
Justus Harris ....Tyler

Raised: Arthur Lockwood Wagner, Charles E. Pettit, William H. Phillips, Lester O. Phillips, Walter D. Strawn, Andrew J. Brown, Charles A. Works, Edward C. Lewis, William O. Gorman.

Affiliated: Henry P. Clark, Wm. L. Phillips, H. W. Smith, John N. Tiffany, Theodore C. Miller, William Stuart Spiers, Cairo D. Trimble and William E. Ensminger.

Demitted: Francis B. Metcalf, Mathew B. Lamb, Frank

J. Warner, James C. Warner, James A. Comstock, R. W. King, W. W. Gardner.

Died: Octavius R. Hanbury.

Thos. J. Wade, District Deputy Grand Master, Ninth Masonic District.

On motion of Bro. Thos. J. Wade, the Grand Lodge at the annual communication in October, 1875, remitted the dues of Occidental Lodge, in view of the loss of their hall by fire during the past year.

During the annual communication of the Grand Lodge, October, 1875, the Grand Lodge by-laws were amended so that one clear ballot entitled a candidate to the three degrees of symbolic Masonry upon his showing a suitable proficiency for advancement. Prior to this a candidate had to be balloted on for each degree.

1876.

OFFICERS.

Henry F. Clark ....Worshipful Master.
Frederick F. Crane ....Senior Warden.
Walter B. Titus ....Junior Warden.
Henry C. Nash ....Treasurer.
Roswell W. Holmes ....Secretary.
Charles E. Pettit ....Senior Deacon.
Alexander Hanna ....Junior Deacon.
Clarence C. Glover ....Senior Steward.
Geo. A. Mills ....Junior Steward.
Justus Harris ....Tyler.

Raised: Thomas A. Smurr.

Affiliated: Wm. E. Codding.

Demitted: James O'Donnell, Edward K. Walbridge, Daniel J. Holmes, William Stuart Spiers, Madison E. Hollister, Charles A. Works, George L. Austin and Charles M. Catlin.

Edward L. Herrick died April 11, 1876. James N. Colwell killed by cars at Streator, October 11, 1876.

Thomas J. Wade was District Deputy Grand Master, Ninth Masonic District.

At the annual communication of the Grand Lodge in 1876, M. W. Bro. Cregier offered the following resolution, which was adopted:

Resolved, That the Grand Lodge of Illinois condemns the prevailing practice of transmitting by "postal card" notice of the business and other doings of Lodges, and it is hereby ordered that all notices emanating from Lodges or their officers shall be sent to members under sealed covers: *Provided,* that the bare notice of time and place of meeting of said Lodge may be sent by postal card.

This law is still in force and a violation of it would subject the guilty party to expulsion from the fraternity.

Occidental Lodge took a prominent part in the centennial celebration in Ottawa, July 4, 1876, Ottawa Commandery, No. 10, K. T., acting as escort to the Masonic bodies. Humboldt Lodge also participated.

1877.

OFFICERS.

Robert Henning .... Worshipful Master.
E. Follett Bull .... Senior Warden.
Solomon Degen .... Junior Warden.
William Stormont .... Chaplain.
Henry C. Nash .... Treasurer.
E. S. Hobert .... Secretary.
William K. Stewart .... Senior Deacon.
Henry P. Clark .... Junior Deacon.
John L. Piergue .... Senior Steward.
Lester O. Phillips .... Junior Steward.
David R. Gregg .... Tyler.

Raised: Samuel Richolson, Samuel Dittenhoffer, Wm. T. Dickey and Asa Mann Hoffman.

Suspended N. P. D.: Moses D. Calkins, Michael Huthmaker, Sidney C. Bates, Obadiah Jennings, John Colwell, Henry Howland, Frank P. Duplain and Sidney V. Wise.

Demitted: William Palmer, James R. Cross, George J. Burgess, William S. Easton, J. O. Glover, William O. Gorman, Dwight W. Fuller, W. L. Gibson, C. S. C. Crane and David Batcheller.

Obadiah Jennings demitted after having been reinstated from suspension for N. P. D.

Died: Henry F. Clark, Jan. 10, 1877; Dr. D. D. Thompson, May, 31, 1877; Thomas Ryburn, —, 1877.

Thos. J. Wade, District Deputy Grand Master, Ninth Masonic District.

1878.

OFFICERS.

Robert Henning .... Worshipful Master.
Solomon Degen .... Senior Warden.
F. P. Childs .... Junior Warden.
H. C. Nash .... Treasurer.
Clarence C. Glover .... Secretary.
James McManus .... Senior Deacon.
Henry P. Clark .... Junior Deacon.
Fred F. Crane .... Senior Steward.
Justus Harris .... Junior Steward.
David R. Gregg .... Tyler.

Raised: Benjamin F. Bole, Lothrop Perkins.

Affiliated: James McManus and David A. Cook.

Demitted: Robert E. Riale, J. M. Crosby, Avon Pearson, Frank J. Crawford, Wm. H. Ensminger.

Died: Hubert A. McCaleb, March 24, 1878.

Thos. J. Wade, District Deputy Grand Master, Ninth Masonic District.

1879.

OFFICERS.

Solomon Degen .... Worshipful Master.
Thomas A. Smurr .... Senior Warden.
James McManus .... Junior Warden.
Wm. Stormont .... Chaplain.
Lothrop Perkins .... Treasurer.
Asa Mann Hoffman .... Secretary.
William K. Stewart .... Senior Deacon.
Benjamin F. Bole .... Junior Deacon.
Patrick Ryan .... Senior Steward.
Henry P. Clark .... Junior Steward.
Justus Harris .... Tyler.

Raised: William L. Milligan, W. W. Arnold and Rev. Francis Burdette Nash, Jr.

Affiliated: Paul Teissedre.

Demitted: Benjamin S. Porter, John F. MacKinlay, Albert E. Gibbs, Andrew J. Brown, Ozell Trask, Walter B. Titus, Franklin P. Childs, John L. Piergue, Benjamin F. Bole and Wm. K. Cash.

Died: Col. Absalom B. Moore, July 7, 1879. Buried with Masonic honors. Allen Jordan, Jr., July 12, 1879.

The third degree was not conferred in Occidental Lodge during 1879 until after the annual communication of the Grand Lodge in October. Occidental Lodge had become financially embarrassed through loss by fire, and its connection with the Masonic building association, and many predicted, and, in fact, were in favor of surrendering the charter. Thirteen of the brethren demitted. Good men refused the responsible position of Worshipful Master during this trying time of Occidental Lodge, but Brother Solomon Degen accepted the office, and at once began the herculean task of bringing order out of chaos. The dues were raised to five dollars per annum. Brother Degen personally attended to the collection of back dues; called personally on members in arrears, wherever meeting them, in their offices or on the streets. Those were the days Masoury was tested in Ottawa; when brethren went down into their pockets and raised funds for Masonic funeral expenses and calls for charity. The brethren who are members of Occidental Lodge to-day should revere the names of Brother Solomon Degen and the loyal band of brethren who stood by the helm of old Occidental, and piloted her to a safe and secure harbor.

1880.

OFFICERS.

Solomon Degen ....Worshipful Master.
James McManus ....Senior Warden.
Lothrop Perkins ....Junior Warden.
Henry C. Nash ....Treasurer.
Asa M. Hoffman ....Secretary.
William L. Milligan ....Senior Deacon.
Henry P. Clark ....Junior Deacon.
William K. Stewart ....Senior Steward.
Paul Teissedre ....Junior Steward.
Patrick Ryan ....Tyler.

Raised: Charles W. Fredenburg, Joseph N. Dunaway and James Rollo Chapman.

Reinstated: Francis P. Duplain.

Suspended N. P. D.: Jesse B. Ruger, Alexander Richards, Robert G. Murphy and William A. Brundage.

Expelled: William L. Phillips, for disobedience of summons to pay dues.

Demitted: John F. Gibson, Elias C. Hatheway, John Morrill, William E. Bowman, Wesley B. Hall, Albert J. Pool, Leman A. Rising, Frederick W. Mattocks, William Thomas, Joel F. Pierce, John N. Tiffany, Henry G. Cotton and William T. Dickey.

Theodore Tuthill Gurney was Grand Master in 1880

WILLIAM OSMAN

Raised in 1846. The oldest living member

and rendered some important decisions, among the most important of which, and which was approved and recognized as the law of the Grand Lodge, and which we deem proper to note herewith, as follows:

That "the Grand Lodge clearly sets forth 'The usages and general regulations of Masonry,' by defining the duties of its Treasurer. We are therefore decidedly of the opinion that a dual custodianship of the fiscal property of the Lodge is not authorized by Masonic usage, neither by any law of the Grand Lodge.

"It is true that a Lodge can direct a treasurer to invest its funds as it may elect, but we are not of the belief that it can create a financial department other than that recognized by 'The usages and general regulations of Masonry.' The treasurer, under our system, is the only lawful custodian of the moneys of the Lodge and his position must be respected in its entirety; otherwise we abandon one of the most prominent features of 'usages' and 'general regulations,' that has been handed down to us by the fathers of our organization."

This decision was referred to the Jurisprudence Committee, who made the following report, which was adopted by the Grand Lodge:

"That in the making of leases, suits, conveyances and other legal transactions, to which the Lodge is a party, the Master and Wardens are the trustees in fact, where action is required to validate such transactions under the civil law." (Pages 26 and 108, G. L. Pro., 1880.)

The following report from the Jurisprudence Committee was also approved by the Grand Lodge:

"Your committee concur in the sentiments expressed, and recommend the approval of the action reported by the Grand Master under this head; and ask your assent to the declaration that the Grand Lodge looks with disfavor upon the practice of renting lodge premises for other than Masonic purposes." (Page 110, G. L. Pro., 1880.)

E

1881.

OFFICERS.

Solomon Degen .... Worshipful Master.
James McManus .... Senior Warden.
Lothrop Perkins .... Junior Warden.
Henry C. Nash .... Treasurer.
Asa Mann Hoffman .... Secretary.
William L. Milligan .... Senior Deacon.
Henry P. Clark .... Junior Deacon.
Wm. K. Stewart .... Senior Steward.
Paul Teissedre .... Junior Steward.
David R. Gregg .... Tyler.

Raised: William H. Gilman, John W. Clegg, Nathaniel McDougall, John W. Green, Thos. W. D. Crane, Walter McDonald Woodward, Thomas E. MacKinlay and James Milligan, Jr.

Affiliated: Henry Peck, W. E. Prichard, R. Farnsworth and William Sheppard.

Demitted: Roswell W. Holmes, Charles E. Pettit, Geo. B. Mitchell, Francis B. Nash and Silas W. Cheever.

Died: Patrick Ryan, June 13, 1881; Samuel Eyster, June 29, 1881; Lorenzo Leland, August 26, 1881; Charles Snow, Sept. 9, 1881.

Suspended N. P. D.: Harry W. Smith.

The corner stone of the new court house of La Salle county was placed in position by the Masonic fraternity July 4, 1881. M. W. Bro. William H. Scott, Grand Master, convened an occasional Grand Lodge, with the assistance of R. W. Bro. H. C. Cleveland, Junior Grand Warden, and other grand officers *pro tem.,* in the presence of many prominent citizens and a large number of Masons, officiated. Occidental and Humboldt Lodges and many visiting Lodges, under escort of St. Bernard Commandery, No. 36, K. T., Ottawa Commandery, No. 10, K. T., and other Commanderies, formed procession and acted as escort to the Grand Lodge on this occasion.

Occidental and Humboldt Lodges also took part in the Garfield memorial services, under escort of Ottawa Commandery, No. 10, K. T., September 26, 1881.

1882.

OFFICERS.

James McManus ....Worshipful Master.
Lothrop Perkins ....Senior Warden.
William K. Stewart ....Junior Warden.
Henry C. Nash ....Treasurer.
Asa Mann Hoffman ....Secretary.
Thomas W. D. Crane ....Senior Deacon.
Alexander Hanna ....Junior Deacon.
Paul Teissedre ....Senior Steward.
John W. Clegg ....Junior Steward.
David R. Gregg ....Tyler.

Raised: Willard S. Wheeler, John Green, John E. V. Morse, John C. Farnsworth, William H. Stead, Jesse E. Morgan, Simeon G. Gay, John S. Ryburn.

Affiliated: Charles E. Pettit.

Suspended N. P. D.: Nathaniel C. Walker.

Demitted: James Rhoads and George N. Cash.

Died: Charles W. Cook and John Powe. John Powe was buried with Masonic honors.

The first Masonic school of instruction ever held in Ottawa was on the 7th, 8th and 9th days of March, 1882.

There were present: M. W. W. H. Scott, Grand Master; R. W. M. D. Chamberlain, president *pro tem.;* R. W. W. B. Grimes, secretary of board; R. W. J. H. C. Dill, assistant; also R. W. L. L. Munn, Grand Secretary, and others. Twenty-nine Lodges were represented.

At each of these schools the opening and closing ceremonies and work in each of the degrees were fully exemplified, a general course of instruction given, the lectures rehearsed and each degree conferred on actual candidates.

During this school certain portions of the ritual alluding to the g—p's were stricken from the work because of supposed interfering with the cosmopolitanism of Freemasonry.

1883.

OFFICERS.

James McManus ....Worshipful Master.
William L. Milligan ....Senior Warden.
William K. Stewart ....Junior Warden.
Henry C. Nash ....Treasurer.
Asa Mann Hoffman ....Secretary.
Thomas W. D. Crane ....Senior Deacon.
Thomas E. MacKinlay ....Junior Deacon.
William H. Stead ....Senior Steward.
Simeon G. Gay ....Junior Steward.
Alexander Hanna ....Tyler.

Raised: Thomas Reedy, John C. Corcoran, Louis W. Hess, Joseph A. Wilson.

Affiliated: John F. Gibson, Garvey Donaldson, Thomas C. Fullerton.

Died: William Stadden, June 15, 1883. Was buried with Masonic honors.

1884.

OFFICERS.

William L. Milligan ....Worshipful Master.
William K. Stewart ....Senior Warden.
Geo. A. Mills ....Junior Warden.
William Stormont ....Chaplain.
Henry C. Nash ....Treasurer.
Asa Mann Hoffman ....Secretary.
Thomas W. D. Crane ....Senior Deacon.

John C. Corcoran ....Junior Deacon
Joseph A. Wilson ....Senior Steward.
Paul Teissedre ....Junior Steward.
Alexander Hanna ....Tyler.

Raised: Rector Cass Hitt, John M. Purrucker, Warren C. Riale, Frederick W. Gay, John Dawdle Hammond, William H. Watts, Martin C. Hodgson and John Wesley Johnson, F. C. only.

Affiliated: Samuel Caldwell and Daniel Fletcher Hitt.

Suspended N. P. D.: Edward S. Hobert.

Demitted: George V. Hull, Edward H. Smith and Wm. L. Dunavan. W. L. Dunavan was made an honorary member.

Died: Lothrop Perkins, September 16, 1884; David P. Jones, November 7, 1884. Both buried with Masonic honors.

M. W. Rob. Morris, Past Grand Master of Kentucky, visited Occidental Lodge during this year and conferred the degrees of Palm and Shell (Arabic Masonry) on quite a number of the brethren. He also delivered his lecture on the Holy Land.

The question of Masonic home was frequently mentioned in Occidental Lodge during the year 1884, and at the annual communication of Occidental Lodge, January, 1885, the Worshipful Master placed special stress on this subject in his address to the Lodge.

1885.

OFFICERS.

William L. Milligan ....Worshipful Master.
Thomas C. Fullerton ....Senior Warden.
William H. Stead ....Junior Warden.
Henry C. Nash ....Treasurer.
Asa Mann Hoffman ....Secretary.
James McManus ....Senior Deacon.

Paul Teissedre ....Junior Deacon.
Joseph A. Wilson ....Senior Steward.
Samuel Caldwell ....Junior Steward.
Alexander Hanna ....Tyler.

Raised: Charles H. Angevine, Charles E. Dunbar, Charles Zeitler, Charles Schaulin, Harry E. Rockwood.

Affiliated: Edward H. Roberts.

Demitted: August Haeberlin, William H. Phillips and Lester O. Phillips.

Died: Washington Bushnell, June 30, 1885; Robert Henning, September 27, 1885. They were both buried with Masonic honors.

William L. Milligan was District Deputy Grand Master in 1885.

The Illinois Masonic Orphans' Home was organized March 11, 1885, and W. L. Milligan elected a member of the visiting committee. Received life membership certificate number one in recognition of having made first contribution to fund for home.

Occidental Lodge was reported in the first annual report of the president of the Illinois Masonic Orphans' Home as the banner Lodge, in point of active and life membership.

Humboldt Lodge was most honorably represented in the organization of the Illinois Masonic Orphans' Home, every member of Humboldt Lodge having contributed and received a certificate of active membership.

1886.

OFFICERS.

William L. Milligan ....Worshipful Master.
Chas. E. Pettit ....Senior Warden.
John C. Corcoran ....Junior Warden.
William Stormont ....Chaplain.
Henry C. Nash ....Treasurer.
Asa Mann Hoffman ....Secretary.

Thos. C. Fullerton ....Senior Deacon.
Paul Teissedre ....Junior Deacon.
Joseph A. Wilson ....Senior Steward.
Samuel Caldwell ....Junior Steward.
Alexander Hanna ....Tyler.

Raised: Joshua P. Rodgers, Daniel E. Daly, George M. Trimble.

Affiliated: W. A. Jeffery and David Batcheller.

Demitted: Garvey Donaldson.

Died: Milton H. Swift, May 14, 1886; Robert M. McArthur, Aug. 12, 1886. Robert M. McArthur was buried by Ottawa Commandery, No. 10, K. T. Thos J. Wade died September 6, 1886, and was buried with Masonic honors.

W. L. Milligan, District Deputy Grand Master, Ninth Masonic District.

The Illinois Masonic Orphans' Home was dedicated by the Grand Lodge October 7, 1886. W. L. Milligan elected member board of trustees, Illinois Masonic Orphans' Home.

1887.

OFFICERS.

Charles E. Pettit ....Worshipful Master.
Wm. K. Stewart ....Senior Warden.
Charles E. Dunbar ....Junior Warden.
Thomas E. MacKinlay ....Treasurer.
Asa Mann Hoffman ....Secretary.
William A. Jeffery ....Senior Deacon.
Samuel Caldwell ....Junior Deacon.
John C. Farnsworth ....Senior Steward.
Charles H. Angevine ....Junior Steward.
Alexander Hanna ....Tyler.

Raised: Charles B. Vosburgh, Charles E. Russell, James Francis Murphy, Charles E. Hook, Ross C. Mitchell, Frank B. Logan.

Affiliated: William McCombs, Daniel J. Holmes, L. A. Rising.

Suspended N. P. D.: Theodore C. Miller, Francis P. Duplain, Samuel S. Dittenhoffer and Henry P. Clark.

Demitted: J. C. Hatheway, James E. Rathburn, Henry A. Shuler, John L. Morrison, J. R. Chapman.

Died: Asa Mann Hoffman, May 4, 1887, and was buried by Ottawa Commandery, No. 10, K. T.; and Ross C. Mitchell, October 6, 1887, and was buried with Masonic honors.

W. L. Milligan, District Deputy Grand Master, Ninth Masonic District.

October 5, 1887, W. L. Milligan was introduced to and received by the Grand Lodge as the first representative of the Grand Lodge of South Australia, near the Grand Lodge of Illinois, with the honorary rank of P. S. G. W. of the Grand Lodge of South Australia.

A Masonic school of instruction was held in Ottawa March 1, 2 and 3, 1887. Fifty-seven Lodges were represented, and two hundred nineteen names registered. There were present M. W. A. T. Darrah, Grand Master; R. W. Bro. L. L. Munn, Grand Secretary; Edward Cook, president; W. B. Grimes, secretary; M. D. Chamberlain, James Douglass and C. F. Tenney, members of the board of Grand Examiners; A. B. Ashley, J. H. C. Dill, H. E. Huston and W. E. Ginther, Deputy Grand Lecturers; Owen Scott and W. L. Milligan, D. D. G. M.'s, and others. At each of these schools the opening and closing ceremonies and work in each of the degrees were fully exemplified.

1888.

OFFICERS.

Charles E. Pettit .... Worshipful Master.
William K. Stewart .... Senior Warden.

GILBERT L. THOMPSON

Worshipful Master 1847

Charles E. Dunbar ....Junior Warden.
Daniel J. Holmes ....Chaplain.
Thomas E. MacKinlay ....Treasurer.
William L. Milligan ....Secretary.
James McManus ....Senior Deacon.
Joseph A. Wilson ....Junior Deacon.
Daniel C. Mills ....Senior Steward.
John C. Farnsworth ....Junior Steward.
Alexander Hanna ....Tyler.

Raised: James E. Cooke, Clarence Griggs, Wm. H. Knowles, Marshall B. Mitchell and Charles E. Fisher.

Affiliated: Louis Degen and A. R. Tressler.

Suspended N. P. D.: Walter M. Woodward.

Demitted: Charles Zeitler, Jr., John R. Cameron and Samuel Poundstone.

Died: Justus Harris, E. Follett Bull. Justus Harris was buried with Masonic honors; E. F. Bull by the Knights Templar.

W. L. Milligan, District Deputy Grand Master, Ninth Masonic District.

1889.

OFFICERS.

Charles E. Pettit ....Worshipful Master.
Wm. K. Stewart ....Senior Warden.
Joseph A. Wilson ....Junior Warden.
Daniel J. Holmes ....Chaplain.
Thomas E. MacKinlay ....Treasurer.
David Batcheller ....Secretary.
James E. Cooke ....Senior Deacon.
Lewis Degen ....Junior Deacon.
Daniel C. Mills ....Senior Steward.
William A. Jeffery ....Junior Steward.
Alexander Hanna ....Tyler.

Raised: Augustus Ives, Jr., William H. Barnard, John James Withrow, Frederick E. Mayo, Abraham Cross Godfrey, Duncan McDougall, George Adams Forbes, Charles Benton Hess, Nathaniel Earl Degen, John J. Carrick.

Admitted: John Haws, Henry G. Cotton, Willis Herbert Ward, Henry R. Turner, John J. Tobias, Alva B. Holmes and Henry Waldecker.

Demitted: John Michael Purrucker, Gilbert Goff and Arthur Lockwood Wagner.

Suspended N. P. D.: Webster Wesley Arnold, Fred F. Crane, Henry Clay Nash, Hosea B. Williams, Samuel Degen and George W. Green.

Died: Thomas Reedy, May 4, 1889; Henry M. Godfrey, June 19, 1889. Both were buried with Masonic honors. Charles Snow also died in 1889.

The fiftieth anniversary of the organization of the Grand Lodge of Illinois was celebrated by the Grand Lodge in Chicago, October 1, 1889.

W. L. Milligan, District Deputy Grand Master, Ninth Masonic District.

1890.

OFFICERS.

Charles E. Pettit .... Worshipful Master.
James E. Cooke .... Senior Warden.
Joseph A. Wilson .... Junior Warden.
Thomas E. MacKinlay .... Treasurer.
David Batcheller .... Secretary.
Willis H. Ward .... Senior Deacon.
William H. Barnard .... Junior Deacon.
Daniel C. Mills .... Senior Steward.
Abraham C. Godfrey .... Junior Steward.
Alexander Hanna .... Tyler.

Raised: William C. Weise, Luman Albert Williams.

Admitted: Hans Gulbronson, P. C. Weaver, Byron F. Maxon, Royal D. McDonald, Charles E. Hills.

Demitted: Daniel J. Holmes, Rector C. Hitt, John J. Tobias, John E. V. Morse and Henry R. Turner.

Died: Nathaniel McDougall, March 5, 1890; Byron F. Maxon, June 22, 1890; and William H. Carey, Sept. 1, 1890.

The corner stone of the Masonic temple in Chicago was laid by the Grand Lodge, November 6, 1890.

1891.

OFFICERS.

James E. Cooke .... Worshipful Master.
Duncan McDougall .... Senior Warden.
William Henry Barnard .... Junior Warden.
James McManus .... Chaplain.
Thomas E. MacKinlay .... Treasurer.
David Batcheller .... Secretary.
Charles E. Hook .... Senior Deacon.
Luman A. Williams .... Junior Deacon.
Clarence C. Glover .... Senior Steward.
P. C. Weaver .... Junior Steward.
Alexander Hanna .... Tyler.

Raised: Adelbert Thomas Olmsted, Clark Brading Provins, Jacob Benner Shuler, Edward Augustus Nattinger, Frank Y. Herbert, David L. Grove and Henry H. Long.

Admitted: Timothy E. Gapen.

Occidental Lodge leased their present quarters from King & Hamilton and moved from the Masonic hall and opera house block in the winter of 1891 and 1892.

1892.

OFFICERS.

James E. Cooke .... Worshipful Master.
Duncan McDougall .... Senior Warden.
William H. Barnard .... Junior Warden.
James McManus .... Chaplain.

Thomas E. MacKinlay ....Treasurer.
David Batcheller .... Secretary.
Frank Y. Herbert ....Senior Deacon.
John J. Carrick ....Junior Deacon.
L. A. Williams ....Senior Steward.
William C. Weise ....Junior Steward.
Foster H. McKenney ....Tyler.

Raised: Edgar G. Dyer, Charles P. Taylor, J. A. Dockter, W. F. Weese, F. M. Yentzer, Mathew Scanlan, John Wesley Hackett, Isaac Baumgardner, William E. W. MacKinlay, John Raymond Hoffman, Charles Sumner Beckwith.

Reinstated: John A. Gray.

Affiliated: Le Roy L. McKinley, Gilbert Goff, Foster H. McKenney, James M. Trenary, James Briggs and John Stout.

Suspended N. P. D.: Fred E. Mayo and Charles Edward Russell.

Demitted: Adelbert T. Olmsted.

Died: John Stuart Ryburn, Sept. 21, 1892; Frederick W. Gay, May 6, 1892.

On March 15, 1892, M. W. Monroe C. Crawford, Grand Master, assisted by R. W. Brother George W. Warvelle, who acted as Grand Orator on the occasion, and R. W. Brother Edward Cook, Junior Grand Warden, and other brothers, organized an occasional Grand Lodge and dedicated the lodge room, ante-room and the other parts of the hall of Occidental Lodge, No. 40, to the purposes of Free Masonry, in due and ancient form. There was a large attendance of not only the brethren of Occidental Lodge and Humboldt Lodge, but from sister Lodges of La Salle and adjoining counties.

1893.

OFFICERS. .

William H. Barnard ....Worshipful Master.
Charles E. Hook ....Senior Warden.
Luman A. Williams ....Junior Warden.
James McManus ....Chaplain.
Thomas E. MacKinlay ....Treasurer.
David Batcheller ....Secretary.
Charles S. Beckwith ....Senior Deacon.
Clarence E. Tryon ....Junior Deacon.
Daniel C. Mills ....Senior Steward.
William E. W. MacKinlay ....Junior Steward.
Foster H. McKenny ....Tyler.

Raised: Kimball White Leland, Henry Edgar Gedney, Clarence Edward Tryon, Jacob Isaac Warner, Albert Burling Cole, Daniel Douglas Saylor, David Refior, Milo Putney, Douglass Lee Dunavan.

Affiliated: Rector Cass Hitt, James Norris Downs, Thomas Wilson Burrows.

Demitted: William E. Codding, Henry Harrison Long.

Died: Benjamin Beach Fellows, March 3, 1893.

A Masonic school of instruction was held in Masonic hall, in Ottawa, Ill., January 24, 25 and 26, 1893.

There were present M. W. Monroe C. Crawford, Grand Master; R. W. Edward Cook, J. G. W.; R. W. L. L. Munn, Grand Secretary; R. W. brethren W. B. Grimes, A. B. Ashley, James John, Jos. E. Evans and John W. Rose, Grand Examiners; R. W. Bro. D. D. Darrah, D. G. L.

There were forty-six Lodges represented and two hundred and eighty-six names registered.

1894.

OFFICERS.

William H. Barnard ....Worshipful Master.

Luman A. Williams ....Senior Warden.
Charles S. Beckwith ....Junior Warden.
James McManus ....Chaplain.
Thomas E. MacKinlay ....Treasurer.
David Batcheller ....Secretary.
Clarence E. Tryon ....Senior Deacon.
David Refior ....Junior Deacon.
Daniel D. Saylor ....Senior Steward.
Douglass L. Dunavan ....Junior Steward.
F. H. McKenney ....Tyler.

Raised: Frederick Lewis Fischer, Matthew W. Bach, Arthur S. Hook.

Affiliated: Charles J. Yockey.

Suspended N. P. D.: Samuel R. Helmick, Matthew Scanlan and W. S. Wheeler.

Demitted: John Green, A. R. Tressler.

Died: William E. Bell, Feb. 12, 1894; Henry E. Gedney, Jan. 31, 1894; Thomas C. Fullerton, Aug. 2, 1894; William Stormont, Oct. 12, 1894; Simon Zimmerman, Oct. 8, 1894.

1895.

OFFICERS.

Luman A. Williams ....Worshipful Master.
Charles S. Beckwith ....Senior Warden.
Clarence E. Tryon ....Junior Warden.
Thomas E. MacKinlay ....Treasurer.
David Batcheller ....Secretary.
James McManus ....Chaplain.
David Refior ....Senior Deacon.
Arthur B. Cole ....Junior Deacon.
Douglass L. Dunavan ....Senior Steward.
Frederick L. Fischer ....Junior Steward.
James M. Trenary ....Tyler.

Raised: Louis Wayland Merrifield, William Dyer Fullerton, Edgar Eldredge and Everett H. Butterfield.

Affiliated: Wilbur F. Heath, E. S. Jacobs and Adelbert J. Newell.

Demitted: John A. Dockter, Thomas E. MacKinlay, Timothy E. Gapen.

Died: David Robbins Gregg, John Dean Caton and Gilbert L. Thompson. Brothers Caton and Thompson were charter members of Occidental Lodge.

1896.

OFFICERS.

Adelbert J. Newell ....Worshipful Master.
Clarence Edward Tryon ....Senior Warden.
David Refior ....Junior Warden.
Charles E. Hook ....Treasurer.
David Batcheller ....Secretary.
James McManus ....Chaplain.
William Dyer Fullerton ....Senior Deacon.
Edgar Eldredge ....Junior Deacon.
Paul Teissedre ....Senior Steward.
Alva B. Holmes ....Junior Steward.
Alexander Hanna ....Tyler.

Raised: Elmer Ellsworth Gladfelter, John Duncan MacKenzie, John Hilliard, Harry Nicholas Weber, Samuel S. Pearson, Albert T. Lardin, Charles W. Campbell, Enos Ephraim Palmer and Elnathan P. Hatheway.

Affiliated: Hazen Hayward, H. L. Cawthorne, Davis N. Shipman, William Briggs Rowe and Samuel H. Heidler.

Demitted: James Briggs.

Suspended N. P. D.: Chas. B. Vosburgh, Jesse Emerson Morgan.

Initiated: Simeon W. Lauck and Wilson Hupp. Neither of these brethren ever took any further steps in Masonry.

Died: David LaFayette Grove, David Batcheller, John

A. Gray, Arthur Lockwood, John Brooks Rice, George Beatty and Reuben F. Dyer.

1897.

OFFICERS.

Adelbert J. Newell ....Worshipful Master.
William Dyer Fullerton ....Senior Warden.
Edgar Eldredge ....Junior Warden.
Charles E. Hook ....Treasurer.
James McManus (by dispensation May 15th.)...Secretary.
William H. Barnard ....Chaplain.
Elmer E. Gladfelter ....Senior Deacon.
Enos Ephraim Palmer ....Junior Deacon.
Alva B. Holmes ....Senior Steward.
Alexander Hanna ....Tyler.

Raised: Calvin D. Phillips, Enoch Yentzer, Jr., Sylvester Canfield, Irving De Forest Vincent, George Craft Dunaway, Edward Webster Bach, Charles Lewis Belrose.

Affiliated: Arthur W. Ladd.

Demitted: Davis N. Shipman, James E. Cooke, Henry G. Cotton, Jr., Frank A. Kendall, Samuel Caldwell, John Wesley Hackett and Edgar G. Dyer.

Suspended N. P. D.: Charles H. Angevine and John D. Hammond.

Died: William C. Weise.

1898.

OFFICERS.

William D. Fullerton ....Worshipful Master.
Joseph N. Dunaway ....Senior Warden.
Charles W. Campbell ....Junior Warden.
Charles E. Hook ....Treasurer.
James McManus ....Secretary.
William H. Barnard ....Chaplain.
James N. Downs ....Senior Deacon.
Alva B. Holmes ....Junior Deacon.

JOSEPH AVERY

Junior Warden 1846

Irving De Forest Vincent ....Senior Steward.
Sylvester Canfield ....Junior Steward.
Alexander Hanna ....Tyler.

Raised: Charles G. Deenis, Henry Phillips, Christian Gasser, Edward Danyel Ross, George John Kruse, Albert Warren Merrifield, Harry Gilman Cook, Angus Ross Mercer, Herbert Charles Wiley.

Affiliated: Harry J. Lee.

Demitted: Samuel H. Heidler, Cairo D. Trimble.

Suspended N. P. D.: John J. Carrick.

Died: James McManus. Was buried with Masonic honors.

1899.

OFFICERS.

Joseph N. Dunaway ....Worshipful Master.
Charles W. Campbell ....Senior Warden.
Walter F. Weese ....Junior Warden.
Charles E. Hook ....Treasurer.
Charles E. Pettit ....Secretary.
William H. Barnard ....Chaplain.
Albert B. Cole ....Senior Deacon.
Enoch Yentzer, Jr. ....Junior Deacon.
Angus R. Mercer ....Senior Steward.
Herbert C. Wiley ....Junior Steward.
Alexander Hanna ....Tyler.

Raised: Albert Clinton Bradish, Samuel Baldwin Bradford, Charles William Weeks, Charles Francis Wilson, William H. Gruhlkey.

Affiliated: William Herbert Higby.

Demitted: Irving De Forest Vincent, David Krouse, Samuel B. Bradford, Wilbur F. Heath.

Died: Daniel Fletcher Hitt, Adelbert J. Newell and Benjamin Padgett.

Reinstated: Samuel Degen.

F

1900.

OFFICERS.

William H. Higby ....Worshipful Master.
Herbert C. Wiley ....Senior Warden.
Angus R. Mercer ....Junior Warden.
Charles E. Hook ....Treasurer.
Charles E. Pettit ....Secretary.
William H. Barnard ....Chaplain.
Edward W. Bach ....Senior Deacon.
George C. Dunaway ....Junior Deacon.
William H. Gruhlkey ....Senior Steward.
Charles F. Wilson ....Junior Steward.
Alexander Hanna ....Tyler.

Raised: John Bergeson, William D. Duncan, Ralph Aylmer Green.

Affiliated: William Raley, William F. Jacobs, J. D. McCaughtry, Christopher J. Byrne, Robert Lucien Smith.

Initiated: John B. Haeberlin. No further record.

Demitted: Albert Warren Merrifield and Kimball White Leland.

Died: Clarence E. Tryon, Willis H. Ward.

Suspended N. P. D.: Charles Schaulin, John D. MacKenzie.

On March 7, 1900, the Grand Master granted a dispensation permitting Occidental Lodge to pass John H. Weaver to the degree of F. C. without having to pass an examination in the E. A. degree.

A Masonic school of instruction was held in Masonic hall, Ottawa, Ill., March 6, 7 and 8, 1900.

There were present M. W. C. F. Hitchcock, Grand Master; George M. Moulton, D. G. M.; W. B. Wright, S. G. W.; C. E. Allen, J. G. W.; J. H. C. Dill, Grand Secretary; Edward Cook, P. G. M.; A. B. Ashley, J. E. Evans, J. R. Ennis, H. T. Burnap and H. S. Hurd, Grand Examiners; S. S. Borden, G. O. Frederick, James John, E. F. Seavey,

J. S. Thomas, H. S. Albin, W. M. Burbank, Herbert Preston, W. B. Iott, James McCredie, J. J. Crowder, R. R. Strickler, D. D. Darrah, Arthur Goodrich and A. O. Novander, D. D. G. L.'s.

Two hundred seventy-eight names were registered, seventy-one Lodges and two grand institutions were represented.

1901.

OFFICERS.

William H. Higby ....Worshipful Master.
Herbert C. Wiley ....Senior Warden.
Harry N. Weber ....Junior Warden.
Charles E. Hook ....Treasurer.
Charles E. Pettit ....Secretary.
William H. Barnard ....Chaplain.
Charles F. Wilson ....Senior Deacon.
William H. Gruhlkey ....Junior Deacon.
George J. Kruse ....Senior Steward.
Albert C. Bradish ....Junior Steward.
Alexander Hanna ....Tyler.

Raised: William Alfred Dunaway, Henry Fehr, Albert Edmund Herzog, Eric Larson, Howard Halsey Bayne, George Grant Galloway, George Philo Hills, William Henry Seward, Otis Bach, Albert Jay Roberts, Samuel Erastus Bergeson and Herbert Le Roy Pettitt.

Affiliated: William Sherman Dick, John L. Clark, Nicholai A. Hauge.

Demitted: Nathaniel Earl Degen, Douglass Lee Dunavan and Henry Fehr.

Died: Joseph Cushman Hatheway, Samuel Degen, Peleg A. Hall and Isaac Reed.

1902.

OFFICERS.

Herbert C. Wiley ....Worshipful Master.

Joshua P. Rodgers ....Senior Warden.
Charles F. Wilson ....Junior Warden.
Charles E. Hook ....Treasurer.
Charles E. Pettit ....Secretary.
William H. Barnard ....Chaplain.
Christopher J. Byrne ....Senior Deacon.
Frederick L. Fischer ....Junior Deacon.
William H. Seward ....Senior Steward.
Otis Bach ....Junior Steward.
Alexander Hanna ....Tyler.

Raised: Richard Daniel Mills, Douglass Low McKenney, Herman Silver Blanchard, Frank Leslie Seward, William Willard Harden, Peter McGilvary Campbell, George Henry Ahlborn, Albert Morton Shaw, Emil J. Hoffman.

Initiated: Edward Justice Belrose. No further record.

Affiliated: Charles M. Buell, Benjamin F. Reeder.

Reinstated: Wesley W. Arnold and John D. Hammond.

Suspended N. P. D.: Warren C. Riale, Frank B. Logan and Abraham C. Godfrey.

Demitted: Charles W. Weeks, William S. Dick, Milo Putney, Louis Degen and Louis W. Hess.

Died: Royal D. McDonald, Charles J. Yockey.

Theodore Roosevelt, then Vice-President of the United States, received the third degree of Masonry in Mantinecock Lodge, No. 806, at Oyster Bay, New York, on April 24, 1902.

William D. Fullerton, appointed in October, 1902, District Deputy Grand Master, Ninth Masonic District.

1903.

OFFICERS.

Joshua P. Rogers ....Worshipful Master.
Edward W. Bach ....Senior Warden.
George P. Hills ....Junior Warden.

Charles E. Hook ....Treasurer.
Charles E. Pettit ....Secretary.
Howard H. Bayne ....Chaplain.
Herman S. Blanchard ....Senior Deacon.
Ralph A. Green ....Junior Deacon.
Emil J. Hoffman ....Senior Steward.
George H. Ahlborn ....Junior Steward.
Leman A. Rising ....Tyler.

Raised: Martin Luther Sample, Travers Herbert Barrett, Fred Andrew Bach, Charles Gideon Kelly, Earl Wayne Zibbell, William Beighel Myers, James Henry Monteith, Edward Holbrook Ashley, Harry Wallace Mitchell.

Affiliated: Robert J. Reid, Samuel Baldwin Bradford.

Reinstated: John D. MacKenzie and Abraham C. Godfrey.

Suspended N. P. D.: James N. Downs.

Demitted: John D. Hammond, George John Kruse, William B. Rowe.

Died: Solomon Degen, Calvin D. Phillips and Edward A. Nattinger.

By request of Occidental Lodge, the Fellow Craft and Master Mason degrees were conferred on Edward Holbrook Ashley by Palace Lodge, No. 765.

Wm. D. Fullerton, District Deputy Grand Master, Ninth Masonic District.

1904.

OFFICERS.

Edward W. Bach ....Worshipful Master.
Samuel B. Bradford ....Senior Warden.
Herman S. Blanchard ....Junior Warden.
Charles E. Hook ....Treasurer.
Charles E. Pettit ....Secretary.
William H. Barnard ....Chaplain.
James H. Monteith ....Senior Deacon.

Emil J. Hoffman ....Junior Deacon.
Earl W. Zibbell ....Senior Steward.
Harry W. Mitchell ....Junior Steward.
Leman A. Rising ....Tyler.

Raised: Charles Samuel Eells, William Scales, John Low Barnard, John Welch Willard, Ralph Melvin Cram, Benjamin Franklin Trumbo, William Huntington Hull, Edgar Freeman Bradford, Walter Garfield Button, Thomas Woods Smurr and Frank Forrest Follett.

Initiated: Albert Freeman Hornung, Lewis Edmond Weidemann and Oscar Frank Weidemann. No further record.

Reinstated: Charles B. Vosburgh, James N. Downs and George W. Green.

Affiliated: R. J. W. Briggs, Ellis Seed, Burdett Elmerine La Due.

Suspended N. P. D.: Charles E. Dunbar.

Demitted: James D. McCaughtry, George W. Green, Angus Ross Mercer.

Died: John Haws and William W. Harden.

Wm. D. Fullerton, District Deputy, Ninth Masonic District.

1905.

OFFICERS.

Samuel B. Bradford ....Worshipful Master.
Herman S. Blanchard ....Senior Warden.
James H. Monteith ....Junior Warden.
Charles E. Hook ....Treasurer.
Charles E. Pettit ....Secretary.
William H. Barnard ....Chaplain.
Emil J. Hoffman ....Senior Deacon.
Earl W. Zibbell ....Junior Deacon.
Harry W. Mitchell ....Senior Steward.
John L. Barnard ....Junior Steward.
Joseph A. Wilson ....Tyler.

Raised: George William Harris Dingman, Charles Wallace Long, William Henry Hinebaugh, Walter Elmer Speckman, Charles Lincoln Gapen, Samuel Emory Clegg, Troy Wilson Appleby.

Affiliated: James Madison McKeel, George John Waters, Walter Stephen Bradford.

Demitted: Harry E. Rockwood, Edward H. Ashley, Nicholai A. Hauge, Eric Larson.

Suspended N. P. D.: Charles M. Buell.

Died: Joanis O. Harris, Daniel C. Mills, Douglas Hapeman, David A. Cook and Frank G. King.

Wm. D. Fullerton, District Deputy Grand Master, Ninth Masonic District.

1906.

OFFICERS.

Herman S. Blanchard .... Worshipful Master.
Richard D. Mills .... Senior Warden.
Emil J. Hoffman .... Junior Warden.
Charles E. Hook .... Treasurer.
Charles E. Pettit .... Secretary.
William H. Barnard .... Chaplain.
Earl W. Zibbell .... Senior Deacon.
Harry W. Mitchell .... Junior Deacon.
John L. Barnard .... Senior Steward.
William Scales .... Junior Steward.
Joseph A. Wilson .... Tyler.

Raised: Elmer Ellsworth Roberts, Silas Eclips Kain, David Arthur Cook, John Sedgwick Rhoads, Carl Moody Provins, Carl Volkenannt.

Affiliated: William Sherman Myers.

Reinstated: Sidney V. Wise.

Demitted: H. L. Cawthorne, Samuel E. Bergeson and Sidney V. Wise.

Died: John F. Gibson, Clark B. Provins and Samuel Richolson.

Wm. D. Fullerton, District Deputy Grant Master, Ninth Masonic District.

THE SIXTIETH ANNIVERSARY

Of Occidental Lodge was appropriately celebrated on October 8, 1906, by a large assemblage of the members and their wives and families, in all more than two hundred being present.

William Osman, the venerable editor of the Ottawa *Free Trader,* who is the only Mason now living who was raised in Occidental Lodge sixty years ago, was to have been present and given some reminiscences of those old days, but, owing to a temporary indisposition, was unable to be present.

Richard D. Mills, acting Master, presided.

The address of John F. Nash, the oldest living Past Master of Occidental Lodge, was rich in historic lore. It was his pleasure to enjoy the personal acquaintance with every Master of the Lodge from date of organization in 1846.

Omitting the topic assigned to Brother Osman, the program, as carried out, was as follows:

Presiding officer, Richard D. Mills.

Called to order, 8:15 P. M.

Music, Oriental Quartet of Chicago.

Presiding officer's address.

"The Genealogy of the Lodge," W. L. Milligan.

Music, Quartet.

"The Early Masters of Occidental Lodge," J. F. Nash.

Music, Quartet.

"The Craft," A. T. Lardin.

"Greeting from our Daughter Lodge," George H. Haight.

Music, Quartet.

After which an elegant repast was served in the banquet room, where a general social good time was had.

BURTON C. COOK

Worshipful Master 1858

Those in charge of the event were congratulated upon the thorough success of the entire affair.

The general committee consisted of brothers J. N. Dunaway, W. D. Fullerton, C. E. Fisher, A. J. Roberts and S. B. Bradford.

The decorations, which were beautiful, consisted of autumn leaves, flags and potted plants, and were under the supervision of brother C. E. Fisher and a special committee.

The reception committee was composed of brother R. D. Mills and sister, Mr. and Mrs. H. W. Mitchell, Mr. and Mrs. J. L. Barnard, Mr. and Mrs. C. E. Pettit, Mr. and Mrs. C. E. Hook and Mr. and Mrs. David Refior.

Six subordinate Lodges, with a membership of one hundred and twenty-seven, owed allegiance to the Grand Lodge of Illinois in 1840. In 1906, the Grand Lodge of Illinois has upon her roll seven hundred and forty-three chartered Lodges, with a membership of more than seventy thousand Free Masons.

THE TYLER'S SWORD

Is of historic origin. It was carried by Lieut. John Gibson, during the war of 1812, at the battle at Lundy's Lane, Bridge Water and the storming of Fort Erie, and was presented to Occidental Lodge by his sons, William L. and Theodore Cunningham Gibson, both of whom saw military service in both the Mexican and Civil wars, truly inheriting the military spirit of their father. Brother Theodore C. Gibson is still a member of Occidental Lodge and one of its oldest members, having been raised in 1856.

TO THE MOCKING BIRD.

Sweet bird! Thou singest in the lonely woods,
  Far from great cities. There men dream of life,
And walk with blinded eyes, while grim care broods
  Upon their withered hearts; and snarling strife,
Flaps her foul wings before the eyes of men.
  Hate gnaws their hearts, and sordid avarice halts
Out from his noisome, miserable den,
  Clutching men's souls with yellow, shriveled hands,
Till each shrinks up; and filthy gods exalt
  To proud dominion, worse than Pagan lands
  Ever bowed down before;
While grasping handfuls of his glittering ore,
  He makes of it, oh wonder! tough strong bands,
To bind them to his sordid service and curst lore.

II.

Thou knowest nought of this, thy home is in
  The thick, green forests. There thou hast thy nest,
Where the leaves whisper with an earnest din,
  And gentle winds cool thy harmonius breast,
And there thy music fills the listening wood,
  And rings among the giant forest trees,
Waking up every slumbering solitude,
  And sending out with never ceasing flow,
A different strain on the wings of every breeze,
  Now loud, now soft, now rapid and then slow,
  With many a merry change;
And causing men, for thy wild, wondrous range,
  Halt in their journeying, and seek to know,
What emulous mad bird pours out a song so strange.

III.

Thou small philosopher, who laughs at
  All troubles of the world. I would that I
Thy mirth and merriment could imitate,
  And high above all care and trouble fly.
Thou art not drunk with rich, rosy wine,
  Joy ever nestles in thy happy heart,
Shaking a dewy influence divine,
  From his soft wings upon it. Thou whose throat
Surpasses in its powers all human art,

Who startles each lone bird with his own note,
As if thou wert his mate.
  Thou, whose fine song is heard, early and late,
Through the thick leaves and flowers to dance and float,
  Teach me the joyful secret of thy happy state!

IV.

It cannot be that thou, who now dost sing
  With so tumultous melody, while round
All spirits of the woods are hovering
  And drinking in with eager ears each sound,—
It cannot be that thou, too, dost conceal
  The sorrows of thy soul in stormy mirth,
Or that thou dost not in good earnest feel
  The joyance of thy song. That is for men
Who walk alone on the pain-peopled earth,
  And pour out melodies with tongue and pen
That all the world admire,
  While they with their own songs grow faint and tire,
And sadly droop and languish, even when.
  Their golden verse burns brightest with poetic fire.

1828.   —ALBERT PIKE.

THE MASONIC TEMPLE AND OPERA HOUSE.

Occidental Lodge held its first communications in the third story of the old Reddick block, on Court street, thence in the third story of the Glover and Cook building, now the Gedney block, at the corner of Court and Madison streets, where the brethren continued the practice of the mystic rites until about the year 1862, when more commodious rooms were secured on the fourth floor of the Hickling building, now owned by the estate of the late Andrew Lynch. (On Mr. Lynch assuming ownership of this building he had the fourth story taken down.) Occidental Lodge was at this time in a flourishing condition, and had accumulated several thousand dollars, which, with funds stored in the treasuries of Shabbona Chapter, R. A. M., and Ottawa Commandery, No. 10, K. T., it was deemed advisable to invest the same in real estate on which to erect at some time in the near future a Masonic home. Accordingly, on the 4th day of June, 1868, William S. Easton, Julius Avery and Samuel C. Walker, as trustees of Occidental Lodge, No. 40, A. F. & A. M., purchased from Abigail Holland and Edward C. Holland, the north sixty feet of lot three, and the north forty feet of lot four, in block eighty-nine, in State's addition to Ottawa, La Salle county, Illinois, for the sum of $4,500.00.

During the winter of 1868 and 1869 the brethren of Occidental Lodge began to devise means whereby they could erect a Masonic temple on the Holland property. It was finally decided that a Masonic association be incorporated for the purpose of constructing and maintaining a Masonic temple in Ottawa. On application to the Secretary of State a charter was duly issued March 26, 1869.

An Act to Incorporate the "Masonic Association of Ottawa."

Section 1. Be it enacted by the people of the state of Illinois, represented in the General Assembly, that William S. Easton, John F. Nash, Henry F. Clark, George J. Burgess, Francis L. Fiske, Thomas J. Wade, Robert McArthur, Robert Henning, William L. Gibson, and their associates and successors, be, and the same are, hereby created a body corporate, by the name and style of the Masonic Association of Ottawa, and by that name shall have perpetual succession, and sue and be sued, plead and be impleaded, may make all needful rules and regulations and by-laws for the government of the said company, and the control of its property, fix the amount of the capital stock of the said company, not exceeding the sum of one hundred thousand dollars, and appoint such officers and agents as it may deem necessary.

Section 2. Said company may receive by donation, buy, lease, mortgage, sell and convey real and personal estate for the purpose only of constructing and maintaining a Masonic temple in the city of Ottawa, in La Salle county, and may have and use a common seal.

Section 3. Said company shall consist of all persons who become stockholders therein, and in managing the affairs of said company each stockholder shall be entitled to one vote for each share owned by him, and shares shall not be less than seventy dollars, and Ottawa Commandery, No. 10, Shabbona Chapter, No. 37, and Occidental Lodge, No. 40, and Humboldt Lodge, No. 555, may each, as a Masonic order, become stockholders in said company. The stock of each of said orders shall be represented by one trustee to be appointed by each of said orders.

Section 4. Said company may organize when three thousand dollars is subscribed to the capital stock.

Section 5. As soon as said company is organized Samuel C. Walker, Julius Avery and William S. Easton shall convey to it all real estate held in trust by them for any of said orders, and each of said orders shall be considered subscribers to said stock for an amount equal to their several amounts advanced by them, respectively, for the purchase of said real estate.

Section 6. In case either of said Masonic orders cease to exist, the interest of said order in said company shall vest in, and belong to, said corporation for the benefit of the same.

Section 7. This act shall be a public act, and shall take effect after its passage.

(Signed)   F. CORWIN,
Speaker of the House of Representatives.
J. DOUGHERTY,
Speaker of the Senate.

Approved March 26, 1869.

JOHN M. PALMER, Governor.

United State of America, State of Illinois, ss.—Office of Secretary.

I, Edward Rummel, Secretary of State of Illinois, do hereby certify that the foregoing is a true copy of an act to incorporate the Masonic Association of Ottawa, approved March 26, 1869, now on file in this office.

In witness whereof, I hereto set my hand and affix the great seal of state, at the city of Springfield, this 10th day of April, A. D. 1869.

(Signed)   EDWARD RUMMEL,
[Seal.]   Secretary of State.

At a stated communication of Occidental Lodge, No. 40, A. F. & A. M., April 4, 1870, on motion of brother Thomas J. Wade, brother John Stout was unanimously chosen trustee to represent the interests of Occidental Lodge, No. 40, in the Masonic Association of Ottawa, in accordance with charter of said association.

THE MASONIC ASSOCIATION OF OTTAWA, ILLINOIS.

At a meeting of the corporators of the Masonic Association, of Ottawa, held at the office of Wm. S. Easton, on Monday evening, May 9, 1870, there were present Wm. S. Easton, Robert M. McArthur, George J. Burgess, Robert Henning, Francis L. Fiske, Thomas J. Wade, Wm. L. Gibson, John F. Nash and Henry F. Clark, corporators of the

Masonic Association of Ottawa, also Edward H. Smith, trustee of Shabbona Chapter, No. 37, R. A. M. W. S. Easton was chosen chairman and H. F. Clark secretary. The object of the meeting being to perfect the organization of the Masonic Association of Ottawa, under the charter from the people of the state of Illinois, Wm. S. Easton, J. F. Nash and H. F. Clark were appointed a committee to prepare and report by-laws, and at an adjourned meeting of the association, held May 23, 1870, Wm. S. Easton, from the committee on by-laws, reported the following, which were unanimously adopted:

By-Laws.

Article 1. The name of this Association shall be the "Masonic Association of Ottawa."

Article 2. The board of directors shall consist of nine persons, one of whom shall be the trustee appointed by Occidental Lodge, No. 40, A. F. & A. M., one the trustee appointed by Shabbona Chapter, No. 37, R. A. M., and one the trustee appointed by Ottawa Commandery, No. 10, K. T., to represent and vote on the stock which each of said Masonic bodies may hold in said association, and six other persons, stockholders in the association, who shall be Master Masons in good standing, who shall be elected on the 23d day of May, 1870, and annually thereafter on the first Monday in January, and shall immediately enter upon the duties of their office, and shall hold the same until their successors shall be elected and qualified. No person shall be declared elected who shall not receive a majority of all the votes cast. Vacancies happening from any cause shall be filled by appointment by the remaining members of the board for the unexpired term. In the case of suspension or expulsion of a member of the board of directors, or an officer of the association, by a Master Mason's Lodge, his official position shall be declared vacant, and the vacancy filled as provided for in Article 4 of these by-laws.

Article 3. All elections shall be by ballot, each share of stock being entitled to one vote, and the number of shares

THE MANSION HOUSE

The meeting place of Ottawa Lodge.   Reddick's Block is shown at the extreme left of the picture, where Occidental Lodge first met

of each stockholder shall be endorsed upon his ballot. Ballots may be cast in person or by proxy appointed in writing, the appointment to be filed with the secretary. Stock owned by Masonic bodies may be voted by the trustee of the body owning the stock.

Article 4. The officers shall consist of a president, vice-president, secretary and treasurer, who shall be chosen by the board of directors at their first regular meeting after their election, and shall hold their offices for one year, or until their successors are elected and qualified. Vacancies from any cause may be filled for the unexpired term by appointment by the board.

Article 5. No person shall be eligible to the office of president unless he be a director. His duties shall be to preside at all meetings of the board of directors, and call special meetings of the board for the transaction of business, to see that the officers perform their duties, and that these by-laws are enforced, and to do such other things as may be required of him by law. He shall not vote except to give the casting vote in case of a tie.

Article 6. The vice-president shall be chosen from the board of directors, and shall perform the duties of president in case of his absence, or inability to perform them from any cause. When acting as president he shall not vote except to give the casting vote in case of a tie.

Article 7. The secretary shall have the care and custody of the records and seal of the association. Shall record the proceedings of all meetings of the board of directors, and perform such other duties as they may direct or as may be required by law.

Article 8. The treasurer shall have the care and custody of the books of accounts and business papers of the association, as well as of all moneys, with authority to collect and receive the same, and shall pay out the same only on the order of the president, countersigned by the secretary, unless otherwise specifically directed by the board of directors. He shall give a bond in the sum of at least twenty thousand dollars, conditioned that he shall faithfully perform the duties of his office, and keep an account of all the moneys of the association which shall come to his hand while he shall

G

hold the office of treasurer, which bond shall be approved by the board of directors.

Article 9. There shall be a finance committee appointed by the president annually, at the first regular meeting of the directors, consisting of three members of the board, who shall serve for one year, and whose duty it shall be to examine all accounts and reports of the officers of the board, and make annual and other reports as directed by the directors.

Article 10. The capital stock shall be fifty thousand dollars, divided into shares of twenty dollars each, and shall be transferable upon the books of the association only upon a surrender of the certificate therefor, and the issuing of a new certificate for the same to the person or persons to whom the same is transferred. In case of the loss or destruction of a certificate of stock, to be established to the satisfaction of the board of directors, a new certificate or certificates may be issued to the person or persons entitled to same.

Article 11. In the case of the failure of any subscriber to the capital stock to pay any call or assessment upon or for any portion of his stock at the time same shall be made payable, the board of directors, at their option, may declare such subscription forfeited, and upon such forfeiture all moneys paid on such subscriptions, or stock, issued to such subscribers, shall become the absolute property of the association.

Article 12. Regular meetings of the board of directors shall be held on the second Monday in April, July, October and January, in each year, at the office of the association. Special meetings may be called at any time by the president or upon the written request of any two directors, left with the secretary, of which he shall give all the directors written notice. For business purposes, a majority of the board shall constitute a quorum, but no officer shall be elected unless by the votes of a majority of all the directors.

Article 13. The compensation of the various officers shall be fixed by the board of directors.

Article 14. These by-laws shall not be altered, amended or repealed except at a regular meeting of the board of directors, and then only when written notice of the proposed action shall have been given to each director at least thirty days previous to the meeting; provided, however, that by a unanimous vote of all the members of the board the same may be altered or repealed without notice.

Adopted May 23, 1870.

The subscription book being opened at this meeting, the following sums were duly subscribed:

Occidental Lodge, No. 40, A. F. & A. M., by John
    Stout, trustee $1,300.00
Shabbona Chapter, No. 37, R. A. M., by E. H.
    Smith, trustee 1,600.00
Ottawa Commandery, No. 10, K. T., by Julius
    Avery, trustee 600.00
John F. Nash 100.00
H. F. Clark 100.00
Wm. S. Easton 100.00
F. L. Fiske 100.00
R. M. McArthur 100.00
W. L. Gibson 100.00

At a meeting of the stockholders of the Masonic Association, held in the office of Wm. S. Easton, on Monday evening, May 23, 1870, Wm. S. Easton, H. F. Clark, J. F. Nash, F. L. Fiske, R. M. McArthur, W. L. Gibson, Julius Avery, E. H. Smith and John Stout were elected directors. R. Henning was afterwards appointed to fill the vacancy caused by the death of Julius Avery.

At a meeting of the directors of the association, Monday evening, May 23, 1870, the following officers were elected:

Wm. S. Easton, President.

R. M. McArthur, Vice-President.

H. F. Clark, Secretary.

John F. Nash, Treasurer.

And the president appointed F. L. Fiske, W. L. Gibson and John Stout to serve on the finance committee, and the by-laws adopted by the corporators were unanimously adopted by the directors.

At a stated communication of Occidental Lodge, No. 40, A. F. & A. M., Monday evening, Feb. 6, 1871, on motion of brother F. L. Fiske, the following preamble and resolution was adopted unanimously:

Whereas, Abigail Holland and Edward C. Holland, by their deed, dated June 4, 1868, did convey to Wm. S. Easton, Julius Avery and Samuel C. Walker, as trustees of Occidental Lodge, No. 40, A. F. & A. M., and the survivor or survivors of them, the north sixty feet of lot three and the north forty feet of lot four in block number eighty-nine, in the State's addition to Ottawa, La Salle county, Illinois, in trust for the uses and purposes following, to-wit: That said trustees, as trustees, shall have and hold said property for the sole and exclusive use, behoof and benefit of said Occidental Lodge, with full power in said trustees to mortgage, sell, convey and lease said property or any part thereof with the consent of said Occidental Lodge, to be expressed by a resolution of said Lodge at any regular meeting thereof. And,

Whereas, By an act to incorporate the Masonic Association of Ottawa, approved March 26, A. D. 1869, it is provided in section five of said act that as soon as said company is organized Samuel C. Walker, Julius Avery and William S. Easton shall convey to it all real estate held in trust by them for any Masonic orders in Ottawa, including Occidental Lodge, No. 40.   Therefore,

Resolved, That Wm. S. Easton (he being the sole survivor of trustees above mentioned) be, and he is, hereby authorized and directed to execute a quitclaim deed, conveying the title held by him, as aforesaid, in the real estate aforesaid, to the Masonic Association of Ottawa.

In compliance with said resolution, Wm. S. Easton executed a trust deed to the Masonic Association of Ottawa, Ill., February 18, 1871.

At a stated communication of Occidental Lodge, No. 40, A. F. & A. M., Tuesday evening, January 15, A. D. 1872, on motion of brother J. F. Nash, it was unanimously resolved that the Masons of Ottawa and vicinity desire the erection this coming season of a Masonic building, and that we make the attempt to raise the money for same, and, on further motion, Bros. W. S. Easton, J. F. Nash and John Stout were appointed a committee to solicit subscriptions for said purpose.

At this time the Masonic Association had subscribed to their capital stock four thousand one hundred dollars.

At an adjourned meeting of the directors of the Masonic Association of Ottawa, Monday evening, April 10, 1872, director Fiske offered the following resolution, which, on motion of director Nash, was unanimously adopted:

Resolved, That a committee of three be appointed by the president to procure plans and specifications for a Masonic hall and opera house. Said plans to be made on the basis of the sketches now in possession of the association, and made by Messrs, Carter & Drake, of Chicago, with such alterations and changes as the committee may suggest, provided that said plans for the building shall be made so that the estimated cost of said building shall not exceed $40,000.

John F. Nash, James N. Colwell and Robert Henning were appointed a committee to procure plans and specifications for building, in accordance with the above resolution, and, on motion of Nash, the president was added to the committee. At the same meeting Article 10 of the by-laws was amended, as follows:

"And no assessment shall be made upon any stock that has been paid in full."

At an adjourned meeting of the Masonic Association, May 3, 1872, the president was directed to take the necessary steps to procure title to the south twenty feet of lot 4, block 89, State's addition to Ottawa.

Director Henning filed his certificate as director from Ottawa Commandery, No. 10, K. T., in place of Julius

Avery, deceased, said appointment bearing date January 12. 1871.

The committee on plans and specifications reported that they had contracted with Carter & Drake for plans and specifications for building, designed for an opera house and Masonic hall, and presented the plan for the stone foundation for inspection. The committee on finance reported $23,000.00 subscribed to the capital stock.

At an adjourned meeting of the Masonic Association, May 7, 1872, president Easton presented a bond for a deed for the south twenty feet of lot 4, block 89, in the State's addition to Ottawa. The proposal of Colwell, Clark & Co. to excavate the cellar and construct the stone work for the Masonic building, according to plans and specifications, for the sum of $3,390.00, was received, and, on motion of Fiske, the work was let to Colwell, Clark & Co. for the above amount, to be performed under the direction of a building committee appointed by the president, consisting of F. L. Fiske, R. Henning and John Stout.

At a meeting of the directors of the Masonic Association, June 5, 1872, director Fiske from committee on building, reported proposals from W. F. Bushnell, Mendota, for a portion of the work for the sum of $39,600.00, and from Colwell, Clark & Co. for the entire work, as specified, for the sum of $44,312.00.

On motion of Fiske both bids were rejected.

At a meeting of the directors of the association, June 10, 1872, on motion of J. F. Nash, the proposition of Colwell, Clark & Co., to make the necessary excavations and erect the building on lots 3 an 4, in block 89, according to the plans and specifications furnished by Carter, Drake & Wright, for the sum of $44,312.00, was accepted. Accordingly a contract was subsequently drawn and signed by the president and secretary for the association.

Twenty per cent. of the capital stock of the association was made payable June 1, 1872, twenty per cent. July 1, 1872, and twenty per cent. every fifteen days after July 1, 1872. On July 16, 1872, the treasurer of the association was ordered to draw an order for $6,000.00, payable August 16, 1872, to be paid the contractors, which amount being due per estimate of the building committee.

At a meeting of the directors, August 10, 1872, it was agreed to execute to Colwell, Clark & Co., notes at sixty days, to the amount of $10,000.00, and that, in final settlement with said Colwell, Clark & Co., the association reimburse to them the discount on said notes.

Subscribers were slow in paying their subscriptions to the capital stock, and an assistant secretary was appointed, at a salary of $50.00 per month, to assist the secretary in collecting assessments. The building being completed, the building committee was directed to procure carpets and necessaries for putting home in order.

At a meeting of the association, October 22, 1872, director J. F. Nash presented a statement of finances, and a list of delinquent subscribers, and, on motion, such delinquent subscriptions, as in the opinion of the secretary and treasurer cannot be collected, were ordered placed in the hands of Messrs. Bushnell & Bull for collection. At this meeting the secretary was empowered to rent hall at such rates as in his discretion may be proper, and the president secretary and building committee were authorized to fix the rent of stores and offices, and to lease the same as may be seen best, and the building committee were authorized to hire a janitor.

On November 6, 1872, at a meeting of the directors of the Masonic Association, the secretary was instructed to procure insurance on Masonic temple building, not to exceed $30,000.00, said insurance to be for the benefit of Colwell, Clark & Co., as contractors and builders, and the cost of said insurance to be allowed to them in final settlement.

The new Masonic temple and opera house was completed late in the fall of 1872. Subscribers failed to come forward with ready cash to satisfy the contractors. The balance due, amounting to many thousands of dollars for extra work and finish, was heavy.

The Masonic association was unable to meet its obligations with the contractors. The association was confronted with a deficit in the treasury. Colwell, Clark & Co. secured the services of Washington Bushnell, and the beginning of the end of the Masonic Association was at hand.

At a meeting of the directors of the Masonic Association, December 31, 1872, Washington Bushnell, attorney for Colwell, Clark & Co., presented and made a statement of the basis of settlement in full for building Masonic temple and opera house, and extras. On January 3, 1873, Washington Bushnell, attorney for Colwell, Clark & Co., presented a written statement to the directors of the association, showing final adjustment of all accounts against the Masonic Association, and, on motion, a committee was appointed to examine the same and report at an adjourned meeting. The meeting then adjourned to meet again at 3 P. M., of the same day, at which meeting, on motion of brother Robert Henning, it was ordered that all former propositions for settlement with Colwell, Clark & Co. by the directors be rescinded, and, on motion of brother Ed. H. Smith, it was ordered that the settlement with Colwell, Clark & Co. be placed in the hands of an attorney, said attorney to be selected by the president and secretary.

At the annual meeting of the Masonic Association, held in the opera house block, January 4, 1873, brothers J. F. Nash, E. F. Bull, R. M. McArthur, George J. Burgess, Wm. S. Easton and E. L. Herrick were elected directors.

"THE EAST" OF OCCIDENTAL LODGE

At the next subsequent meeting of the directors, held in January, 1873, on motion of brother E. H. Smith, W. S. Easton was elected president for the ensuing year. On motion of brother J. F. Nash, brother John Stout was elected secretary for the ensuing year, and on motion of brother W. S. Easton, brother J. F. Nash was elected treasurer for the ensuing year. On motion of brother J. F. Nash, it was ordered that a settlement be made with Colwell, Clark & Co., upon the basis reported by director E. F. Bull, and, on motion of brother E. H. Smith, the following preamble and resolutions were adopted:

Resolved, Whereas, it appears upon the adjustment and settlement of the matters of differences between the Masonic Association of Ottawa, and John Colwell, Henry F. Clark and James N. Colwell, composing the firm of Colwell, Clark & Co., that there is now due said firm of Colwell, Clark & Co., upon their contract for building the opera house and Masonic hall building, and for their bill of extras (after allowing all proper deductions), the sum of twenty-two thousand three hundred and ninety-five and 50-100 dollars, upon which sum said Colwell, Clark & Co. are entitled to interest at the rate of ten per cent. from the first day of November, A. D. 1872, which would make the amount, principal and interest, due said firm on the first day of January, A. D. 1873, the sum of twenty-two thousand seven hundred and sixty-eight and 75-100 dollars;

And, whereas, on the first day of January, A. D. 1873, there was due Henry Smeeton, the sum of five hundred sixty-seven and 02-100 dollars for work done and material furnished to said Masonic Association, and to George J. Burgess, the sum of one thousand seventy and 47-100 dollars for plumbing, gas fitting and labor and material, and to Messrs. Carter & Drake, the sum of twelve hundred dollars for services as architects, and on note at National City Bank, balance due fifteen hundred dollars, all of which said sums so due said Smeeton, Burgess, Carter & Drake, and on said note, said Colwell, Clark & Co. have assumed and agree to pay, and which sums so assumed by them, added to the amount found due upon their contract, makes the sum total of twenty-seven thousand one hundred six and 24-100 dollars, now due them, on which they are justly entitled to interest from the first day of January, A. D. 1873;

And, whereas, the said Masonic Association are unable to pay the sum at present, and said Colwell, Clark & Co. have agreed to take notes, secured by a trust deed upon the real estate and buildings owned by said Association, for the sum so due, drawing interest at the rate of ten per cent. per annum, payable semi-annually, and notes and trust deed to bear date January 1, 1873, and to become due eighteen months after date; therefore, be it

Resolved, By the board of directors of said Masonic Association, that the president and secretary be, and they are, hereby authorized and directed to make, execute and deliver to said Colwell, Clark & Co. the notes of said association, amounting in the aggregate to the sum of twenty-seven thousand one hundred six and 24-100 dollars, dated January 1, 1873, to be due in eighteen months from date, drawing interest at the rate of ten per cent. per annum, interest payable semi-annually, and containing a provision that upon a failure to pay either installment of interest the whole of the principal sum and interest shall immediately become due and payable, and that in order to secure the payment of said notes they execute and deliver to E. Follett Bull, for the association, a trust deed upon the following described lots or parcels of real estate, situated in the city of Ottawa, county of La Salle and state of Illinois, viz.:

The north sixty (60) feet of lot No. three (3), all of lot No. four (4), in block No. eighty-nine (89), State's addition to Ottawa, including the stage scenery in the opera house and other fixtures, containing power of sale in the usual form, authorizing said trustee to sell and convey said premises, and all equity of redemption for the whole of said principal sum and interest, or either installment of interest, and also providing that said association shall keep the building situated upon said premises insured for the full amount due said Colwell, Clark & Co., and for their benefit, in first class companies, and that said association shall pay all taxes assessed against said real estate from time to time in due season, and that in default thereof the said Colwell, Clark & Co. may pay the same and add the amount so paid, either for taxes or insurance, to the sum due on said notes, and thereupon the principal sum and interest due upon said notes shall become immediately payable, and the provision of said trust deed enforced to secure its payment.

Resolved, That said trust deed shall contain all the provisions usually required by persons loaning money on real estate security, and inserted in trust deed or sale mortgage given to secure the re-payment of money loaned.

On motion of Herrick ordered that the committee appointed to rent the building be authorized to purchase coal, etc., that may be necessary for the opera house, and the clerk ordered to draw orders for same.

JOHN STOUT, Secretary.

In compliance with the above resolution, the Masonic Association of Ottawa executed trust deed to E. Follett Bull, dated January 1, 1873.

COPY OF ARTICLE OF AGREEMENT.

Article of Agreement, made this 13th day of January, A. D. 1873, between the Masonic Association of Ottawa, of the one part, and Colwell, Clark & Co., of the other part.

Witnesseth, That said association will reserve and pay to Colwell, Clark & Co. the net proceeds arising from the rent of their buildings, situated on the north sixty feet of lot No. three, and all of lot four, in block No. eighty-nine, in State's addition to the city of Ottawa, La Salle county, Illinois, and all moneys collected and stock subscriptions remaining unpaid, after paying the taxes and insurance, and all necessary repairs and expenses on said building, first to be applied to the payment of the semi-annual interest on their claims against the association, and the balance, if any, to be indorsed on the notes held by them at the expiration of each six months. Said Colwell, Clark & Co., hereby agree to raise the chimneys on the main buildings, as soon as practicable, two feet higher than now, to give the cornice over store front and north entrance one coat of pure white lead and oil paint, to grain the doors and woodwork in the vestibule, to paint the iron steps, to place two shelves in each closet and strips for clothes hooks and hooks therefor (hooks to be ten inches apart), to fill in with brick work from the storm wall to the chimneys in opera house, to properly brick up and cement the pediment and inside of iron cornice, to oil the main stair rail in the vestibule, to place such fastenings on all the windows as per specifications, to pay the following claims and debts against the association, viz.:

To Henry Smeeton ....$ 567.02
To Geo. J. Burgess......................... 1,070.47
To Messrs. Carter & Drake 1,200.00
On note at National City Bank, balance due.... 1,500.00
Dated at Ottawa, the day and year above written.

MASONIC ASSOCIATION OF OTTAWA,
By Wm. S. Easton, its President.
John Stout, Secretary.
COLWELL, CLARK & CO.

COPY OF RECEIPT.

Received of the Masonic Association of Ottawa, notes to the amount of $27,106.24, dated January 1, 1873, due in eighteen months, with interest at ten per cent., payable semi-annually, in full payment and satisfaction of all claims against said association for work done on opera house building, including contract and extras, and also including our responsibility in assuming the payment of the above receipted indebtedness, said notes secured by a trust deed to E. F. Bull, on north sixty feet lot No. 3, and whole of lot No. 4, in block 89, State's addition to Ottawa, January 15, 1873.

COLWELL, CLARK & CO.,
By Bushnell & Bull, their attorneys.

Four notes at $2,500.00, dated Jan. 1, 1873, due in 18 months, $10,000.00.

Two notes at $5,000.00, dated Jan. 1, 1873, due in 18 months, $10,000.00

Three notes at $1,500.00, dated Jan. 1, 1873, due in 18 months, $4,500.00.

One note, dated Jan. 1, 1873, due in 18 months, $2,-606.24.

Total, $27,106.24.

Interest on the above notes at ten per cent. per annum, payable semi-annually.

The new Masonic temple being completed, Occidental Lodge began to make arrangements for leasing the Masonic hall, and properly apportioning the amount of lease among the different Masonic bodies which were to meet in the hall. The question of appropriately furnishing the new hall was a momentous question for Occidental Lodge to handle, with their exchequer now empty, their cash assets having been invested in the stock of the Masonic Association of Ottawa.

At a stated communication of Occidental Lodge, No. 40, A. F. & A. M., Monday evening, October 21, 1872, brother W. S. Easton presented the following resolution in writing, as an amendment to our by-laws, by adding Section 5 to Article 2, which section reads as follows:

"There shall be appointed by the Worshipful Master, at each annual election, one trustee to represent and vote on the stock which this Lodge holds in the Masonic Association of Ottawa."

At a stated communication, November 15, 1872, the above amendment was adopted, and, on motion of brother B. S. Porter, it was ordered that the Worshipful Master appoint a committee of one, to confer with a like committee from Shabbona Chapter and Ottawa Commandery, to arrange for the rent of the new hall, and also for the frescoing of the same. Whereupon the Worshipful Master appointed brother Ed. H. Smith such committee.

At the annual communication of Occidental Lodge, No. 40, A. F. & A. M., Monday evening, December 2, 1872, brother John Stout was appointed trustee to represent Occidental Lodge in the Masonic Association of Ottawa.

At a stated communication of Occidental Lodge, No. 40, A. F. & A. M., Monday evening, December 16, 1872, on motion of brother E. L. Herrick, it was ordered that the Worshipful Master, Senior and Junior Wardens secure a lease of the new Masonic hall of the Masonic Association of Ottawa, for a term of ten years from January 1, 1873, at an annual rental not to exceed $500.00. Said officers were also authorized to loan from Shabbona Chapter, No. 37, R. A. M., two hundred and fifty dollars for one year, at ten per cent. interest.

During the winter of 1873 a social party was given by the Lodge, which netted them $51.00, also a Masonic dramatic association was organized and gave performances of a highly creditable character in the Masonic opera house, which netted Occidental Lodge $200.00.

At a stated communication of Occidental Lodge, No. 40, A. F. & A. M., Monday evening, February 17, 1873, brother Ed. H. Smith, who was appointed to arrange for frescoing, furnishing and adjusting rent of Lodge rooms as between the other Masonic bodies, reported as follows:

1872.
Nov. 22.	Smith and Cameron, fare to Chicago	$ 12.00
Nov. 25.	Moving stove	.75
Nov. 27.	Cover for flue	.12
Nov. 30.	Carrying coal	.60
Dec. 3.	Carrying coal	.60
Dec. 6.	A. Anderson, night watch	12.00
Dec. 14.	Wire cloth for ventilators	.50
Dec. 18.	Coal	3.50
Dec. 19.	Help moving furniture	1.00
Dec. 20.	Tacks	1.00
Dec. 20.	Cleaning floors, etc	8.45

1873.
Jan. 17.	Coal	3.75
Jan. 22.	Freight on carpet	1.50

	Thread for carpet	.25
	Taking up and cleaning old carpet	2.25
Nov. 6.	Dewey's bill, putting up stoves, etc.	3.05
Nov. 13.	Tacks, thread, etc	.35
Nov. 17.	Platt's bill, cleaning Lodge...	12.00
	Sewing and putting down carpet	8.00
	Planing floor	5.00
	T. B. Lauderback, keeping fires	20.00
	S. H. Reade, carpet	278.31
	J. Gaul, upholstering furniture	18.90
	H. Smeeton, stoves	74.70
	D. R. Gregg, putting down carpets	15.00
	G. J. Burgess, gas fitting.....	274.98
	Schobert & Knoeing, frescoing	550.00

$928.04

By cash $180.52
By cash 200.00

$380.52

List of creditors:
Schobert & Knoeing $210.00
G. J. Burgess 274.98
S. H. Peck 178.31
D. R. Gregg 15.00
H. Smeeton 74.70
J. Gaul 18.90
I. B. Lauderback 33.00
E. H. Smith, advanced 123.15

$928.04

Report of rent adjusted:
Humboldt Lodge $100.00
Ottawa Commandery 100.00
Shabbona Chapter 150.00

(Signed) E. H. SMITH, Com.

Which report was received and, on motion, adopted, and

brother Smith discharged from further duties in the premises, with the thanks of the Lodge.

On motion of brother Easton, it was ordered that orders
upon the treasurer be drawn for amounts reported by said
committee to be due from the Lodge, as follows:

Schobert & Knoeing $210.00
George J. Burgess 274.98
S. H. Peck 178.31
D. R. Gregg 15.00
H. Smeeton 74.70
J. Gaul 18.90
I. B. Lauderback 33.00
E. H. Smith 123.15
                                          ─────────
                                           $928.04

At the annual communication of Occidental Lodge, No.
40, A. F. & A. M., Monday evening, December 1, 1873,
brother Robert M. McArthur was elected Worshipful Master. John Stout was again appointed trustee to represent
Occidental Lodge in the Masonic Association of Ottawa for
the ensuing year.

At the following stated communication, the following
communication was received from brother R. M. McArthur,
which was accepted, and ordered that a dispensation for an
election of Worshipful Master be procured:

Ottawa, Ill., Dec. 15, 1873.
Worshipful Master, Wardens and Brothers of Occidental
    Lodge, No. 40, A. F. & A. M.:

I have the honor to acknowledge the official notice of
your action at the late annual election of officers of Occidental Lodge, No. 40, on the evening of the 1st inst., at which
time it was your pleasure to elect me as Worshipful Master
for the ensuing Masonic year. While I acknowledge the
high compliment thus conferred, I must say that it would
afford me much pleasure to serve you in that capacity, but

"THE WEST" OF OCCIDENTAL LODGE

Showing the finest Masonic Pillars in the United States

circumstances, which I cannot control, will compel me to decline that distinguished honor.

Very respectfully, your brother fraternally,

ROBT. M. McARTHUR.

Accordingly a dispensation was duly received from the Grand Master, a special election held, and Worshipful Brother H. F. Clark was elected Worshipful Master for the ensuing Masonic year.

The Masonic Association having failed to meet their financial obligations, entered into with Colwell, Clark & Co., in January, 1873, trustee E. Follett Bull was required to execute a trust deed to Colwell, Clark & Co., dated Jan. 17, 1874, consideration the amount of four notes due Colwell, Clark & Co., $27,106.24. This was the last transaction of the Masonic Association of Ottawa, and we trust that the Masonic bodies may never have such another experience in their efforts to secure a home.

At a stated communication of Occidental Lodge, No. 40, A. F. & A. M., May 4, 1874, a committee of three, consisting of brothers John F. Nash, Geo. J. Burgess and E. H. Smith, was appointed to confer with Colwell, Clark & Co., to whom the Masonic temple was transferred, in regard to leasing the lodge rooms.

At the following stated communication, May 18, 1874, the above committee reported that the proprietors had suggested to them the following terms for a new lease, viz., a lease for the term of six years from Jan. 1, 1874, at an annual rental of $300.00 for the first three years, and an annual rental of $500.00 for the last three years, and agreed, upon the execution of said new lease, to remit to the Lodge all back rent due up to the 1st day of January, A. D. 1874. On motion, the report was received and the committee discharged.

At a stated communication of the Lodge, August 17,

H

1874, a communication from Colwell, Clark & Co. was presented, notifying the Lodge that they had become proprietors of the building in which the lodge room of Occidental Lodge was situated, and that they did not consider the existing lease between the Lodge and the Masonic Association binding upon them.

At the stated communication of Occidental Lodge, No. 40, A. F. & A. M., September 21, 1874, it was ordered that the Worshipful Master and Secretary, under seal of the Lodge, or the Worshipful Master and Wardens, be authorized and directed to execute on behalf of Occidental Lodge a lease from the proprietors of the Masonic building, for the Masonic rooms, for six years from January 1, 1874, at a rental of $300.00 per year for the first three years and $500.00 per year for the next three years, rent payable quarterly. The said proprietors guaranteeing the Lodge from any payment for rent prior to said January 1, 1874. At the next stated communication the new lease was presented and accepted.

At the annual communication of Occidental Lodge, December 7, 1874, the Worshipful Master elect appointed brother Chas. M. Catlin trustee, to represent Occidental Lodge in the Masonic Association of Ottawa, for the ensuing Masonic year.

The last communication of Occidental Lodge held in the new Masonic Temple, before it was destroyed by fire, was Monday evening, December 21, 1874.

The temple was destroyed by fire on the night of December 27, 1874. On January 4th, following the loss of their temple by fire, Occidental Lodge secured a lease of the Metropolitan hall from Andrew Lynch, for an annual rental of $100.00, where they continued to meet until Colwell, Clark & Co., who began at once the rebuilding of the Masonic temple and opera house block, had same ready for occupancy, during the winter of 1875-6.

Occidental Lodge began preparing to put their new home in order as soon as Colwell, Clark & Co. began rebuilding, as will be observed from the following extracts from their records during the summer and fall of 1875.

At a stated communication, June 7, 1875, on motion, brothers F. L. Fiske, W. B. Titus and Ed. H. Smith were appointed a committee to confer in relation to the purchase of an organ.

At a stated communication, June 21, 1875, the committee, to whom was referred the matter of the purchase of an organ, made their report, and the committee was discharged, and, on motion, further action was posponed.

NEW HALL, 1875.

The pillars, "Jachim and Boaz," at the entrance to the middle chamber, were made by Colwell, Clark & Co., at a cost of $235.98, which amount was ordered paid at a stated communication, July 19, 1875. They are said to be the finest pillars for Masonic purposes in the United States.

At this same communication, the Worshipful Master appointed brothers J. F. Nash, F. L. Fiske, J. H. Widmer, W. B. Titus and E. L. Herrick a committee to examine into the condition of the finances of the Lodge, and also to see what furniture will be necessary for the new lodge room, and the probable cost of the same, including the frescoing of the hall, with a request that they report at the next regular communication of the Lodge.

At a stated communication, September 6, 1875, the above named committee made their report in the above premises, and, on motion, the Worshipful Master was added to said committee, and full power given them to fresco and furnish the new lodge room for occupancy, and the Secretary was ordered to draw orders on the Treasurer for such sums as may be certified as necessary by said committee in frescoing and furnishing said hall.

On motion of brother Thos. J. Wade, for the purpose of raising funds for frescoing and furnishing said hall, a loan was authorized of twelve hundred dollars, for a term of three years, at ten per cent. interest per annum, payable annually, for which the bonds of this Lodge shall be issued, with interest coupons attached, said coupons when due to be receivable for the dues of this Lodge. On further motion, brothers T. J. Wade, L. A. Rising and W. B. Titus were appointed a committee to solicit subscriptions for said loan.

At this meeting brother Wade was authorized to invite brother Robert Morris to be present at some future meeting and deliver his lecture upon "The Holy Land under the light of Freemasonry."

At a stated communication, Sept. 20, 1875, brother T. J. Wade, as chairman of the committee to solicit a loan of twelve hundred dollars, reported his progress, whereupon brother E. F. Bull presented the following preamble and resolutions, which were adopted:

WHEREAS, Several persons, members of Occidental Lodge, No. 40, A. F. & A. M., and others, have subscribed and promised to subscribe various sums of money for the purpose of assisting Occidental Lodge, No. 40, A. F. & A. M., in frescoing, painting and furnishing and otherwise improving the new lodge room of said Lodge, in the opera house block, for which said sums so subscribed, it is proposed to issue to each person so subscribing the obligations of the Lodge for the sums so subscribed and paid, such obligations to be made payable in three years, to draw interest at ten per cent. per annum, interest payable annually; and,

WHEREAS, It is desired on the part of said Lodge to secure the persons who may contribute funds for the purpose aforesaid; therefore, be it

Resolved, That the title of the furniture of the said Lodge, now owned by it, and that which shall be hereafter purchased, be, and the same is hereby vested in the Master of the said Lodge, and in his successors in office, and that the title thus vested in the Master be held for him in trust for the benefit of the persons contributing to the purposes set forth in the preamble.

Resolved, That the title of the said furniture continue to be vested in the Master of this Lodge and his successors in office until said sums shall be fully repaid with interest.

Resolved, That the Master and his successors be, and he is hereby directed to keep such furniture fully insured, and in case of loss to pay said persons so contributing the several sums due them, with interest, the balance of the insurance, if any, to accrue to the benefit of the Lodge.

At this communication, the Worshipful Master was instructed to secure a loan of $500.00 from Shabbona Chapter, No. 37, R. A. M., at ten per cent. interest per annum, and execute a note in the name of the Lodge, as security therefore.

At a stated communication, October 18, 1875, the Worshipful Master reported to the Lodge that he had secured a loan of $400 from Shabbona Chapter, No. 37, R. A. M., due in one, two, three and four years, with interest at the rate of ten per cent., and executed the notes of the Lodge as security therefor. At this same communication, brothers F. F. Crane, C. E. Pettit and J. E. Rathbun were appointed a committee to confer with the other Masonic bodies and with Ottawa Commandery, No. 10, who contemplated occupying the new hall, for the purpose of apportioning the rent to be paid by them for its use and occupancy, and report this action to the Lodge for confirmation. Upon the approval by the Lodge of said committee's action, the three principal officers were ordered to execute leases to the several bodies so occupying the hall, for the same time and upon the same conditions as the lease from Colwell, Clark

& Co. A committee was also appointed at this communication, consisting of brothers Jas. E. Rathbun, C. C. Glover, B. S. Porter, Solomon Degen and Fred F. Crane, to make arrangements for a social entertainment, to be held at some future time in the new lodge room, at the discretion of said committee.

Occidental Lodge moved into the new temple during the winter of 1875-'6, and continued making it their home until 1892, when, owing to their inability to make a satisfactory renewal of lease with F. A. Sherwood, who had purchased the property from Colwell, Clark & Co., secured a lease from King & Hamilton for their present home, which they moved into in 1892.

The Masonic bodies purchased the Columbus street school property from the Board of Education in 1906, the title running to brother Wm. D. Fullerton, in trust, on which they hope to be able to erect a Masonic temple in the near future.

CHAPTER II.

TO THE LIVING AND THE DEAD.

Let us drink together fellows, as we did in days of yore,
And still enjoy the golden hours that fortune has in store,
The absent friends remembered be, in all that's sung or said,
And love immortal consecrate the memory of the dead.

Fill every goblet to the brim—let every heart be filled
With kindly recollections, and all bitter ones be stilled.
Come round me, dear old fellows, and in chorus as we sing,
Life's autumn days shall be as glad as were its days of spring.

Drink, brothers, to the absent who are living, first of all,
While each familiar name and face we lovingly recall;
The generous and brave and good; the kind and frank and true,
Who knew not how false word to speak or what was base to do.

We see the faces of the dead, they hover in the air,
And looking on us lovingly, our mirth they seem to share.
O dearly loved, though ye have gone to other stars or spheres,
We still have for you thoughts of love and consecrated tears.

Pour a libation rich with love upon the graves that hold
The ashes of the gallant hearts that long ago grew cold;
And swear that never party feuds or civil war shall break
Our bonds of love, and enemies of friends and comrades make.

The dead are with us always; friends, let us their teachings heed.
"Forgive thy brother, if he err," they eloquently plead;
"Let bygones be bygones," they cry, "let the old love revive,
And on the altars of your heart keep friendship's fire alive."

It is better far to love than hate, for nations as for me.
Let us hope the old good humor soon will bless the land again,
But if the politicians still should wrangle, scold and fight,
Their quarrels shall not break the ties that we re-knit to night.

Our autumn days of life have come, the frosts begin to fall,
Beyond the dark, deep river, hark! we hear old comrades call.
To the dead and living, whom each loves, let each his goblet fill,
And the memory of the dead shall make the living dearer still.

—ALBERT PIKE.

119

Col. D. F. Hitt. He was a physician and a zealous Mason, and was the first among the brethren to suggest the organization of a Masonic Lodge in Ottawa, and was the chief factor in obtaining a dispensation from Grand Master Breckenridge of Kentucky in 1839, and was elected the first Secretary. He died December 3, 1840. Col. Hitt said he was a noble and generous man.

DAVID WELLS. Proprietor of Mansion house, in partnership with the firm of Wells & Fulton. It was in this historic hostelry that Ottawa Lodge held their meetings. Was Treasurer of Ottawa Lodge, No. 114, Grand Lodge of Kentucky, in 1840. Moved to Galena, Illinois, and affiliated with Far West Lodge, No. 29, June 18, 1842.

LUCIUS WOODRUFF. No authentic records, but is supposed to have been the father of Alson Woodruff, and came here from New York in 1834. He was Senior Deacon of Ottawa Lodge in 1839-'40, and died August 29, 1840.

HENRY J. REID came from Pennsylvania in 1834. Was a carpenter by trade. Stepfather of the late George Hayward. Rode on horseback from Ottawa, Ill., to Louisville, Ky., to session of the Grand Lodge of Kentucky in August, 1840, and brought the charter of Ottawa Lodge, No. 114, back with him. Was Junior Deacon in 1839-'40. Died about 1892. Was Second Lieutenant in Dickey's company during war with Mexico.

WILLIAM K. BROWN kept hotel near the acqueduct at time of building. Was known as "Billy-K.-Brown." Was Steward and Tyler in 1840. Affiliated with Occidental Lodge, No. 40, and was Tyler of No. 40 in 1848 and 1849.

LUTHER WOODWARD. Came from Taunton, Mass., and set-

tled in Deer Park township in 1836. Built
a dam and saw-mill on the Vermillion river.
Was justice of the peace several years.
Went to California in 1850; returned in 1853
to Deer Park, and died in 1857. He demitted from Ottawa Lodge at the organization
of St. John's Lodge, No. 13, at Vermillionville, and was Master of St. John's Lodge in
1841, 1842 and 1845.

THOMAS RUSSELL. Could only learn that brother Russell
(a merchant) lived in South Ottawa. No
record of his membership since 1841.

JABEZ FITCH came from Plattsburg, N. Y., in 1835, and located in South Ottawa. He was a merchant,
and County Treasurer of La Salle county
from 1839 to 1846. He moved to New
York, where he died.

SETH B. FARWELL came from New York to Ohio, thence to
Ottawa in 1835. Lawyer. Was State's Attorney for La Salle county in 1838. Went
to Sacramento, Cal., where he was elected
judge. Died on the plains.

CHARLES G. MILLER came to Ottawa in 1836 from Cumberland county, Pa. Was justice of the peace
in Ottawa several years. Lived on west side,
near Catholic church. Affiliated with Occidental Lodge, No. 40, in 1846.

JONATHAN STADDEN, son of Wm. Stadden, Dayton. Miller.

JOHN R. HALL. No record showing him a member of Ottawa Lodge since 1840. He was named in
petition for dispensation for Master of Ottawa Lodge, but records from Grand Lodge
of Kentucky show H. D. Gorbett named as
such in the dispensation granted December
19, 1839, by George Breckenridge, Grand
Master of Kentucky.

G. F. WEAVER, associated with John Hise as editor Ottawa *Free Trader.* Returned to Harrisburg, Pa.

ASA HOLDRIDGE came from New York in 1833, and settled near Bailey's Point, on the Vermillion river, in Eden township. Was a successful farmer. Demitted from Ottawa Lodge, No. 114, to organize St. John's Lodge, No. 13, at Vermillionville, Ill. Was Junior Deacon of St. John's Lodge in 1842. Was Treasurer in 1843. Senior Warden in 1844. Died in 1866.

WILBUR F. WALKER came from Virginia to Ottawa in 1825. Brought up the first keelboat on the Illinois river. Son of Dr. David Walker and brother of George E. Walker, first Sheriff of La Salle county, and of David Walker of Occidental Lodge. W. F. Walker never affiliated with Occidental Lodge. He resided in Ottawa until 1857, when he moved to Union county, Ill. Wilbur F. Walker was an Indian trader, and kept a general store on what was known at that time as Water street.

CHAMPLIN R. POTTER came from New York to Eden township in 1834. He was a farmer and surveyor. Held office of justice of the peace several years, and was member of the Legislature in 1853. He died September 27, 1860.

BENJAMIN THOMPSON came from Massachusetts in 1834. Merchant and partner of W. H. W. Cushman. Died in Massachusetts in 1846.

WILLIAM L. DUNAVAN came from Licking county, Ohio, in 1830. Settled in Rutland township in 1831. Affiliated with Occidental Lodge in 1848.

REUBEN MILLER, brother of Charles Miller, and of "Uncle" John Miller, of Freedom township. Came from Cumberland county, Pa., to Dayton township in 1834. Moved to Salt Lake in an early day, and became an elder in the Mormon church.

T. BOLE.   No record since 1840.

GILBERT L. THOMPSON became charter member of Occidental Lodge (see record of Occidental Lodge).

WILLIAM STADDEN came from Lucas county, Ohio, to Dayton in May, 1830.   Built a flouring mill in 1831.   Was Sheriff of La Salle county 1834 and 1835.   State Senator 1839-1840-1841. He was a prominent and useful citizen.   He died in 1848.   His son, Richard Stadden, was a member of Occidental Lodge, No. 40.

JAMES CLARK came from England to Ohio and thence to Utica in 1833.   Contractor on Illinois and Michigan canal, and was the pioneer manufacturer of hydraulic lime from the Trenton limestone, and greatly enriched himself.   He was a member of the Legislature in 1871. He never affiliated with Occidental Lodge. Assisted in organizing Cement Lodge, at Utica, in 1859, and became a member thereof.

J. COOPER.   No record other than his membership in Ottawa Lodge.   There are strong probabilities that this is Jesse Cooper, who at one time was Secretary of Western Star Lodge, organized at Kaskaskia, Ill., in 1805, and came to this part of Illinois with Warren Brown, who was also a member of Western Star Lodge, and in 1841 was charter member of St. John's Lodge, No. 13, organized at Vermillionville, 1841.   He was raised in Western Star Lodge June 6, 1818.   Demitted March 6, 1819.

JAMES ARMOUR.   Confectionery and bakery.   Affiliated with Far West Lodge, No. 29, at Galena, Ill., in 1844, and was one of the Deacons in 1848. Demitted and affiliated with Acacia Lodge,

No. 67, La Salle, in the 50s. He was a brother of John Armour, a prominent grain merchant in Ottawa during the 50s and 60s, and father of Mrs. Dr. Ryburn.

ALSON WOODRUFF came from Onondago county, New York, in 1834. County Commissioner in 1840. Sheriff in 1836 and 1837. Affiliated with Occidental Lodge, No. 40.

ABRAM R. DODGE, lawyer. Boarded at Fox River house. No record since record of Ottawa Lodge. Was member of the Legislature in 1840-'41.

AARON DANIELS received F. C. degree in Ottawa Lodge. Went to California in 1849; returned and received M. M. degree in Occidental Lodge, No. 40.

WALTER LAMB. No record since 1841.

JOHN J. HILL. No record except received the E. A. degree in 1840, and was on the roll as such in 1841.

L. W. LISKE. No record except received the E. A. degree in 1840.

THOMAS W. HENNESSEE came from Ireland to La Salle in 1837. Was a practicing physician in La Salle for twenty years. Then moved to a farm in Dimmick township. Was initiated in Ottawa Lodge in 1840 and raised in St. John's latter part of 1841. Treasurer of St. John's Lodge in 1842. Junior Deacon 1844-'45.

GEORGE H. NORRIS. Worshipful Master in 1841. (See record in Occidental Lodge with which he affiliated.)

LORENZO P. SANGER came from Ohio to Ottawa in 1838. Member of David Sanger & Sons, who had contract and built the aqueduct across Fox river for Illinois and Michigan canal. Was Senior Warden Ottawa Lodge in 1841. No record since.

MARSHALL MILLER. Shoemaker. Treasurer of Ottawa
Lodge in 1841. Affiliated with Occidental
Lodge.

JAMES W. ROBERTS. Senior Deacon in 1841. No other
record. Civil engineer at building of Illinois
and Michigan canal.

THOMAS A. HENRY. Carpenter. Tyler 1841.

PATRICK M. KILDUFF came from Harper's Ferry, Va., to
Peru, Ill., in 1838. Was mayor of Peru, Ill.,
in 1838. Was mayor of Peru, magistrate and
County Commissioner in 1849. Affiliated
with St. John's Lodge, No. 13. (His widow
died February, 1907.)

Z. H. BAXTER. No record since 1841.

SAMUEL RODEKER. No record since 1841.

ADAM LAMB. No record since 1841.

HERMAN WHITEHEAD. Affiliated with St. John's Lodge,
No. 13, in 1842, and on December 15th
was elected Senior Warden, and the year following elected Treasurer of St. John's
Lodge. He died in 1849.

CHRISTIAN H. CHARLES, and wife, Juliet Mann, came from
Tioga county, Pa., to Peru, Ill., in 1837.
Was a merchant in partnership with John
Hoffman, brother-in-law and father of Asa
Mann Hoffman, who was Secretary of Occidental Lodge several years. Brother Charles
was the father of Mrs. Washington Bushnell,
one of Ottawa's most estimable ladies, now
residing on the east side. He died July 20,
1840.

WILLIAM CHUMASERO came from New York to Peru, Ill.,
in 1838. A lawyer of fine ability. Initiated
in Ottawa Lodge, No. 114, in 1841. Raised
in St. John's Lodge, No. 13, at Peru, Ill.,
April 29, 1847, and on June 13, 1847, was
elected Junior Warden.

JOHN H. McFARREN (or McFARRAND) came from Tioga
county, New York, to La Salle in 1837. Railroad contractor. Was contractor on Illinois
and Michigan canal and on the Illinois Central railroad. Was postmaster several years;
also member board of supervisors. No Masonic record since 1841.

THE GOLDEN WEDDING.

O Love, whose patient pilgrim feet
    Life's longest path have trod,
Whose ministry hath symboled sweet
    The dearer love of God;
The sacred myrtle wreaths again
    Thine altar as of old
And what was green with summer then
    Is mellowed now to gold.

Not now as then the future's face
    Is flushed with fancy's light,
But memory, with a milder grace,
    Shall rule the feast to-night.
Blest was the sun of joy that shone,
    Nor less the blinding shower,
The bud of fifty years agone
    Is love's perfected flower.

O memory! Ope the mystic door!
    O dream of youth return!
And let the light that gleamed of yore
    Beside this altar burn.
The Past is plain; 'twas love designed
    E'en sorrow's iron chain;
And mercy's shining thread has twined
    With the dark warp of pain.

So be it still! O thou who hast
    That younger bridal blest
Till the May morn of love has passed
    To evening's golden rest,
Come to this later Cana, Lord,
    And at thy touch divine,
The water of that earlier board
    To-night shall turn to wine.

—DAVID GRAY.

LORENZO LELAND

Treasurer in 1846

PERSONNEL OF OCCIDENTAL LODGE,
No. 40, A. F. & A. M.

GEORGE H. NORRIS came to Ottawa in 1835. Owned ferry on Illinois river. County Surveyor ten years. Justice of the peace. Admitted to the bar in 1839. Established the bank of Ottawa, now the First National bank. Helped to build the Ottawa starch factory. Moved to Colorado, thence to Florida. Was Worshipful Master of Ottawa Lodge, No. 114, Grand Lodge of Kentucky. Charter member and first Worshipful Master of Occidental Lodge, U. D., 1845. Demitted 1859.

REV. CHARLES V. KELLEY. Episcopalian minister. Was member of Ottawa Lodge, No. 114, Grand Lodge of Kentucky. Was charter member of Occidental Lodge, No. 40, and Senior Warden and Chaplain 1845. Demitted in 1859.

ALSON WOODRUFF came from New York in 1834. Was County Commissioner in 1840. Sheriff in 1836-'37. Member of Ottawa Lodge, No. 114, Grand Lodge of Kentucky. Charter member of Occidental Lodge, No. 40, and Junior Warden while Lodge worked under dispensation in 1845. Died in 1856.

GILBERT L. THOMPSON came to Ottawa in 1840. Kept a drug store a number of years. Was member of Ottawa Lodge, No. 114, Grand Lodge of Kentucky. Was charter member of Occidental Lodge, No. 40, and at an election of officers held June 23, 1846, was elected Senior Warden. Was Worshipful Master in 1847. He died October 26, 1895, and was buried by Occidental Lodge, according to his wish. He was held in high esteem as a citizen and a Mason.

MARSHALL MILLER was a shoemaker. Member Ottawa
Lodge, No. 114, Grand Lodge of Kentucky.
Charter member Occidental Lodge, No. 40,
and Senior Deacon in 1846. Expelled June
21, 1867, for disobedience of summons to
pay dues.

JOSEPH AVERY was a carpenter. Member of Ottawa Lodge,
No. 114, Grand Lodge of Kentucky. Char-
ter member Occidental Lodge. Junior Warden in 1846. Demitted in 1850.

WILLIAM K. BROWN. Hotel-keeper. Member of Ottawa
Lodge, No. 114, Grand Lodge of Kentucky.
Was charter member of Occidental Lodge.
Was Tyler Occidental Lodge in 1848-'49.
Died August 16, 1850. Is buried in Ottawa
avenue cemetery, and his marble tombstone
has square and compass engraved on it.

MILTON H. SWIFT came to Ottawa in 1838. Lawyer and
financier. President First National bank several years. Raised in Occidental Lodge December 11, 1845. Secretary in 1846. Died
May 14, 1886.

JOHN DEAN CATON came to Ottawa in 1842. Was among
the first lawyers in Chicago. Circuit Judge
of circuit embracing La Salle county, and,
subsequently, Chief Justice of the Supreme
Court of Illinois. Accumulated a fortune.
Raised in Occidental Lodge December 11,
1845. Was installed Worshipful Master of
Occidental Lodge October 10, 1846, the day
Occidental Lodge was constituted; also Worshipful Master in 1851 and 1852. He continued his membership until July 20, 1895,
when he died in Chicago, and is buried in
Ottawa avenue cemetery.

LORENZO LELAND came to Ottawa July, 1835. Lawyer.
Clerk Circuit Court 1842-'49, and Supreme
Court 1848-'67. Raised in Occidental Lodge

January 2, 1846. Elected Treasurer June 23, 1848; also Treasurer 1847-'48. Died August 26, 1881.

THEOPHILUS LYLE DICKEY came to Ottawa in 1839. Lawyer. Elected Judge Circuit Court 1842; also Judge Supreme Court 1875. Captain in Mexican war. Colonel Fourth Illinois cavalry during Rebellion, and chief of cavalry on Gen. Grant's staff. Raised in Occidental Lodge January 17, 1848. Was Steward in 1853. Demitted 1855, when he moved to Chicago, where he had opened a law office in 1854, to enable him to pay off his old debts contracted during the financial panic of 1837. At the expiration of twenty-one years he paid all his debts with interest. Of him, the Hon. Leonard Swett said before the U. S. Circuit Court, Northern District of Illinois: "Judge Dickey and his sons and sons-in-law have rendered marked services to their country, and deserve a monument more enduring than brass." * * * "In all that adorns a man, Judge Dickey was as bright as a new blade. He was quick and bright in his standard of honor. His professional and judicial character was pure, and was never even sullied by suspicion or accusation."

JOSEPH OTIS GLOVER came to Ottawa in 1835. Lawyer. United States District Attorney 1869. Ex-mayor of Ottawa. Raised January 17, 1846. Elected Secretary June 23, 1846. Demitted July 5, 1877.

MAURICE MURPHY. Nursery. Raised in Joliet Lodge, No. 10, May 20, 1841, while working U. D. Was one of the brethren to whom the Grand Master granted a dispensation to form and open Occidental Lodge, U. D., and was named as Senior Warden, but no further record of his membership can be found, and the returns of Occidental Lodge, U. D., 1846, show Rev. Chas. V. Kelley Senior Warden.

BURTON C. COOK came to Ottawa in 1835. Lawyer. State's Attorney 1846-1850. State Senator 1852 and 1856. Member of Peace Conference in 1861 at Washington. Elected to Congress 1864, 1866, 1868 and 1870. Raised in Occidental Lodge February 24, 1846. Senior Deacon 1846. Junior Warden 1847. Senior Warden 1848. Worshipful Master 1858. Demitted April 21, 1873.

WILLIAM OSMAN came to Ottawa from Dauphin county, Pa., where he was born June 18, 1820. Veteran Mexican war. Editor Ottawa *Free Trader* since 1840. Is now the oldest editor in the United States, as well as the oldest living member of Occidental Lodge, having been raised June 13, 1846, and continued his membership to the present time, 1906. A member sixty years. Secretary 1848-'49. He was clerk of Illinois House of Representatives 1851-'56. Postmaster 1856-'58 and 1886-'90. And now, nearly 90 years of age, continues to write editorials for his paper, and attends divine services at the Episcopal church, of which he has long been a member and warden over forty years, every Sunday morning.

JAMES LAFFERTY. Carpenter. Made a Mason in Pittsburg, Pa. Affiliated with Occidental Lodge in 1846, and was appointed Tyler August 21, 1846. Was Junior Warden 1847-'48. Demitted in 1850. Affiliated with Humboldt Lodge, No. 555, in the 80s. Died May 25, 1900.

JACOB B. RICH. Tinsmith for John Manley. Affiliated 1846. Died at sunrise October 23, 1849. Buried with Masonic honors in Ottawa avenue cemetery.

THOMAS TRACY lived in South Ottawa. Farmer. Came there in 1831. Affiliated in 1846. Demitted in 1853, and removed to Michigan, where he died.

JOHN PALMER. Millwright. Affiliated 1846. Died July 22, 1852. Buried in Ottawa avenue cemetery.

DANIEL LYONS. Reported as member in 1846, but no further record can be found.

SHELBY DOOLITTLE. Lawyer. Raised November 30, 1846. Died at Princeton, Ill., January 9, 1848.

WILLIAM REDDICK. Merchant, capitalist and politician. Came from Fayette county, Pennsylvania, 1835. Settled on the Vermillion river. Sheriff La Salle county in 1838. Was also State Senator several terms. Raised November 30, 1846. Demitted February 2, 1871. Father of the Reddick liquor law. Bequeathed to the city of Ottawa his homestead, valued at $60,000, and a fund of $125,000 for a public library (Reddick's library); also to La Salle county one hundred acres of fine land adjoining the county asylum.

DANIEL F. NEWTON. Hardware merchant. Affiliated 1846. Demitted 1859. Moved to Ohio.

EDWARD BACON. Affiliated in 1846 while Lodge was working U. D. No further record.

DAVID WALKER. Came to Ottawa in 1826 with his father, Dr. David Walker. Druggist. Was mayor of Ottawa and president Board of Education. Member Ottawa Lodge, No. 114, Grand Lodge of Kentucky. Affiliated in 1846. Demitted January 16, 1865.

WILLIAM HENRY LAMB WALLACE. Son of John Wallace, of Deer Park. Lawyer. State's Attorney 1852-'57. Served in Mexican war. Colonel Eleventh Illinois infantry, and Brigadier General at Pittsburg Landing, where he was killed, April 10, 1862. Raised 1846. Worshipful Master 1848-1849. (See obituary.)

MATHEW DIAMOND. Affiliated 1846. Demitted same year, and affiliated with St. John's Lodge, No. 13, Peru, Ill.

H. W. HOPKINS. Physician. Raised 1847. Junior Warden 1848. Demitted 1855.

WILLIAM BALDWIN. Merchant at Rockwell. Came to Farm Ridge in 1837. Affiliated with Occidental Lodge in 1847. No further record.

WILLIAM RICHARDSON came from New York in 1837. Kept hotel in Peru several years, then bought a farm in South Ottawa. Dealt largely in cattle. Affiliated in 1847. Suspended N. P. D. 1851. Was father of Wm. Capron Richardson, grain merchant in 50s and 60s.

WILLIAM PALMER came to Ottawa in 1836. Wagonmaker. Raised 1847. Demitted February, 1877.

MADISON E. HOLLISTER came to Ottawa in 1836. Lawyer. Circuit Judge. Postmaster under President Van Buren. Consul Buenos Ayres 1866. Chief Justice Supreme Court Idaho Territory 1871-1877. Raised April 6, 1847. Demitted March 6, 1876.

A. KEEFER. Hotel-keeper at Norway. Affiliated in 1847. Suspended N. P. D. 1851. Went to California, via Isthmus of Panama, in 1849.

Extract from letter to Mr. Phelps, of Ottawa, from A. Keefer: Panama, December 7, 1849. Dear Sir: I met Mr. Clark, of Chicago, to-day, and as he will pass through Ottawa, I seize the opportunity to drop you a few lines. I arrived here about the first of last month, and found about 1,200 persons here, waiting passage through to San Francisco. The fare is very high. Cabin passage on board the steamers is utterly out of the question, while steerage passage tickets sell as high as $600.00, and they are paying $300.00 passage on sail vessels. * * * I would advise all who think of going to California to stay at home. If they could see the misery I have seen they would not think of going. * * * My respects to all.

A. KEEFER.

Again, December 3, 1849, he writes: Dear Sir: I have purchased a ticket for a passage on the Unicorn, which leaves for San Francisco on the 15th of January. I paid $350.00 for my ticket, which is fifty dollars less than I have heard of them being sold since I left the Isthmus. I will get to San Francisco on the 10th of February. * * * With respects to all, etc.

A. KEEFER.

THOMAS L. BOUGHTON. Merchant. Initiated in 1847. Died May 31, 1850. Buried in Ottawa avenue cemetery.

JOHN S. DILLON. Raised November 5, 1847. Connected with building of Illinois and Michigan canal. No further record.

GEORGE W. HYDE. Civil war veteran. Raised November 5, 1847. Demitted 1851.

BENJAMIN BEACH FELLOWS. Civil war veteran. Came to Mission township in 1835. Elected County Treasurer 1851. Moved to Ottawa. Raised August 7, 1848. Killed by railroad train March 3, 1893.

JOHN M. QUIMBY. Merchant. Raised October 15, 1849. Tyler 1851. Worshipful Master 1853. Demitted 1859.

A. DELANO. Affiliated 1848. Went to Sacramento in 1849. Suspended N. P. D. 1851.

From Sacramento, California, A. Delano wrote a letter to Judge Caton March 12, 1850, in which occurred the following passage: * * * "During my uncertain absence I commend my family to the care of my brethren, and I doubt not they

will receive from you such attention as your kindness of heart will prompt you to bestow. * * *
Fraternally yours,   A. Delano."

F. Mandelbaum. Merchant. Affiliated 1848. Junior
Warden 1849-'50. Demitted 1852, and
moved to California.

Nelson Knickerbocker. Proprietor country tavern on
Chicago road. Raised April 2, 1849. No further record.

N. P. Heath. Affiliated 1849. Senior Deacon 1850. Demitted 1859.

Henry Beach. Merchant. Affiliated 1849. Secretary
1850. Demitted 1851.

Philo Lindley. Clerk of Circuit Court 1849 to 1856, inclusive. Raised December 23, 1850. Secretary 1851. Worshipful Master 1856. Killed
near Altoona, Ga., June 24, 1864. Was
Quartermaster of Fifty-third Illinois regiment at time of his death.

George S. Fisher. Banker. Initiated 1851. No further
record.

Arthur Lockwood. Dry goods merchant and justice of the
peace. Raised 1851. Died November 18,
1896.

Edward C. Henshaw. Retired. Captain Henshaw's battery during Civil war. Raised 1851. Demitted 1852.

William L. Gibson. Furniture, drugs and grain. In
Mexican war. Colonel Fifty-third Illinois
during Civil war. Raised 1851. Senior
Warden 1861. Demitted October 1, 1877.

William I. Moore. Raised 1851. Demitted and affiliated
with Bureau Lodge, No. 112, Princeton, Ill.,
February 19, 1853. Was farmer near Princeton, Ill.

JOHN FISKE NASH. Born in Massachusetts, December 24, 1824. Came to Ottawa, 1847. Admitted to the bar in 1849. Clerk of the Circuit Court and Recorder of Deeds from 1855 to 1861. Was clerk of the Senate of State of Illinois 1861-1865. Assisted in organizing the First National bank in 1865. Was cashier thirty-five years. Is now retired, and passing his declining years most happily with his family at his beautiful home on Illinois avenue, where the social element of his nature is frequently exemplified in entertaining his host of friends. The oldest living Past Master of Occidental Lodge. He was raised 1851. Senior Deacon 1853, '54, '55. Junior Warden 1856. Senior Warden 1857. Worshipful Master 1863-'64. Was Grand Commander Grand Commandery Knights Templar 1877. He has discharged every duty assigned him with marked ability.

CHARLES G. MILLER. Justice of the peace. Member Ottawa Lodge, No. 114, Grand Lodge of Kentucky. Affiliated 1851. Demitted February 18, 1867.

A. N. TUTTLE. Merchant. Affiliated 1851. Demitted 1855.

H. M. KELLOGG. Affiliated 1851. Died 1855.

DANIEL D. THOMPSON. Physician. Raised 1852. Died May 31, 1877. Worshipful Master Occidental Lodge 1861-'62.

R. EATON GOODELL. Raised 1852. Demitted 1855. Came to La Salle county in 1834 with his parents and settled near Buffalo Rock. Sheriff 1851-'53. Married daughter of Governor Matteson and moved to Springfield.

LIPMAN RAUGH. Clothier. Raised 1852. Secretary 1855. Demitted May 6, 1867.

WILLIAM P. THOMAS (or THOMPSON). Raised 1852. Died 1855.

A. VOGLE. Raised 1852. No record since 1856, when his name appeared among the list of members.

J. J. FINLEY. Marble cutter. Raised 1852. No record since 1853, when his name appeared among list of members.

DAVID McINTOSH. Raised 1852. Demitted 1855. Clerk for Walker & Hickling. Moved on farm near Mud Creek, Livingston county, Illinois.

P. V. N. SMITH. Raised 1852. No record since 1853. when his name appeared among the list of members.

WILLIAM MASTERS. Affiliated 1853. Tyler 1853. No further record.

ALEXANDER W. MAGILL. Grain merchant. Raised 1853. Died July 9, 1867.

IRA POTTER. Veterinary surgeon. Civil war veteran. Affiliated 1852. Suspended N. P. D. November 18, 1867.

BRADFORD C. MITCHELL. Mexican war veteran. Served with Colonel Dickey in Mexican war. Gunsmith and ammunition store. A valued citizen, and father of brother Marshall B. Mitchell. Raised 1853. Died September 18, 1858, and buried with Masonic honors.

JARED B. FORD. County Treasurer 1851-'54. Raised 1853. Died November 9, 1862.

ISAAC V. WATERMAN. Insurance and real estate. Raised 1853. Secretary 1853. Demitted December 1, 1863.

GEORGE CHURCHILL. Stonemason. Raised 1853. Demitted January 4, 1869.

JOSHUA WHITMORE. Clerk. Affiliated 1853. Junior Warden 1854. Demitted 1860 and affiliated with Pontiac Lodge, No. 294.

HENRY MOORE. Merchant. Affiliated 1853. Demitted 1856.

ISAAC REED. Farmer. Affiliated 1853. Died November 11, 1901.

DAVID ROBBINS GREGG. Veteran Mexican war. Musician for Fifty-third Illinois during the Rebellion. Raised 1854. Tyler 1854-'56, and several years during the 70s and 80s. Died March 23, 1895.

WM. C. SMITH. Lawyer. Raised 1854. Junior Deacon 1856. Demitted 1860.

W. W. CAVARLY. Physician. Son of Lyman D. Cavarly and son-in-law of A. W. Cavarly. Raised 1854. Died 1855.

AVON PEARSON. Clerk in postoffice. Civil war veteran. Raised 1854. Secretary 1858. Demitted October 6, 1865. Reaffiliated June 3, 1867. Demitted November 4, 1878.

THEODORE HAY. Physician. Raised 1854. Died September 26, 1860.

AZRO C. PUTNAM. Physician. Raised 1854. Civil war veteran. Demitted October 2, 1865.

SILAS W. CHEEVER. General store. Raised 1854. Demitted May 16, 1881.

REUBEN SHERMAN. Plasterer. Raised 1854. Suspended N. P. D. November 18, 1867.

ROBERT HICKLING. Merchant. Raised 1854. Demitted in 1858, and moved to Kansas.

WESLEY B. HALL. Engineer. Civil war veteran. Raised 1854. Senior Deacon 1858. Demitted January 5, 1880.

JOHN STOUT. Dry goods merchant. Insurance. Affiliated 1854. Demitted October 19, 1874. Reaffiliated May 16, 1892.

OLIVER CROMWELL GRAY. Lawyer. Veteran Mexican

war. Affiliated 1854. Worshipful Master
1854. Died July 31, 1871. Was a prominent
lawyer and brilliant man.

JOHN MORRILL. Farmer. Veteran Mexican war. Colonel
Sixty-fourth Illinois, Civil war. Brevet Brigadier General. Raised 1854. Demitted January 5, 1880.

THOMAS JEFFERSON WADE. Hotel proprietor. Affiliated
1854. Worshipful Master 1855, 1857 and
1859. Was Grand Lecturer for several years.
Died September 6, 1886.

MOSES R. BROWN. Grain merchant. Raised 1854. Demitted October 1, 1866.

DANIEL C. STONE. Physician. Affiliated 1854. Demitted
1855. Reaffiliated 1857. Demitted April 6,
1868.

RICHARD STADDEN. Attorney. Affiliated 1854. Demitted
1859.

HENRY P. BRUNKER. Gunsmith. Civil war veteran. Raised 1854. Died February 20, 1872.

CHAUNCEY U. WADE. Livery stable. Affiliated 1854. Died
February 15, 1863.

WILLIAM FRY. Cabinet-maker. Raised 1854. No record
since 1858, when his name appeared among
list of members.

FRANK C. FLORY. Meat market. Affiliated 1854. Died
1863.

S. F. DENNING. Minister. Raised 1854. Chaplain 1855.
Demitted 1857.

JOHN D. MORGAN. Dry goods merchant. Affiliated 1854.
Suspended N. P. D. 1873.

FRANCIS WARNER. Sheriff La Salle county 1854-'55, 1858-
'59. Raised 1854. Demitted April 19, 1875.
Moved to Chicago.

DANIEL FLETCHER HITT. Came to Ottawa 1830. Civil

engineer. In Blackhawk and Mexican wars. Colonel Fifty-third Illinois during Rebellion. Became a member of Far West Lodge, No. 29, Galena, Ill., July 31, 1841. Affiliated Occidental Lodge 1854. Demitted 1857, and assisted in organizing Cement Lodge, at Utica, 1859. Reaffiliated with Occidental Lodge January 7, 1884. Died May 11, 1899. A brave, noble and generous man.

RICHARD THORNE. Sheriff 1853-'54. Received E. A. degree 1855. No further record.

ELI PLUMB was initiated 1854. No further record.

CHARLES TURK. Farmer. Raised 1855. Died 1863.

AARON DANIELS. Came from Ohio in 1831. Farmer Rutland township. Received Fellow Craft degree in Ottawa Lodge, No. 114, Grand Lodge of Kentucky. Raised Occidental Lodge 1855. Demitted same year. Moved to Kansas.

R. W. BATCHELLER. Farmer. Raised 1855. Demitted 1856. Reaffiliated June 6, 1865. Demitted October 16, 1865.

WILLIAM P. GREGG. Civil war veteran. Printer. Raised 1855. Demitted June 6, 1870.

EDWARD L. HERRICK. Quartermaster One Hundred Fourth Illinois in Civil war. Deputy County Clerk. Raised 1855. Treasurer 1856-'57. Senior Warden 1862. Died April 11, 1876.

JAMES HATHEWAY. Proprietor Geiger house. Raised 1855. Demitted 1857.

HENRY G. COTTON, SR. Probate Judge 1847. Probate and County Judge to November, 1856. Raised 1855. Died November 1856.

JOSEPH WARE. Storekeeper. Raised 1855. Demitted 1856.

CASPER MEYER. Brewer. Record shows initiated 1855, and no further record at hand.

OCTAVIUS R. HANBURY. Brewer. Affiliated 1855. Returned to England. Died 1875.

CHARLES PHILLIPS. Affiliated 1855. Demitted 1855.

F. S. McNAMARA. Physician. Affiliated 1855. Suspended N. P. D. 1860.

WILLIAM BERG (or BREG or BERGE). Affiliated 1855. Demitted 1861.

R. F. TAYLOR. Initiated 1856. No further record. Farmer near Newark.

WILLIAM L. F. JONES. Initiated 1856. Raised in, or affiliated with, Meteor Lodge, No. 283, Sandwich. Was a farmer and blacksmith, living near where Millington is now located, only on west side of Fox river.

LEVI MASON. Superintendent Gas Co. Raised 1856. Junior Deacon 1857. Junior Warden 1858. Senior Warden 1859. Worshipful Master 1860. Demitted April 17, 1865.

THEODORE CUNNINGHAM GIBSON. Furniture dealer. Elected member Legislature 1862. County agent for several years. Insurance. In Mexican war. Major Fifty-third Illinois during the Civil war. Raised 1856. Junior Deacon 1861. Senior Warden 1863. A continuous member for fifty years, with honors worthily worn.

WILLIAM C. FASH. Shoemaker. Raised 1856. Suspended N. P. D. 1860.

ORVILLE L. MOORE. Telegraph operator. First to receive messages by sound. Fellow Craft only 1856. Died January 14, 1859.

GEORGE M. DUNAVAN. Farmer. Raised 1856. Demitted May 5, 1873.

GEORGE W. FUCHS. Civil war veteran. Groceries. Raised 1856. Demitted November 18, 1867. Charter member Humboldt Lodge, No. 555.

WARREN R. BRUNDAGE. Farmer. Initiated 1856. No further record.

HENRY D. GORBETT. Farmer and preacher. Lived in South Ottawa. (See record Ottawa Lodge, Grand Lodge of Kentucky.) Affiliated 1856. Demitted 1859, to assist in organizing Cement Lodge, at Utica.

WILLIAM L. DUNAVAN. Came to La Salle county from Ohio in 1830. Farmer in Rutland township. Was a member of Ottawa Lodge, No. 114, Grand Lodge of Kentucky. Affiliated with Occidental Lodge 1856. Demitted September 15, 1884. Made honorary member on same date. Moved to Texas and died there.

QUINCY D. WHITMAN. Civil war veteran. Revenue collector. Affiliated 1856. Secretary 1860. Demitted June 3, 1872.

EDWARD M. WADE. English capitalist. Affiliated 1856. Demitted September 20, 1871. Lived on west bluff. Returned to England.

JOSEPH FORD. Farmer. Civil war veteran. Raised 1857. Suspended N. P. D. April 5, 1875.

JOHN M. EARLE. Wagonmaker. Firm, Slack & Earle. Raised 1857. Demitted 1861.

MOSES D. CALKINS. Proprietor Farmers' house, South Ottawa. Raised 1857. Suspended N. P. D. April 4, 1875.

JEREMIAH ABBEY. Raised 1857. Demitted April 5, 1869.

ERASMUS N. JENKS. Farmer. Raised 1857. Demitted 1866.

WILLIAM K. STEWART. Civil war veteran. Contractor. Raised 1857. Demitted November 1, 1869. Affiliated May 6, 1878. Tyler 1859. Senior Deacon 1877, 1879. Senior Warden 1884, '87, '88, '89. Junior Warden 1882-'83.

JOSEPH CUSHMAN HATHEWAY. Physician. Raised 1857.

Senior Steward 1860. Demitted April 18, 1887. Affiliated May 3, 1897. Died January 21, 1901.

C. H. FROESE. German teacher in old Mechanics hall. Initiated and passed 1857. No further record.

ADOLPH HOFFMAN. Affiliated 1857. Suspended N. P. D. 1860.

SAMUEL EYSTER. Carpenter. Affiliated 1857. Died June 29, 1881.

COLEMAN OLMSTEAD. Came to Ottawa 1835. Farmer. Affiliated 1857. Demitted September 5, 1881.

HOLMES SLADE. Raised 1858. Demitted 1860.

HOSEA B. WILLIAMS. Paper manufacturer. Raised 1858. Suspended N. P. D. May 4, 1889.

SIMON ZIMMERMAN. Furniture. Raised 1858. Died October 8, 1894.

SOLOMAN DEGEN. Stock dealer. Raised 1858. Worshipful Master 1878, '79 and '80· Died January 4, 1903.

NELSON CONARD. Farmer. Raised 1858. Demitted 1860.

JULIUS CAESAR AVERY. Lawyer. Member firm Gray, Avery & Bushnell. Ex-mayor of Ottawa. Democratic candidate for Congress 1870. Raised 1858. Senior Deacon 1859. Died November 22, 1870.

FRANKLIN D. SWEETZER. Agricultural implements. E. A. 1858 only.

SAMUEL A. W. JEWETT. Methodist minister. Raised 1858. Chaplain 1859. Demitted December 17, 1866.

SAMUEL C. WALKER. Lawyer. Son of George E. Walker, the first Sheriff of La Salle county. Raised 1858. Died October 23, 1869.

REUBEN SHERMAN. Plasterer. Raised 1858. Suspended N. P. D. November 18, 1867.

WILLIAM REDDICK

Who, by will, endowed Reddick's Library

DANIEL H. ASHTON. Clothier. Affiliated 1858. Suspended July 5, 1867.

HENRY F. CLARK. Contractor. Member firm Colwell, Clark & Stebbins. Affiliated 1858. Secretary 1859. Junior Warden 1861. Worshipful Master 1874, '75 and '76· Died January 10, 1877.

THERON JOHNSON. Clerk in store. Affiliated 1858. Demitted 1864.

JAMES RUSS MURPHY. Druggist. Affiliated 1858. Died 1859.

JOHN F. LAMB. Farmer Rutland township. Raised 1859. Demitted December 9, 1863, to become charter member of Marseilles Lodge, No. 417.

ISAAC R. HILL. Carpenter. Raised 1859. Demitted May 20, 1867.

S. O. WADE. Livery. Raised 1859. Demitted April 7, 1862.

WILLIAM G. EARLE. Civil war veteran. Painter. Raised 1859. Suspended N. P. D. April 5, 1875.

WILLIAM A. McCULLOM. Farmer. Raised 1859. Demitted June 6, 1865.

SAMUEL D. COLE. Retired farmer. Raised 1859.

JAMES KEELER. Miller. Raised 1859. Demitted 1860.

HENRY GONDOLF. Harnessmaker. Raised 1859. Demitted November 18, 1867, to become charter member of Humboldt Lodge, No. 555.

CALVIN WILSON. Carpenter. Raised 1859. Junior Steward 1860. Demitted July 21, 1862.

SAMUEL THANHAUSER. Clothier. Raised 1859. Senior Deacon 1860-'61. Demitted December 6, 1869.

R. P. VORCE. Superintendent Cushman foundry. Raised 1859. Demitted 1861.

FRANK J. CRAWFORD. First lieutenant Company E, Fifty-third Illinois, Civil war. Lawyer. Raised 1859. Demitted November 18, 1878.

GEORGE H. WALKER. Justice of the peace. Raised 1859. Demitted 1862.

HERMAN ALSCHULER. Clothier. Affiliated 1859. Demitted November 18, 1867, to become charter member of Humboldt Lodge, No. 555.

ROBERT H. PIERCE. Miller. Affiliated 1859. Demitted March 20, 1865.

WELLS WAITE. Farmer. Affiliated 1859. Demitted January 7, 1867.

J. W. FAY. Banker and lawyer. Affiliated 1859. Demitted March 20, 1865.

GEORGE J. BURGESS. Machinist and plumber. Affiliated 1859. Tyler 1863-'64. Senior Warden 1868. Worshipful Master 1869. Senior Deacon 1871. Demitted October 2, 1876.

OLIVER P. STUMPH. Druggist. Raised 1860. Demitted November 6, 1865.

SAMUEL R. LEWIS. Farmer. Treasurer La Salle county 1855-'58. State Senator 1878-'80. Initiated 1860. No further record.

GEORGE B. SCHNEIDER. Cigar and tobacconist. Raised 1860. Died April 11, 1872.

CORNELIUS CLAGGETT. Cabinetmaker. Raised 1860. Demitted June 21, 1867.

JOHN BROOKS RICE. Ex-mayor of Ottawa. Lawyer. Raised 1860. Died February 24, 1896. Brother Rice was one of the beacon lights of the La Salle county bar. Was honored in his profession and a friend to the lawyer student.

JOEL F. PIERCE. Meat market. Raised 1860. Demitted May 3, 1880.

GEORGE W. ADAMS. Clerk City bank. Nephew L. H. Eames. Board of Trade, Chicago. Raised

1860. Treasurer 1861. Senior Deacon 1862. Demitted April 7, 1862.

C. A. MATHEWSON. Initiated 1860. No further record.

C. S. C. CRANE. Detective. Tyler 1861-'62. Affiliated 1860. Demitted October 15, 1877.

JOHN POWE. Farmer. Raised 1861. Died May 26, 1882.

ELIAS C. HATHEWAY. Merchant and fruit grower. Deputy Sheriff 1882-'86. Raised 1861. Demitted January 5, 1880.

N. A. HEINFARETER. Raised 1861. Demitted September 7, 1863.

A. H. STROBEL. Harnessmaker, and toll-keeper Fox river bridge. Raised 1861. Demitted November 18, 1867, to become charter member Humboldt Lodge, No. 555.

THOMAS H. CLARK. Principal Columbus street school. Raised 1861. Demitted December 16, 1872.

WM. S. EASTON. Insurance. Raised 1861. Secretary 1863. Senior Warden 1864. Worshipful Master 1865, '66, '67, '68 and '70. Demitted June 2, 1877. District Deputy Grand Master 1868.

ALBERT WOLFORD. Meat market, southwest corner La Salle and Madison streets. Raised 1861. Demitted April 16, 1866.

DOUGLAS HAPEMAN. Editor and book store. Colonel One Hundred Fourth Illinois during Civil war. Raised 1861. Died June 3, 1905.

E. J. CAMPRELL. Merchant. Raised 1861. Demitted June 6, 1865.

CHARLES STOUT. Dry goods merchant. Raised 1861. Demitted July 3, 1871.

D. M. CLARK. Dry goods merchant. Raised 1861. Demitted November 20, 1871.

GEORGE CLOUD. Son of Joseph Cloud. Raised 1861. Demitted May 19, 1862.

CHARLES HUSTON. Druggist. Clerk for E. Y. Griggs. Resides Columbus, Ohio. Raised 1861. Demitted March 16, 1868.

SHELDON B. GRISWOLD. First lieutenant Company B, Fifty-third Illinois, Civil war. Grain dealer. Raised 1861. Suspended N. P. D. November 18, 1867.

E. G. HALBERT. Shoe merchant. Raised 1861. Demitted October 2, 1865.

S. B. OLMSTEAD. Affiliated 1861. Demitted February 7, 1865.

E. S. HOBERT. Dentist. Affiliated 1861. Suspended N. P. D. August 18, 1884.

JOHN COLWELL. Contractor. Firm Colwell, Clark & Stebbins. Affiliated June 17, 1861. Suspended N. P. D. August 21, 1876.

HENRY C. NASH. Bank teller. Raised 1861. Treasurer several years. Suspended N. P. D. March 4, 1889.

JOHN R. CAMERON. Dry goods and postmaster. Raised 1861. Demitted February 6, 1888.

J. O. HARRIS. Surgeon Fifty-third Illinois, Civil war. Physician, insurance and real estate. Raised January 13, 1862. Died January 10, 1905.

DAVID P. JONES. Lawyer. Ex-mayor of Ottawa. Raised February 17, 1862. Died November 7, 1884. Was State's Attorney 1861-'64.

EDWARD L. ARMSTRONG. Clothier. Raised February 22, 1862. Suspended N. P. D. March 17, 1873.

GUSTAVE KOCH. Brass worker. Raised March 3, 1862. Demitted March 5, 1866.

MOSES OSMAN. Bookstore. Veteran Mexican war. Raised March 10, 1862. Demitted March 5, 1866.

P. S. McKay (or Mackey). Raised March 17, 1862. Demitted July 7, 1862.

G. B. Morgan. General store. Raised March 24, 1862. Demitted November 6, 1865.

F. F. Maybury. Druggist. Firm Dimmick & Maybury. Raised April 7, 1862. Demitted December 3, 1866.

Frank F. Brower. Lawyer. Ex-mayor of Ottawa. Raised April 28, 1862. Died April 8, 1870.

George B. Mitchell. Restaurant. Raised June 2, 1862. Demitted March 21, 1881.

Absalom B. Moore. Methodist minister. Colonel One Hundred Fourth Illinois during the Civil war. Clerk County Court 1865-'68. Affiliated June 2, 1862. Died July 7, 1879.

George S. Stebbins. County Treasurer 1859-'62. Raised July 7, 1862. Died November 29, 1867.

Samuel Harvey. Lawyer. Affiliated January 27, 1862. Demitted July 7, 1862.

David H. Porter. Merchant. Affiliated July 21, 1862. Demitted October 18, 1869.

W. H. Williams. English capitalist. Raised September 30, 1862. Demitted April 8, 1864. Returned to England.

Christian Irion. Grocer. Raised November 17, 1862. Demitted November 18, 1867.

John A. Carton. Farmer. Raised December 1, 1862. Demitted July 15, 1867. Moved to Ackley, Iowa.

Samuel Poundstone. Farmer. Raised February 2, 1863. Demitted February 6, 1888.

Charles Houghtaling. Captain Houghtaling's Battery during the Civil war. Raised February 16, 1863. Demitted February 18, 1867.

W. W. GARDNER. Civil war veteran. Toll-keeper Illinois river bridge. Raised March 2, 1863. Demitted December 20, 1873.

T. Y. MICKLE. Traveling salesman. Raised March 7, 1863. Now resides in St. Louis, Mo.

GEORGE BEATTY. Dry goods merchant. Firm, Lynch, Beatty & O'Kane. Raised March 9, 1863. Died February 25, 1896.

RICHARD W. KING. Box manufacturer. Raised March 23, 1863. Demitted November 15, 1873.

ROBERT M. MCARTHUR. Physician. Raised April 6, 1863. Died August 12, 1886.

GEORGE WOEFEL. Farmer. Raised April 13, 1863. Demitted September 19, 1864.

JOSEPH GONDOLF. Harness manufacturer. Raised June 1, 1863. Demitted November 18, 1867, to become charter member of Humboldt Lodge, No. 555.

JAMES C. WARNER. Telegraph instrument manufacturer. Raised June 8, 1863. Demitted June 19, 1866. Affiliated November 16, 1868. Junior Warden 1871. Demitted June 21, 1875.

JUSTUS HARRIS. City marshal and deputy Sheriff. Raised August 7, 1863. Tyler 1872-1875. Died November 27, 1888.

SYLVANUS H. HILL. Raised September 7, 1863. Demitted November 21, 1870.

THOMAS C. FULLERTON. Farmer. Lawyer. Captain in Sixty-fourth Illinois during Civil war. Raised February 25, 1864. Demitted February 25, 1866. Affiliated December 3, 1883. Senior Warden 1885. Senior Deacon 1886. Died August 2, 1894. Was Republican candidate for Congress, and died during the campaign.

THOMAS I. CONGER. Farmer. In Sixty-fourth Illinois during the Civil war. Raised February 25, 1864. Killed at battle of Atlanta, Ga., 1804.

FRANK G. KING. Pump manufacturer. In Fifty-third Illinois during Civil war. Raised April 21, 1864. Died October 30, 1905.

SAMUEL I. HANEY. Farmer. Raised April 21, 1864. Killed in battle during the Civil war in 1864.

S. M. PETTINGILL. Farmer. Raised July 19, 1864. Died January, 1865.

J. B. SMITH. First Lieutenant Company B, Fifty-third Illinois, Civil war. Received E. A. degree April 4, 1864, and died the same month. Clerk in Kimball's hardware store.

JAMES SPENCER. Farmer. Received E. A. degree August 3, 1863. No further record.

DANIEL WAY. Received E. A. degree March 21, 1864. Received second and third degrees in Marseilles Lodge, No. 417, A. F. & A. M.

C. G. LUTZ. Bookbinder. Raised July 18, 1864. Demitted November 18, 1867, to become charter member of Humboldt Lodge, No. 555.

HERMAN WARLICK. Painter. Raised August 1, 1864. Demitted November 18, 1867, to become charter member of Humboldt Lodge, No. 555.

J. F. MARRINER. Civil war veteran. Painter. Dentist. Raised August 15, 1864. Expelled May 17, 1869.

EDWARD C. MILLS. Farmer. Raised September 5, 1864. Suspended N. P. D. December 4, 1871.

HENRY BILHARZ. Farmer. Raised September 5, 1864. Demitted October 1, 1867.

LEWIS N. KENNEDY. Merchant. Raised October 1, 1864. Demitted January 6, 1868.

SAMUEL DEGEN. Stock dealer. Was in Confederate service during Rebellion. Raised November 28, 1864. Suspended N. P. D. September 16, 1889. Reinstated August 7, 1899. Died April 24, 1901.

WASHINGTON BUSHNELL. Was born in Madison county, New York. Graduated at the National Law School, Poughkeepsie, N. Y., 1853. Was admitted to the bar, and came to Ottawa the same year, and was a member of the law firm of Gray, Avery & Bushnell, the strongest law firm then in Illinois. Elected State Senator 1860-'64. Elected Attorney General of Illinois in 1868 for four years. Was city attorney three years and State's Attorney for four years. Married Phœbe M. Charles, daughter of Christian H. Charles, who was a member of Ottawa Lodge, No. 114, Grand Lodge of Kentucky. Raised December 12, 1864. Died June 30, 1885.

OSCAR H. MANN. Inventor of safety valve for steam engines. Affiliated November 21, 1864. Demitted February 21, 1868.

CHARLES P. STIMPSON. E. A. degree December 3, 1864. No further record.

A. E. GIBBS. Dentist. Affiliated November 21, 1874. Demitted March 17, 1879.

WILLIAM E. BELL. Bridge builder. Affiliated December 19, 1864. Died February 12, 1894.

FRANCIS P. CHILDS. Shoe merchant. Affiliated January 2, 1865. Demitted July 21, 1879.

J. M. CROSBY. Carpenter. Affiliated January 5, 1865. Demitted October 2, 1878.

HENRY M. GODFREY. Physician. Raised January 16, 1865. Died June 9, 1889.

SIDNEY C. BATES. Painter. Raised January 23, 1865. Suspended N. P. D. June 4, 1876.

JACOB HESS. Miller. Raised February 11, 1865. Demitted December 2, 1867. Affiliated with Humboldt Lodge, No. 555, March 20, 1868.

SIMON ALSCHULER. Clothier. Raised February 12, 1865. Died in Colorado February 13, 1873.

MATTHEW B. LAMB. Farmer. Raised March 7, 1865. Demitted April 5, 1875.

WILLIAM H. CAREY. Grain dealer. Raised April 24, 1865. Died September 1, 1890.

CHAMPLAIN C. CHESTER. Raised April 24, 1865. Died February 26, 1871. Buried at Monmouth, Illinois.

JOHN FLETCHER GIBSON. Farmer. Veteran Mexican war. Raised April 24, 1865. Demitted October 6, 1879. Affiliated February 19, 1883. Died February 24, 1906.

FRANCIS L. FISKE. Clothing. Firms of Fiske, Strickland & Wing, and Fiske & Beem. Raised May 1, 1865.

FRANK B. CHAPMAN. Express agent. Raised May 1, 1865. Demitted December 4, 1871.

THOMAS RYBURN. Grain dealer. Raised May 15, 1865. Died 1878.

M. F. GOOODSPEED. Grain dealer. Affiliated June 6, 1865. Demitted February 5, 1872.

WARREN V. COOLEY. School teacher. Raised June 19, 1865. Demitted December 4, 1871.

ALBERT P. BARNES. Printer. Raised July 3, 1865. Demitted August 6, 1866. Affiliated June 17, 1867. Suspended N. P. D. 1873.

RANDALL LYNNE. Raised August 21, 1865. Demitted December 7, 1868.

H. D. WILLIAMS. Paper manufacturer. E. A. degree October 16, 1865. Passed and raised in Polar Star Lodge, No. 113, Iowa, in 1867.

JACOB SCHMIDT. Wagonmaker. Raised November 20, 1865. Demitted November 18, 1867, to become charter member of Humboldt Lodge, No. 555.

JOHN L. MORRISON. Clerk for Wm. Reddick, general store. Veteran Civil war in Henshaw's Battery. Raised November 27, 1865. Demitted September 19, 1887.

ALBANUS E. GROW. Deputy Sheriff under Sheriff Waterman. Raised January 1, 1866. Suspended N. P. D. March 15, 1875.

OZELL TRASK. Jeweler. Raised February 17, 1866. Demitted April 17, 1879.

WILLIAM N. RICHARDSON. Grain dealer. E. A. degree February 26, 1866. No further record.

PELEG A. HALL. Bookkeeper. Raised April 4, 1866. Killed by falling off building June 28, 1901.

WILLIAM H. CUSHMAN. Bank teller. Raised April 4, 1866. Demitted February 4, 1867. Moved to Colorado. Died in New York.

JESSE B. CHARLES. Printer. E. A. degree April 23, 1866. No further record.

LEMAN A. RISING. Cigar manufacturer. Firm, Smith & Rising. Veteran Civil war. Affiliated April 2, 1866. Demitted February 16, 1880. Affiliated November 21, 1887. Tyler 1903-'04.

ROBERT HENNING. Telegraph instrument manufacturer. Raised April 16, 1866. Worshipful Master 1871, '72 and '73. Moved to Chicago. Died September 27, 1885. Was buried in Ottawa avenue cemetery with Masonic honors.

FRANCIS B. METCALF. Raised August 24, 1866. Demitted April 5, 1875.

ROBERT Y. MURPHY. Furniture. Raised October 15, 1866. Suspended N. P. D. June 7, 1880.

HENRY KOCH. Bookkeeper. Raised November 19, 1866. Demitted November 18, 1867. Charter member Humboldt Lodge, No. 555.

WILLIAM S. JACKSON. Farmer, speculator, banker. Affiliated November 19, 1866. Demitted 1869. Charter member Seneca Lodge.

EDWARD H. SMITH. Cigar manufacturer. Firm of Smith & Rising. Deputy Sheriff 1881-'82. Civil war veteran. Affiliated December 3, 1866. Demitted February 2, 1884.

WILLIAM CULLEN. Farmer. Sheriff 1865-'66. Editor Ottawa *Republican* several years. Elected to Congress 1880 and re-elected in 1882. Affiliated January 1, 1867.

CHARLES HENRY NATTINGER. Carpenter. Raised February 18, 1867. Died December 9, 1870.

EBENEZER E. LEWIS. Lawyer. Raised March 23, 1867. Demitted May 19, 1873.

ROSS DENNY. Plasterer. Affiliated February 4, 1867. Demitted April 5, 1869.

JAMES RHOADS. Farmer. Affiliated February 18, 1867. Demitted January 2, 1882.

WILLIAM H. LONG. Farmer. Raised April 6, 1867. Demitted June 5, 1871.

GEORGE W. CUMMINGS. Wagonmaker. Raised April 8, 1867. Demitted October 8, 1868. Charter member Streator Lodge.

ABRAM CUMMINGS. Wagonmaker. E. A. degree April 22, 1867. Passed and raised in Streator Lodge.

GILBERT GOFF. Dry goods merchant. Raised April 13, 1867. Demitted December 16, 1889. Affiliated June 3, 1892. Lives at Goodland, Ind.

BENJAMIN PADGETT. Tailor. Raised May 13, 1867. Died September 28, 1899.

WILLIAM E. BOWMAN. Photographer. Affiliated May 6, 1867. Demitted January 7, 1880.

ROBERT E. RIALE. Grocer. Affiliated June 3, 1867. Demitted June 13, 1878.

FRANK B. STEARNS. Hotel. Affiliated June 15, 1867. Demitted February 2, 1884.

JOSEPH W. DOW. Postmaster during the 60s. Raised June 15, 1867. Demitted January 2, 1871.

GEORGE W. FRANCIS. Received E. A. and F. C. degrees in Occidental Lodge in 1864. Received M. M. degree in some other Lodge and affiliated with Occidental Lodge June 15, 1867. Demitted June 5, 1871.

ALEXANDER HANNA. Farmer and collector. Resided in South Ottawa. Raised June 15, 1867. Tyler 1883 to 1891, inclusive, and 1895 to 1904, inclusive.

JOHN A. GRAY. Minister. Raised June 17, 1867. Suspended N. P. D. April 5, 1875. Reinstated July 6, 1892. Died September 29, 1896.

HARRY J. LOGAN. Millwright. Initiated July 15, 1867. No further record.

FREDERICK F. CRANE. Grain-buyer and bookkeeper. Raised July 22, 1867. Senior Steward 1878. Suspended N. P. D March 4, 1889.

ANDREW J. SAWYER. School teacher. Raised July 22, 1867. Demitted, May 4, 1868.

JOHN H. DRUITT. Lawyer. Raised August 16, 1867. Demitted August 6, 1872.

FRANCIS P. DUPLAIN. Telegraph instrument maker. Raised October 12, 1867. Senior Deacon 1872-'73. Suspended N. P. D. 1877. Reinstated July 1, 1895.

NATHANIEL C. WALKER. Clerk. Raised October 12, 1867. Suspended N. P. D. June 5, 1882.

DAVID BATCHELLER. Clerk. Civil war veteran, Henshaw's Battery. Raised November 4, 1867. Demitted June 3, 1878. Affiliated February 15, 1886. Secretary from 1888 to time of his death, December 28, 1896.

SEWARD THORSON. Dry goods merchant. Firm, Hull & Thorson. Raised December 16, 1867. Demitted December 4, 1871.

WILLIAM J. PIGOTT. School teacher. Initiated December 23, 1867. No further record.

FREDERICK MARCH. Clerk. Raised January 6, 1868. Demitted February 21, 1870.

GEORGE J. RUNDELL. Affiliated January 20, 1868. Demitted January 17, 1870.

ISAAC N. BEEM. Clothing merchant. Firm, Fiske & Beem. Affiliated February 17, 1868.

AUSTIN G. CREGAR. Raised January 20, 1868. Suspended N. P. D. 1877.

JOHN F. MACKINLAY. Banker. Raised February 24, 1868. Demitted February 27, 1879.

JOHN H. SHEPHERD. County Treasurer. Civil war veteran. Raised March 23, 1868. Died June 27, 1872.

EDWARD COAN. Episcopal minister. Raised May 13, 1868. Demitted April 19, 1869.

FRANCIS M. ROSE. Druggist. Raised May 11, 1868. Demitted April 19, 1869.

WALTER TODD. Miller. Raised May 25, 1868. Demitted October 4, 1869.

JOHN W. COLLINS. Raised October 19, 1868. Demitted September 19, 1870.

WILLIAM STADDEN. Miller at Dayton. Raised March 25, 1868. Died June 5, 1883.

ANTHONY D. SIMON. Music teacher. Raised October 21, 1867.

DANIEL J. HOLMES. Methodist minister. Affiliated August 17, 1868. Demitted February 21, 1876. Reaffiliated February 7, 1887. Chaplain 1888-'89. Demitted February 3, 1890.

FERNANDO C. PRESCOTT. Gents' furnishings. Raised November 23, 1868. Died February 22, 1874.

JAMES N. COLWELL. Contractor. Firm, Colwell, Clark & Stebbins. Raised December 21, 1868. Senior Steward 1871. Junior Deacon 1872. Killed by the cars at Streator, October 10, 1876.

WILLIAM A. BRUNDAGE. Carpenter. Raised December 28, 1868. Suspended N. P. D. January 7, 1880.

JAMES R. CROSS. Constable. Civil war veteran. Raised April 5, 1869. Demitted February 9, 1877.

CHARLES M. CATLIN. Bookkeeper. Raised May 10, 1869. Senior Warden 1875. Suspended for un-masonic conduct in August, 1875, and reinstated January 3, 1876. Demitted January 17, 1876.

SAMUEL W. PORTER. United States express agent. Civil war veteran. Raised June 14, 1869.

WILLIAM W. ESTABROOK. Minister. Affiliated August 2, 1869. Senior Warden 1871. Demitted December 4, 1871.

OBADIAH JENNINGS. Farmer. Raised October 4, 1869. Demitted December 3, 1877.

JAMES O'DONNELL. Lawyer. Raised October 4, 1869. Junior Warden 1874. Demitted January 17, 1876.

JOHN BOHLANDER. Telegraph instrument maker. Raised October 11, 1869. Demitted February 2, 1873.

PHILIP R. MARTIN. Affiliated November 15, 1869. Demitted January 2, 1871.

WILLIAM K. CASH. Book store. Raised August 15, 1870. Demitted December 1, 1879.

AMASA C. CHILDS. Shoe store. Raised December 19, 1870. Died May 18, 1874.

HENRY STEAD. Farmer. Raised March 21, 1870. Father of brother W. H. Stead.

EDWARD K. WALBRIDGE. Farmer. Raised April 2, 1870. Demitted January 17, 1876.

GEORGE G. WENTZ. Merchant. Raised May 7, 1870. Demitted January 19, 1874.

HENRY A. HOWLAND. Son of Dr. Howland. Raised January 20, 1870. Suspended N. P. D. August 20, 1876.

BENJAMIN S. PORTER. Carriagemaker. Affiliated December 5, 1870. Senior Warden 1873. Demitted February 2, 1879.

ELISHA SMITH. Received Fellow Craft degree April 18, 1870; received Master Mason degree in Rockton Lodge, No. 316, Kent, Ohio.

DWIGHT W. FULLER. C., B. & Q. station agent. Affiliated December 5, 1870. Demitted September 17, 1877.

ALBERT J. POOL. Farmer. Raised February 20, 1871. Demitted January 19, 1880.

THOMAS THOMELEY. Raised May 22, 1871. Demitted July 6, 1874.

JAMES W. KELLOGG. Lawyer. Raised July 19, 1871. Demitted August 1, 1872.

CHARLES W. COOK. Millwright. Raised November 20, 1871. Senior Steward 1873. Died January 10, 1882.

MICHAEL HUTHMAKER. Affiliated December 4, 1871. Suspended N. P. D. January 4, 1876.

GEORGE V. HULL. Salesman. Raised January 22, 1872. Demitted January 7, 1884.

ALEXANDER RICHARDS. Farmer. Raised February 5, 1872. Suspended N. P. D. January 10, 1880.

JESSE C. ALLEN. Affiliated February 5, 1872. Demitted May 18, 1874.

REUBEN F. DYER. Physician and surgeon. Veteran Civil war. Raised June 17, 1872. Died January 25, 1896.

SIDNEY V. WISE. Raised November 25, 1872. Junior Deacon 1873. Suspended October 2, 1876. Reinstated April 16, 1906. Demitted May 7, 1906.

PATRICK RYAN. Bookkeeper. Veteran Civil war. Captain. Raised January 20, 1873. Tyler 1880. Died January 3, 1881.

JOHN LAWRENCE STEELE. Minister. Raised May 12, 1873. Chaplain 1874. Demitted April 19. 1876.

DAVID KROUSE. Gunsmith. Veteran Civil war. Raised July 7, 1873. Demitted January 16, 1899.

ENOCH S. YENTZER. Tailor. Raised July 14, 1873.

CHARLES SNOW. Moulder. Raised August 4, 1873. Died September 9, 1881.

GEORGE N. CASH. Bookstore. Affiliated May 19, 1873. Demitted January 5, 1882.

HUBERT A. McCALEB. Colonel Sixth United States Colored artillery in Civil war. Affiliated January 6, 1873. Died March 24, 1878. Was Sheriff La Salle county 1866-'68. County Clerk 1873-'74.

GEORGE L. AUSTIN. Machinist. Affiliated September 1, 1873. Demitted January 7, 1876.

SAMUEL R. HELMICK. Machinist. Affiliated January 19, 1874. Suspended N. P. D. March 5, 1894.

JOHN H. WIDMER. Lawyer. Major One Hundred Fourth Illinois, Civil war. Raised January 26, 1874.

HENRY MAYO. School teacher, lawyer. State's Attorney 1872-'80. Postmaster since 1896. Civil war veteran. Raised February 2, 1874.

THEODORE CUNNINGHAM GIBSON

A member over fifty years

E. FOLLETT BULL. Lawyer. Affiliated February 16, 1874. Senior Warden 1877. Died December 4, 1888.

JAMES A. COMSTOCK. Tinsmith. Affiliated February 16, 1874. Demitted September 20, 1875.

DANIEL C. MILLS. Retired farmer. Raised May 4, 1874. Senior Steward 1888-'89. Died May 2, 1905. Brother Mills was one of La Salle county's early settlers and most prosperous farmers and substantial citizens. He was of decided opinions and strict integrity.

HENRY G. COTTON. Druggist. Raised May 11, 1874. Demitted June 7, 1880. Affiliated February 4, 1889. Again demitted April 5, 1879.

WILLIAM THOMAS. Canal superintendent. Raised July 20, 1874. Demitted April 19, 1880.

JAMES E. RATHBUN. Grain dealer. Raised July 27, 1874. Demitted April 18, 1887.

WILLIAM STORMONT. Foundry and machine shop. Raised July 27, 1874. Chaplain 1877-'79. Died October 12, 1894.

FREDERICK W. MATTOCKS. Traveling salesman. Raised August 3, 1874. Demitted February 16, 1880.

AUGUST HAEBERLIN. Hardware. Affiliated August 3, 1874. Demitted February 16, 1885.

JOHN L. PIERGUE. Cafe. Raised August 10, 1874. Senior Steward 1877. Demitted July 21, 1879.

CHARLES BLANCHARD. Lawyer. State's Attorney. Judge Circuit Court. Affiliated August 17, 1874.

ALLEN JORDAN, JR. Manufacturer. Raised September 21, 1874. Died July 12, 1879.

ROSWELL W. HOLMES. Circuit Clerk. Raised October 5, 1874. Secretary 1875-'76. Demitted January 3, 1881.

K

HENRY A. SHULER. Grain dealer. Raised October 12, 1874. Demitted April 18, 1887. [The beautiful clock that hangs upon the wall of Occidental Lodge was presented to Occidental Lodge by brother Shuler.]

FRANK A. KENDALL. Hardware. Raised October 19, 1874. Demitted April 5, 1897.

CLARENCE C. GLOVER. Collector Illinois and Michigan canal. Raised November 9, 1874. Secretary 1878.

GEORGE A. MILLS. Farmer. Raised November 11, 1874. Junior Steward 1876.

WALTER BRIGGS TITUS. Contractor. Raised November 23, 1874. Senior Deacon 1875. Junior Warden 1876. Demitted March 13, 1879.

JESSE B. RUGER. Lawyer. Raised November 30, 1874. Suspended N. P. D. January 7, 1880.

JOHN N. TIFFANY. Wagonmaker. Affiliated January 4, 1875. Demitted May 18, 1880.

CHARLES E. PETTIT. Printer. Associate editor *Republican-Times*. Civil war veteran. Raised February 22, 1875. Demitted March 21, 1881. Affiliated August 7, 1882. Senior Warden 1885. Worshipful Master 1887 to 1890, inclusive. Secretary 1899 and consecutive years since.

THEODORE C. MILLER. Clerk. Affiliated March 1, 1875. Suspended N. P. D. April 4, 1887.

WILLIAM STUART SPIERS. Minister. Affiliated March 1, 1875. Demitted February 21, 1876.

WILLIAM H. PHILLIPS. Grocer. Raised April 12, 1875. Demitted February 16, 1885.

LESTER O. PHILLIPS. Grocer. Raised April 26, 1875. Junior Steward 1877. Demitted April 20, 1885.

WALTER D. STRAWN. Farmer. Director National City bank. Raised June 14, 1875.

EDWARD C. LEWIS. Farmer and stockman. Chairman Board of Supervisors La Salle county several years. Now manufacturing heating furnaces in Chicago. Raised June 28, 1875.

CHARLES A. WORKS. Lawyer. Raised July 5, 1875. Demitted August 7, 1876.

ANDREW J. BROWN. Pump manufacturer. Raised July 12, 1875. Demitted April 7, 1879.

CAIRO D. TRIMBLE. Clerk Supreme Court. Affiliated July 24, 1875. Demitted December 19, 1898.

WILLIAM O. GORMAN. Bookkeeper. Raised August 9, 1875. Demitted February 19, 1877.

HENRY P. CLARK. Painter. Affiliated September 6, 1875. Junior Deacon 1877-'78. Suspended N. P. D. April 18, 1887.

ARTHUR LOCKWOOD WAGNER. General regular army, U. S. A. Raised September 13, 1875. Demitted May 30, 1889.

W. L. PHILLIPS. Merchant. Affiliated September 20, 1875. Expelled January 7, 1880.

HARVEY W. SMITH. Hotel-keeper, Clifton. Affiliated September 20, 1875. Suspended N. P. D. January 1, 1881.

WILLIM H. ENSMINGER. Affiliated November 1, 1875. Demitted November 18, 1878.

WILLIAM E. CODDING. Canal collector. Affiliated January 17, 1876. Demitted December 19, 1893.

THOMAS A. SMURR. Physician. Raised August 20, 1876. Junior Warden 1879.

SAMUEL RICHOLSON. Lawyer. Ex-mayor of Ottawa. Raised May 7, 1877. Died June 24, 1906.

SAMUEL DITTENHOFFER. Clothier. Raised October 1, 1877. Suspended N. P. D. April 4, 1887.

WILLIAM T. DICKEY. Jeweler. Raised November 5, 1877.

Demitted June 21, 1880. Moved to California, where he died.

ASA MANN HOFFMAN. Deputy County Treasurer. County Treasurer 1886. Raised December 24, 1877. Died May 4, 1887. Secretary 1877 to 1887, inclusive.

BENJAMIN F. BOLE. Painter. Raised May 20, 1878. Junior Deacon 1879. Demitted August 18, 1879.

LOTHROP PERKINS. Superintendent Gas & Coke Co. Raised July 1, 1878. Treasurer 1879. Junior Warden 1880-'81. Senior Warden 1882. Died September 16, 1884.

JAMES MCMANUS. Deputy County Clerk. Affiliated December 17, 1877. Senior Warden 1880-'81. Worshipful Master 1882-'83. Secretary 1897-'98. Died September 23, 1898.

DAVID A. COOK. Lawyer. Bank examiner 15 years. Civil war veteran. Past Master Mendota Lodge. Affiliated January 1, 1878. Died September 21, 1905.

PAUL TEISSEDRE. Clerk. Affiliated July 21, 1879. Junior Steward 1881 and 1884. Senior Steward 1882. Junior Deacon 1885-'86.

WILLIAM LEE ROY MILLIGAN. Farmer. Deputy Sheriff 1883-'86. Traveling salesman. Raised October 13, 1879. Senior Deacon 1880-'81. Senior Warden 1882-'83. Worshipful Master 1884-'86.

WEBSTER W. ARNOLD. Warden county asylum. Raised November 3, 1879. Suspended N. P. D. March 4, 1889. Reinstated January 6, 1902.

FRANCIS BURDETT NASH, JR. Minister. Raised December 15, 1879. Demitted April 18, 1881.

CHARLES WILLIAM FREDENBURG. Traveling salesman. Raised April 12, 1880.

JOSEPH NEWTON DUNAWAY. Farmer. Grain merchant.

Raised August 2, 1880. Senior Warden 1889. Worshipful Master 1899.

JAMES ROLLA CHAPMAN. Officer U. S. army. Raised September 20, 1880. Demitted August 3, 1887.

RICHARD FARNSWORTH. Farmer and stockman. Affiliated April 3, 1881.

HENRY PECK. Farmer and stockman. Affiliated April 3, 1881.

WILLIAM H. GILMAN. Painter and contractor. Raised April 11, 1881.

JOHN W. GLEGG. Plumber. Raised June 20, 1881. Junior Steward 1882.

WILLIAM E. PRICHARD. Horse dealer. Vice-president Ottawa Banking & Trust Co. Civil war veteran. Affiliated October 13, 1881. Past Master Marseilles Lodge, No. 417.

WILLIAM SHEPPARD. Veterinary surgeon. Affiliated October 17, 1881.

THOMAS WILSON DORR CRANE. Lawyer. Raised November 28, 1881. Senior Deacon 1882-'84.

WALTER McDONALD WOODWARD. School teacher. Lawyer. Raised December 10, 1881. Suspended N. P. D April 2, 1888.

NATHANIEL McDOUGALL. Drug clerk. Raised December 19, 1881. Died March 5, 1890.

THOMAS E. MacKINLAY. Lawyer. Raised December 19, 1881. Junior Deacon 1883. Treasurer 1887 to 1895, inclusive. Demitted December 10, 1895.

JAMES MILLIGAN. Merchant tailor. President Ottawa Tailoring Co. Raised December 19, 1881.

GEORGE W. GREEN. Tile manufacturer. Raised December 26, 1881. Suspended N. P. D. November 18, 1889. Reinstated July 4, 1904. Demitted December 19, 1904.

JOHN E. V. MORSE. U. S. railway mail clerk. Raised February 4, 1882. Demitted January 20, 1890.

WILLARD S. WHEELER. Photographer. Civil war veteran. Raised March 6, 1882. Suspended N. P. D. June 4, 1894.

JOHN GREEN. Tile manufacturer. Raised March 9, 1882. Demitted March 5, 1894.

JOHN C. FARNSWORTH. Carriage maker. Raised October 2, 1882. Senior Steward 1887.

WILLIAM H. STEAD. Lawyer. State's Attorney. Elected Attorney-General of Illinois in 1904. Raised October 7, 1882. Junior Warden 1885.

JESSE EMERSON MORGAN. Clerk. Raised October 16, 1882. Suspended N. P. D. March 2, 1896.

SIMEON G. GAY. Carriage manufacturer. One of the leading manufacturers of Ottawa. Raised December 16, 1882.

JOHN S. RYBURN. Physician. Raised December 18, 1882. Died September 21, 1892.

GARVEY DONALDSON. Photographer. Affiliated February 19, 1883. Demitted November 15, 1886.

THOMAS REEDY. Warden county asylum. Civil war veteran. Raised April 7, 1883. Died March 4, 1889.

JOHN C. CORCORAN. Harness manufacturer. Raised May 7, 1883. Junior Warden 1886.

LOUIS W. HESS. Baker. Superintendent electric street car line. Ex-mayor of Ottawa. Raised October 1, 1883. Demitted March 17, 1902.

JOSEPH A. WILSON. Photographer. Raised November 19, 1883. Junior Deacon 1888. Junior Warden 1889-'90. Tyler since 1905.

RECTOR CASS HITT. Son of Col. D. F. Hitt. Lawyer. Raised January 21, 1884. Demitted February 17, 1890. Affiliated January 16, 1893.

SAMUEL CALDWELL. Carpenter. Affiliated February 7, 1884. Junior Steward 1886. Junior Deacon 1887. Demitted April 18, 1897.

JOHN MICHAEL PURRUCKER. Carpenter. U. S. railway mail clerk. Civil war veteran. Raised February 11, 1884. Demitted February 4, 1889.

WARREN C. RIALE. Grocer. Raised April 7, 1884. Suspended N. P. D. May 19, 1902.

FREDERICK W. GAY. Traveling salesman. Raised April 12, 1884. Died May 6, 1892.

MARTIN C. HODGSON. Farmer and stock raiser. Raised May 19, 1884.

JOHN WESLEY JOHNSON. Received Fellow Craft degree September 1, 1884.

JOHN DAWDLE HAMMOND. Traveling salesman. Raised September 15, 1884. Suspended N. P. D. June 7, 1897. Reinstated January 6, 1902. Demitted February 16, 1903.

WILLIAM H. WATTS. Farmer. Raised December 1, 1884.

EDWARD H. ROBERTS. Clerk. Affiliated June 1, 1885. Demitted February 1, 1897.

CHARLES H. ANGEVINE. Farmer. Raised November 2, 1885. Suspended N. P. D. January 7, 1897.

CHARLES E. DUNBAR. Farmer. Raised November 16, 1885. Junior Warden 1887. Suspended N. P. D. September 19, 1904.

CHARLES ZEITLER. Silversmith. Raised November 21, 1885. Demitted January 16, 1888.

CHARLES SCHAULIN. Farmer. Raised November 28, 1885. Suspended N. P. D. July 16, 1900.

HARRY E. ROCKWOOD. Farmer. Raised December 5, 1885. Demitted March 6, 1905.

JOSHUA P. RODGERS. Retired farmer. Raised March 1, 1886. Senior Warden 1902. Worshipful Master 1903.

DANIEL E. DALY. Traveling salesman. Raised May 17, 1886.

GEORGE M. TRIMBLE. Bookkeeper and insurance. Raised June 21, 1886.

WILLIAM A. JEFFERY. Carpenter and contractor. Affiliated August 16, 1886. Senior Deacon 1887.

CHARLES B. VOSBURGH. Clerk. Raised February 3, 1887. Suspended N. P. D. March 2, 1896. Reinstated February 1, 1904.

CHARLES E. RUSSELL. Insurance agent. Raised March 3, 1887. Suspended N. P. D. May 7, 1892.

JAMES FRANCIS MURPHY. Mechanic. Raised April 4, 1887.

CHARLES E. HOOK. Cashier First National bank. Ex-mayor of Ottawa. Raised April 26, 1887. Senior Deacon 1891. Senior Warden 1893. Treasurer 1896 to 1906, inclusive.

ROSS C. MITCHELL. Clerk. Raised May 25, 1887. Died October 6, 1887.

WILLIAM McCOMBS. Janitor Reddick's library. Civil war veteran. Affiliated October 3, 1887.

FRANK B. LOGAN. Carpenter and contractor. Raised October 17, 1887. Suspended N. P. D. May 19, 1902.

LOUIS DEGEN. Stock dealer; electrician. Affiliated February 6, 1888. Demitted March 3, 1902.

JAMES E. COOKE. Insurance agent. Raised April 30, 1888. Senior Deacon·1889. Senior Warden 1890. Worshipful Master 1891-'92. Demitted January 21, 1897.

CLARENCE GRIGGS. Lawyer. Raised May 14, 1888. Has served as County Attorney for La Salle county for several years.

A. R. TRESSLER. Clerk. Affiliated June 4, 1888. Demitted January 1, 1894.

WILLIAM H. KNOWLES. Foundry and machine shop. Raised June 9, 1888.

MARSHALL B. MITCHELL. Cigar manufacturer. Son of Bradford C. Mitchell. Raised June 11, 1888.

JOHN HAWS. Retired. Affiliated January 7, 1889. Died January 8, 1904.

AUGUSTUS IVES, JR. Physician. Raised January 21, 1889.

CHARLES E. FISHER. Merchant. Firm, Fisher, Myers & Co. Raised February 11, 1888.

WILLIS HERBERT WARD. Telephone superintendent. Affi!-iated February 18, 1889. Senior Deacon 1890. Died May 27, 1900.

JOHN JAMES WITHROW. Merchant. Raised February 18. 1889.

WILLIAM HENRY BARNARD. China store. Raised February 23, 1889. Junior Deacon 1890. Junior Warden 1891-'92. Worshipful Master 1893.

HENRY R. TURNER. Upholsterer. Affiliated March 18, 1889. Demitted January 6, 1890.

JOHN J. TOBIAS. Clergyman. Affiliated April 1, 1889. Demitted March 3, 1890.

FREDERICK E. MAYO. Bookkeeper. Raised April 1, 1889. Suspended N. P. D. March 7, 1892.

ABRAM CROSS GODFREY. Grocer. Raised April 29, 1889. Suspended N. P. D. May 19, 1902. Reinstated May 4, 1903. Junior Steward 1890.

ALVA B. HOLMES. Carriagemaker. Affiliated May 6, 1889. Senior Steward 1896. Junior Deacon 1897-'98·

DUNCAN McDOUGALL. Lawyer. Raised May 28, 1889. Senior Warden 1891-'92.

HENRY WALDECKER. Cigar manufacturer. Affiliated June 3, 1889.

GEORGE ADAMS FORBES. Traveling salesman. Vice-president Ottawa Tailoring Co. Raised June 22, 1889.

CHARLES BENTON HESS. Capitalist. Raised June 29, 1889.

NATHANIEL EARL DEGEN. Lawyer. Raised July 2, 1889. Demitted January 7, 1901.

JOHN J. CARRICK. Clerk. Raised November 25, 1889. Junior Deacon 1892. Suspended N. P. D. March 7, 1898.

HANS GULBRONSON. Piano tuner. Affiliated January 6, 1890.

PHILO C. WEAVER. Piano tuner. Affiliated January 6, 1890.

BYRON F. MAXON. Bookkeeper. Affiliated January 6, 1890. Died June 22, 1890.

ROYAL D. McDONALD. Lawyer. Affiliated February 17, 1890. Past Master Acacia Lodge at La Salle, Ill. Died January 11, 1902.

CHARLES E. HILLS. Druggist. Affiliated February 17, 1890.

WILLIAM C. WEISE. Miller. Raised March 17, 1890. Died February 6, 1897.

LUMAN ALBERT WILLIAMS. Lawyer and city editor. Raised March 31, 1890. Junior Deacon 1891. Senior Steward 1892. Junior Warden 1893. Senior Warden 1894. Worshipful Master 1895.

FRANK YOUNG HERBERT. Dentist. Raised November 9, 1891. Senior Deacon 1892.

DAVID LAFAYETTE GROVE. Implements. Raised November 30, 1891. Died December 14, 1896.

HENRY HARRISON LONG. Bookkeeper. Raised November 23, 1891. Demitted December 18, 1893.

MATHEW SCANLAN. Contractor. Raised March 28, 1892. Suspended N. P. D. June 4, 1894.

TIMOTHY E. GAPEN. Druggist. Affiliated April 20, 1891. Demitted November 18, 1895.

ADELBERT THOMAS OLMSTED. Dentist. Raised April 27, 1891. Demitted November 21, 1892.

CLARK BRADING PROVINS. Physician. Raised May 4, 1891. Died June 4, 1906.

JACOB BENNER SHULER. Coal dealer. Raised May 18, 1891.

EDWARD AUGUSTUS NATTINGER. Editor; postmaster. Civil war veteran. Raised June 1, 1891. Died September 1, 1903.

ISAAC B. BAUMGARDNER. Tinner. Raised April 11, 1892.

WILLIAM E. W. MACKINLAY. Student. Veteran Spanish-American war. Raised April 25, 1892. Is now a commissioned officer in U. S. army.

CHARLES SUMNER BECKWITH. Traveling salesman. Raised April 30, 1892. Senior Deacon 1893. Junior Warden 1894. Senior Warden 1895.

JAMES BRIGGS. Druggist. Affiliated May 16, 1892. Demitted March 16, 1896.

JOHN RAYMOND HOFFMAN. Son of Asa Mann Hoffman. Physician. Raised May 28, 1892.

LEROY L. MCKINLEY. Lawyer; school teacher. Affiliated July 6, 1892.

EDGAR GOODRICH DYER. Student. Raised September 12, 1892. Demitted October 18, 1897.

CHARLES PHILANDER TAYLOR. Vice-president National City bank. Raised September 26, 1892.

FOSTER H. MCKENNEY. Retired. Affiliated October 19, 1892. Tyler 1892-'94.

JAMES M. TRENARY. Retired. Affiliated November 16, 1892. Tyler 1895.

WALTER F. WEESE. Veterinary surgeon. Raised November 28, 1892.

JOHN WESLEY HACKETT. Glass blower. Raised December 3, 1892. Demitted February 15, 1897.

JOHN ALBERT DOCKTER. Glass blower. Raised December 19, 1892. Demitted March 18, 1895.

FRANCIS MARION YENTZER. Traveling salesman. Sales manager J. E. Porter Co. Raised December 31, 1892.

HENRY EDGAR GEDNEY. Horse buyer. Raised January 9, 1893. Died January 31, 1894.

JACOB ISAAC WARNER. Real estate and insurance. Raised January 26, 1893.

KIMBALL WHITE LELAND. Physician. Raised March 13, 1893. Demitted September 3, 1900, and assisted in organization of Utica Lodge, No. 858, Utica, Ill.

JAMES NORRIS DOWNS. Physician. Affiliated March 20, 1893. Suspended N. P. D. May 4, 1903. Reinstated Nov. 21, 1904.

ARTHUR BURLING COLE. C., B. & Q. station agent. Raised April 23, 1893. Junior Deacon 1895. Senior Deacon 1899.

DANIEL DOUGLASS SAYLOR. Glass packer. Raised April 24, 1893. Senior Steward 1894.

THOMAS WILSON BURROWS. Physician. Affiliated July 3, 1893.

DAVID REFIOR. Hardware merchant. Raised September 25, 1893. Junior Deacon 1894. Senior Deacon 1895. Junior Warden 1896.

MILO PUTNEY. Jeweler. Raised November 13, 1893. Demitted December 16, 1901.

CLARENCE EDWARD TRYON. Insurance. Raised November 21, 1893. Senior Deacon 1894. Junior Warden 1895. Senior Warden 1896. Died June 20, 1900.

DOUGLÀSS LEE DUNAVAN. Lawyer. Raised November 27, 1893. Demitted January 21, 1901.

CHARLES J. YOCKEY. Sheriff La ¡Salle county 1894-'97. Civil war veteran. Affiliated April 16, 1894. Died December 27, 1902.

FREDERICK LEWIS FISCHER. Hardware merchant. Raised November 12, 1894.

MATTHEW W. BACH. · Collar manufacturer. Raised December 1, 1894.

ARTHUR S. HOOK. Teller and bookkeeper. Raised December 15, 1894.

WILBUR F. HEATH. Clerk. Affiliated March 3, 1895. Demitted December 18, 1899.

LOUIS W. MERRIFIELD. Salesman. Raised May 4, 1895.

WILLIAM D. FULLERTON. Son of Thos. C. Fullerton. Lawyer. Raised June 1, 1895. Senior Deacon 1896. Senior Warden 1897. Worshipful Master 1898. District Deputy Grand Master since 1902.

E. S. JACOBS. Farmer. Affiliated June 17, 1895.

EDGAR ELDREDGE. Lawyer. Raised September 21, 1895. Junior Deacon 1896. Junior Warden 1897. Elected Judge Circuit Court October, 1906.

EVERETT H. BUTTERFIELD. Physician. Raised November 23, 1895.

ELMER E. GLADFELTER. Furniture dealer. Raised February 24, 1896. Senior Deacon 1897.

JOHN D. MACKENZIE. Harnessmaker. Raised March 16, 1896. Suspended N. P. D. September 3, 1900. Reinstated April 20, 1903.

JOHN HILLIARD. Merchant. Retired. Civil war veteran. Raised March 21, 1896.

HARRY N. WEBER. Tinner. Raised March 23, 1896. Juniar Warden 1901.

ADELBERT J. NEWELL. Grain merchant. Affiliated Nov. 18, 1895. Worshipful Master 1896-'97. Died April 9, 1899. During his short residence in Ottawa he had endeared himself to the brethren.

HAZEN HAYWARD. Farmer. Affiliated February 17, 1896.

H. L. CAWTHORNE. Clergyman. Affiliated March 16, 1896. Demitted February 19, 1906.

DAVIS N. SHIPMAN. Paper dealer. Affiliated March 16, 1896. Demitted June 7, 1897.

SAMUEL S. PEARSON. Hardware merchant. Civil war veteran. Raised April 13, 1896.

ALBERT T. LARDIN. Lawyer. Judge Probate Court. Raised April 27, 1896.

CHARLES W. CAMPBELL. Livery. Raised May 11, 1896. Junior Warden 1898. Senior Warden 1899.

JOHN L. MORRISON. Clerk. Affiliated September 7, 1896.

SIMEON WASHINGTON LAUCK. Minister. Initiated September 14, 1896. No further record.

SAMUEL H. HEIDLER. Teacher. Affiliated October 5, 1896. Demitted June 19, 1898.

ELNATHAN P. HATHEWAY. Physician. Raised November 23, 1896.

ENOS EPHRAIM PALMER. Physician. Raised November 30, 1896.

WILLIAM BRIGGS ROWE. Railway mail clerk. Affiliated December 7, 1896. Demitted October 19, 1903.

WILSON HUPP. Retired farmer. Initiated March 8, 1897. No further record.

CALVIN D. PHILLIPS. Merchant. Raised March 29, 1897. Died August 7, 1903.

SYLVESTER CANFIELD. Blacksmith and farmer. Raised June 14, 1897.

GEORGE CRAFT DUNAWAY. Grain buyer. Raised March 5, 1897. Junior Deacon 1900.

EDWARD WEBSTER BACH. Bookkeeper. Raised March 14, 1897. Senior Warden 1903. Worshipful Master 1904.

ENOCH YENTZER, JR. Electrician. Raised April 26, 1897.

IRVING DE FORREST VINCENT. Bookkeeper. Flour and feed merchant. Firm, Hamilton & Vincent. Raised October 18, 1897. Demitted January 2, 1899. Affiliated September 4, 1899.

CHARLES LOUIS BELROSE. Grain buyer, Wedron, Ill. Raised November 29, 1897.

ARTHUR W. LADD. Foreman. Affiliated December 20, 1897.

HARRY J. LEE. Organ tuner. Affiliated May 2, 1898.

CHARLES G. DEENIS. Veterinary surgeon. Raised May 9, 1898.

HENRY PHILLIPS. Circuit Clerk. Raised August 1, 1898.

CHRISTIAN GASSER. Engineer. Raised October 1, 1898.

EDWARD DANYAL ROSS. Merchant. Raised October 24, 1898.

GEORGE JOHN KRUSE. Plumber. Raised October 31, 1898. Demitted October 5, 1903.

ALBERT WARREN MERRIFIELD. Bookkeeper. Raised November 14, 1898. Demitted January 1, 1900.

ANGUS ROSS MERCER. Superintendent Silica sand works. Raised November 28, 1898. Senior Steward 1899. Junior Warden 1900. Demitted December 19, 1904.

HERBERT CHARLES WILEY. Attorney. Raised December 2, 1898. Junior Steward 1899. Senior Warden 1900. Worshipful Master 1902.

HARRY GILMAN COOK. Attorney. Raised December 2, 1898.

ALBERT CLINTON BRADISH. Lumber dealer. Raised February 27, 1899. Junior Steward 1901.

SAMUEL BALDWIN BRADFORD. Cashier Ottawa Banking & Trust Co. Raised March 13, 1899, Demitted November 20, 1899. Affiliated March 2, 1903. Worshipful Master 1905. Commissioned Grand Lecturer 1906.

WILLIAM HERBERT HIGBY. Druggist. Captain infantry during war with Spain. Affiliated May 15, 1899. Worshipful Master 1900-'01.

CHARLES WILLIAM WEEKS. Music teacher. Raised May 29, 1899. Demitted October 21, 1901.

CHARLES FRANCIS WILSON. Civil engineer. Raised June 12, 1899. Junior Steward 1900. Senior Deacon 1901. Junior Warden 1902.

WILLIAM H. GRUHLKEY. Railroad section foreman. Raised July 10, 1899. Senior Steward 1900. Junior Deacon 1901.

JOHN BERGESON. Oculist. Raised June 15, 1900.

WILLIAM RALEY. Upholsterer. Affiliated February 19, 1900.

WILLIAM F. JACOBS. Manufacturer. Secretary J. E. Porter Co. Affiliated March 5, 1900.

J. D. McCAUGHTRY. Minister. Affiliated March 19, 1900. Demitted March 7, 1904.

WILLIAM D. DUNCAN. Druggist. Raised April 23, 1900.

CHRISTOPHER J. BYRNE. Teacher and superintendent of schools. Affiliated July 16, 1900. Senior Deacon 1902.

RALPH AYLMER GREEN. Railway mail agent. Raised September 24, 1900. Junior Deacon 1903.

ROBERT LUCIEN SMITH. Railroad freight agent, now Deputy County Treasurer. Affiliated November 5, 1900.

JOHN STUART RYBURN

To whose memory Ryburn Memorial Hospital was erected
by his widow

JOHN HENRY WEAVER. Insurance agent. Raised January 14, 1901.

WILLIAM ALFRED DUNAWAY. Civil engineer and County Surveyor. Raised February 18, 1901.

HENRY FEHR. Physician. Raised February 21, 1901. Demitted June 17, 1901.

WILLIAM SHERMAN DICK. Engineer. Affiliated March 4, 1901. Demitted December 2, 1901.

ALBERT EDMUND HERZOG. Physician. Raised March 18, 1901.

ERIC LARSON. Piano maker. Raised April 29, 1901. Demitted December 18, 1905.

HOWARD HALSEY BAYNE. Attorney. Raised May 6, 1901. Chaplain 1903.

GEORGE GRANT GALLOWAY. Electrician. Raised May 20, 1901.

GEORGE PHILO HILLS. Attorney. Raised September 25, 1901. Junior Warden 1903.

WILLIAM HENRY SEWARD. Clerk. Raised October 14, 1901. Senior Steward 1902.

ALBERT JAY ROBERTS. Physician. Raised November 11, 1901.

JOHN L. CLARK. Retired. Affiliated November 18, 1901.
OTIS BACH. Bookkeeper. Raised October 28, 1901.

SAMUEL ERASTUS BERGESON. Merchant. Raised November 25, 1901. Demitted March 19, 1906.

NICHOLAI A. HAUGE. Dentist. Affiliated December 16, 1901. Suspended N. P. D April 17, 1905. Reinstated October 16, 1905. Demitted November 20, 1905.

HERBERT LEROY PETTITT. Druggist. Raised December 30, 1901.

DOUGLAS LOW MCKENNEY. County Clerk La Salle county. Raised February 10, 1902.

CHARLES M. BUELL. Farmer. Affiliated February 17, 1902. Suspended N. P. D. June 5, 1905.

RICHARD DANIEL MILLS. Attorney. Assistant State's Attorney. Raised March 24, 1902. Senior Warden 1906. Acting Master, Master-elect having moved from jurisdiction.

HERMAN SILVER BLANCHARD. Attorney. Raised April 14, 1902. Worshipful Master 1906. Commissioned Grand Lecturer 1906.

FRANK LESLIE SEWARD. Druggist. Raised April 28, 1902.

WILLIAM WILLARD HARDEN. Druggist. Raised May 5, 1902. Died September 7, 1904.

BENJAMIN F. REEDER. Carpenter. Affiliated June 16, 1902.

PETER McGILVARY CAMPBELL. Farmer. Ice dealer. Raised September 20, 1902.

GEORGE HENRY AHLBORN. Carriage trimmer. Raised October 7, 1902. Junior Steward 1903.

ALBERT MORTON SHAW. Physician. Raised October 13, 1902.

EDWARD JUSTICE BELROSE. Clerk. Initiated October 20, 1902. No further record.

EMIL J. HOFFMAN. Manufacturer. Raised October 27, 1902. Senior Steward, 1903. Junior Deacon 1904. Senior Deacon 1905. Junior Warden 1906.

MARTIN LUTHER SAMPLE. Hotel-keeper. Raised February 9, 1903.

TRAVERS HERBERT BARRETT. Dentist. Raised April 27, 1903.

FRED ANDREW BACH. Bookkeeper. Raised June 1, 1903.

EARL WAYNE ZIBBELL. Bank clerk. Raised June 22, 1903. Senior Steward 1904. Junior Deacon 1905. Senior Deacon 1906.

CHARLES GIDEON KELLY. Grocer. Raised June 29, 1903.

ROBERT J. REID. Commission agent. Affiliated July 6, 1903.

WILLIAM BEIGHEL MYERS. Merchant. Firm, Fisher, Myers & Co. Raised July 13, 1903.

JAMES HENRY MONTIETH. Insurance superintendent. Raised September 28, 1903. Senior Deacon 1904. Junior Warden 1905.

EDWARD HOLBROOK ASHLEY. Dentist. Raised October 1, 1903. Demitted March 20, 1905.

HARRY WALLACE MITCHELL. Electrician. Raised November 9, 1903. Senior Steward 1905. Junior Deacon 1906.

WILLIAM SCALES. Piano maker. Raised February 8, 1904. Junior Steward 1906.

CHARLES SAMUEL EELLS. Farmer. Raised February 8, 1904.

JOHN LOW BARNARD. Bookkeeper. Raised March 14, 1904. Senior Steward 1906.

JOHN WELCH WILLARD. Insurance superintendent. Raised March 28, 1904.

ALBERT FREDERICK HORNUNG. Farmer. Initiated April 18, 1904. No further record.

LOUIS EDMUND WEIDMANN. Merchant. Initiated May 9, 1904. No further record.

OSCAR FRANK WEIDMANN. Merchant. Initiated May 9, 1904. No further record.

RALPH MELVIN CRAM. Traveling salesman. Raised May 16, 1904.

ROBERT J. W. BRIGGS. Veterinary surgeon. Affiliated June 6, 1904.

ELLIS SEED. Retired. Affiliated June 6, 1904.

WILLIAM HUNTINGTON HULL. Merchant. Firm, Irion & Hull. Raised October 10, 1904.

EDGAR FREEMAN BRADFORD. Laundryman. Raised October 10, 1904.

WALTER GARFIELD BUTTON. Bookkeeper. Raised October 31, 1904.

BENJAMIN FRANKLIN TRUMBO. Farmer. Sheriff La Salle county 1903-'06. Raised November 28, 1904.

TOM WOODS SMURR. Lawyer. Raised November 28, 1904.

BURDETTE ELMERIN LA DUE. Specialist. Affiliated December 5, 1904.

FRANK FOREST FOLLETT. Lawyer. Raised December 26, 1904.

GEORGE WILLIAM HARRIS DINGMAN. Farmer. Raised January 9, 1905.

JAMES MADISON MEKEEL. Contractor. Affiliated January 16, 1905.

CHARLES WALLACE LONG. Farmer. Raised January 23, 1905.

WILLIAM HENRY HINEBAUGH. Lawyer. Judge County Court. Raised February 20, 1905.

GEORGE JOHN WATERS. Traveling salesman. Affiliated April 3, 1905.

WALTER ELMER SPECKMAN. Printer. Raised April 10, 1905.

WALTER STEPHEN BRADFORD. Confectioner. Affiliated June 5, 1905.

CHARLES LINCOLN GAPEN. Druggist. Lieutenant Company C, war with Spain. Raised June 26, 1905.

SAMUEL EMORY CLEGG. Steam fitter. Raised June 26. 1905.

TROY WILSON APPLEBY. Secretary insurance company. Raised November 13, 1905.

ELMER ELLSWORTH ROBERTS. Attorney. Raised January 29, 1906.

WILLIAM SHERMAN MYERS. Salesman. Affiliated April 2, 1906.

SILAS ECLIPS KAIN. Farmer. Raised April 9, 1906.

DAVID ARTHUR COOK. Attorney. Cashier Central Title & Trust Co., Geneseo, Ill. Raised April 23, 1906.

WILLIAM SUMNER WATSON. Mechanic. Raised April 30, 1906.

JOHN SEDGWICK RHOADS. Jeweler. Raised September 3, 1906.

CHARLES WESLEY NICHOLS. Piano maker. Initiated December 18, 1905.

CARL VOLKENANNT. Blacksmith. Raised September 3, 1906.

CARL MOODY PROVINS. Farmer. Raised October 1, 1906.

RECAPITULATION.

John Dean Caton and Milton H. Swift, father of our esteemed townsman, Edward C. Swift, were raised December 11, 1845. This was the first work in Occidental Lodge, and it was done while the Lodge was working under dispensation. Since that time, to October 10, 1906, four hundred and fifty-six brethren were raised and one hundred and seventy affiliated in Occidental Lodge, making a total membership in sixty years of six hundred and thirty-three, an average increase of more than eleven members each year. The average raising in the sixty years is more than seven and two-thirds, a record not excelled outside of Chicago Lodges. Of this fraternity of men, two hundred and fifty-three demitted, fifty-one were suspended for non-payment of dues, and three were expelled. Two of those expelled were for failure to answer summons to pay dues. Death claimed one hundred and eleven members, which left eleven of the brethren of whom I was unable to discover how their membership with Occidental Lodge was cancelled. With these deductions, Occidental Lodge had, on the tenth day of October, 1906, a membership of one hundred and ninety-seven.

Raised 456
Affiliated 170
                      —— 626

Demitted 253
Suspended N. P. D. 51
Expelled 3
Dead 111
No record 11
Membership October 10, 1906 197
                      —— 626

In the above tabulation we do not count those E. A.s or F. C.s who never advanced.

POLITICAL AND CIVIL OFFICES

HELD BY MEMBERS OF OCCIDENTAL LODGE, No. 40, A. F. & A. M.

JUDGES SUPREME COURT.

John Dean Caton, Chief Justice.

Theophilus Lyle Dickey, Judge.

Madison E. Hollister, Chief Justice of the Supreme Court of Idaho.

JUDGES OF THE CIRCUIT COURT.

John Dean Caton, 1843-'48.

Theophilus Lyle Dickey, 1849-'52.

Madison E. Hollister, 1855-'66.

Charles Blanchard, 1887-1906.

Edgar Eldredge, 1906 and present time.

JUDGES OF THE COUNTY COURT.

Henry G. Cotton, Sr., 1847.

Patrick M. Killduff, Associate, 1847.

William Henry Hinebaugh, 1892 to present time.

JUDGES OF THE PROBATE COURT.

Henry G. Cotton, Sr., ex-officio, 1847.

Albert T. Lardin, 1894 to present time.

ATTORNEY GENERALS STATE OF ILLINOIS.

Washington Bushnell, 1868-'72.

William H. Stead, 1904, present incumbent.

MEMBERS OF NATIONAL CONGRESS.

Burton C. Cook, 1864 to 1871, when he resigned to become solicitor for the Chicago & Northwestern railroad.

William Cullen, 1880-'84.

Burton C. Cook was a member of the Peace Commission that met in Washington in 1861 to try to avert the Civil war.

STATE SENATORS.

William Stadden, 1839, 1840, 1841.
William Reddick, 1847, 1849, 1851, and in the 80s.
Burton C. Cook, 1853, 1855, 1857, 1859.
Washington Bushnell, 1861, 1863, 1865, 1867.

MEMBERS OF THE LEGISLATURE.

Abram R. Dodge, 1840-'41.
Joseph Otis Glover, 1847.
Champlin R. Potter (Ottawa Lodge), 1853.
Theodore C. Gibson, 1863.
James Clark, 1871.

STATE'S ATTORNEYS.

Seth B. Farwell, 1838, 1841, 1842.
Burton C. Cook, 1846 to 1852.
W. H. L. Wallace, 1852 to 1857.
Washington Bushnell, 1857 to 1861.
O. C. Gray, substitute, 1858.
David P. Jones, 1861 to 1864.
Charles Blanchard, 1865 to 1873.
Henry Mayo, 1872 to 1880; also County Attorney several years.
W. H. Stead, 1896 to 1900.
Clarence Griggs has been elected County Attorney by the Board of Supervisors for several years past.

SHERIFFS.

William Stadden, 1834-'35.
Alson Woodruff, 1836-'37.
William Reddick, 1838-'39.
R. Eaton Goodell, 1851-'53.
Francis J. Warner, 1854, '55, '58, '59.
William Cullen, 1865-'66.
Hubert A. McCaleb, 1867-'68.

THEOPHILUS LYLE DICKEY

Benjamin Franklin Trumbo, 1903-'06.

W. L. Milligan was chief Deputy Sheriff under his father, W. R. Milligan, 1883-'86.

CLERKS CIRCUIT COURT.

Lorenzo Leland, 1841-'48.

Philo Lindley, 1846-'56.

John F. Nash, 1857-'61.

Absalom B. Moore, 1862-'64.

Roswell W. Holmes, 1876-'80.

Henry Phillips, 1896-'04.

CLERKS COUNTY COURT.

David Walker, 1831-'32.

Maurice Murphy, vice Joseph Cloud, deceased, 1842.

Philo Lindley, 1857-'60.

A. B. Moore, 1865-'68.

H. A. McCaleb, 1873-'77.

Douglas L. McKenney, 1898, present incumbent.

COUNTY TREASURERS.

Lorenzo Leland, 1836.

Jabez Fitch, 1839-'46.

B. B. Fellows, 1852-'53.

Jared B. Ford, 1854-'55.

Samuel R. Lewis, E. A., 1856-'59.

George S. Stebbins, 1860-'62.

Asa Mann Hoffman was elected Treasurer in 1886, and died May 4, 1887.

MAYORS.

Patrick M. Killduff, Mayor of Peru, 1838.

David Walker, Mayor of Ottawa.

J. O. Glover, Mayor of Ottawa.

Milton H. Swift, Mayor of Ottawa.

Julius Avery, Mayor of Ottawa.

John Brooks Rice, Mayor of Ottawa.
Frank F. Brower, Mayor of Ottawa.
David P. Jones, Mayor of Ottawa.
Samuel Richolson, Mayor of Ottawa.
Louis W. Hess, Mayor of Ottawa.
Charles E. Hook, Mayor of Ottawa.

COUNTY COMMISSIONERS.

Benjamin Thurston, 1835.
Alson Woodruff, 1840.
Henry G. Cotton, 1849.
Champlain R. Potter and Israel C. Cooper were commissioners who divided La Salle county into townships, 1850.

MY OLD HUNTING HORN.

[Written in 1878 by W. L. Milligan, as his farewell to the chase, a sport he was endeared to while on the farm, and which charms were lost with the death of his hunting horse, Frank.]

I.

Your mouthpiece is gone and your luster is dim,
Your sides are all dented and bad broken in,
'Twould be a vain effort to waken the morn,
With such a cracked instrument, old hunting horn.

II.

Thro' forests and wild-woods, your echoes have dwelled,
Along rolling waters your anthems have swelled;
To call from pursuit the hounds all forlorn,
Or cheer up the chase, my old hunting horn.

III.

'Way over green fields and seared meadows you've sang,
Far over the hills and thro' valley you've rang;
And from rock to rock on the night air you've borne
The sweetest of music, my old hunting horn.

IV.

For a moment you'd kiss the wild ledges on high,
And then your soft cadence would soar to the sky,
And sing songs to the stars—returning at morn,
To waken "old Theron,"—my old hunting horn.

V.

Your clear ringing notes that once swelled to the skies,
Are now, my old horn, but low whispering sighs.
Ah, yes, you've grown old; the Vermillion would scorn
To prolong your faint echoes, my old hunting horn.

VI.

I'll wind you no more, you're faltering in sound,
You've lost your rich tenor to call in the hound,
Your strains so elysian, no more on the morn,
Will startle old Reynard, my old hunting horn.

THE WHITE APRON AND THE SWORD.

Major General Joseph Warren, who was slain at the battle of Bunker Hill, was a Freemason and the Grand Master of the Grand Lodge of Massachusetts, and it is significant that this was the first grand offering of American Freemasonry at the altar of liberty, and the ground floor of the temple of the American union was bloodstained at the *eastern gate.* On this same day, Washington was elected commander-in-chief of the American army. Washington was made a Mason in Frederickburg's Lodge, Virginia, in August, 1753. He was offered the Grand Mastership of the Grand Lodge of Virginia in 1779, but declined the honor. He, however, accepted the office of Master of Alexandria Lodge, No. 22, in 1788. On the 30th day of April, 1789, he was sworn in as President of the United States on the bible of St. John's Lodge, New York. He officiated as Grand Master pro tem. in laying the corner stone of the capitol at Washington in 1793. He died in.1799, and was buried with Masonic honors December 18, 1799.

The familiar words, "First in war, first in peace, and first in the hearts of his countrymen," which described the estimation in which he was regarded by his countrymen, were expressed by Major General Henry Lee, a Member of Congress, and a Freemason, in his Masonic oration on December 26, 1799, the day Congress paid a national tribute to the memory of Washington.

General Washington presided and conferred the degrees of symbolic Masonry on General LaFayette, in a military Lodge at Valley Forge, in the winter of 1777.

Brigadier General Richard Montgomery was a Freemason. He entered the American army as Brigadier General, and was killed at the battle of Quebec December, 1775.

Major General David Wooster was a Freemason. He was both a naval and military hero for over forty years. He served in the armies and navies of Spain, France and England, and as Major General in the American army was mortally wounded while leading an attack on the British troops in 1777.

Richard Caswell led the troops under General Gates at the battle of Camden in 1780. He was a Freemason, and afterwards Governor of North Carolina, and Grand Master of the Grand Lodge of Freemasons of the same state.

Mordecai Gist was a Freemason. He fought for his country from the commencement to the close of the Revolutionary war. He was Master of Army Lodge, No. 27, and president of the convention of Masons from the Military Lodge of Morristown, New Jersey, and finally Grand Master of the Grand Lodge of Georgia.

James Jackson served with distinction in the continental army. He afterwards became Governor and Grand Master of Georgia.

Morgan Lewis, who as chief of the staff of General Gates accompanied him in the campaign of 1776 and in the war of 1812, commanded a division of the American army, was Governor of New York in 1804, and Grand Master of Masons of New York from 1830 until his death in 1844.

Irsael Putnam commanded a regiment in the expedition which captured Havana, and was a prominent figure in the war of the Revolution. His tombstone bears the inscription: "He dared to lead where any dared to follow."

Rufus Putnam, "the father of the northwest," was for some time chief engineer of the American army, and commanded a brigade under General Wayne in 1792. He was made a Mason in "American Union Lodge" in 1779, and elected Grand Master of Ohio in 1808.

John Sullivan, one of the most famous of the Generals of the Revolution, was elected Governor of New Hampshire in 1786, and Grand Master in 1789.

Anthony Wayne, whose popular title was "Mad Anthony," won great renown by his capture of Stony Point, New York, only bayonets being used. He succeeded St. Clair in command of the Western army and gained a brilliant victory over the Miami Indians in 1794. A monument to his memory was erected by the Masonic fraternity at Stony Point in 1857.

The Baron de Kalb, mortally wounded at the battle of Camden, was buried with military and Masonic honors by his victorious enemies.

Count Casimir Pulaski, the famous cavalry leader, killed at Charleston in 1779, was a Mason.

Commodore James Nicholson, an active member of the fraternity, was placed in 1776 at the head of the list of captains in the Continental navy, a position which he retained until the close of the war. His brothers, Samuel and John, were also Masons and naval captains.

Stephen Decatur was a member of the same Lodge as Commodore James Nicholson, and, like the latter, a captain in the United States navy from its first establishment.

Commodore Edward Preble, a member of the "Ancient Landmark Lodge," in Portland, Maine, entered the navy in 1779, and commanded the American squadron at the bombardment of Tripoli in 1804.

Commodore Whipple was a member of the "American Union Lodge" during the early days at Marietta. He burned the Gaspe in 1772, and was one of the most brilliant officers of the land or sea service.

General Andrew Jackson at various times commanded armies in the field, but is best known in connection with his decisive victory over the British at New Orleans in 1815, which put an end to the war. He subsequently became President of the United States and Grand Master of Tennessee.

General William H. Winder, who commanded on the losing side at Blandensburg, the other eventful battle of the war of 1812, was elected Grand Master of Maryland in 1821.

General Stephen Austin, the liberator of Texas, and "Sam" Houston, the recognized hero of the Texas war of independence, were Freemasons; also Colonel David Crockett, backwoodsman and Member of Congress, who fought on the same side, and after a hard siege, surrendered to General Santa Anna, by whose order he was put to death with the other survivors in 1836. [Robert Yates Gibson, brother of Bro. Theodore C. Gibson, of Occidental Lodge, was slain with Crockett and his brave followers at the massacre of the Almo.]

William J. Worth served during the last war with England, and was present at the actions of Chrystler's Farm, Chippewa and Lundy's Lane. In 1842 he commanded the army which defeated the hostile savages in Florida, and subsequently distinguished himself in the battles of the Mexican war. A monument was dedicated to his memory by the Grand Lodge of New York in 1857.

John A. Quitman, Grand Master of Mississippi, commanded a division of General Scott's army, and when the city of Mexico was taken, he was made its Governor until peace was proclaimed.

The brethren holding high rank during the Civil war were very numerous. Among them were John A. Rawlins, Eli S. Parker, a Seneca Indian, and William R. Rowley, on the staff of General Grant; John Corson Smith, Lieutenant-

Governor and Grand Master of Illinois; and the following brethren commanded armies in the field: George B. McClellan, Winfield Scott Hancock, whose bayonet charge at Williamsburg won from McClellan the compliment, which became proverbial, that "Hancock was superb," N. P. Banks, John A. McClernand, John A. Logan, George E. Pickett, who led the famous final assault on the Union lines at Gettysburg in 1863; Robert E. Patterson and Benjamin F. Butler, against whose life a plot was formed by Confederate prisoners, but given up on their learning that he was a Freemason. Among the Masonic veterans of the war, General James A. Garfield and Major William McKinley were elected Presidents of the United States. General Robt. Anderson, of Fort Sumpter fame, and Albert Pike, scholar, orator, poet and man of letters, were also of the fraternity. The valuable library of the latter, at Little Rock, Arkansas, was about to be destroyed by the Federal troops during the Civil war, but General Thomas H. Benton (Grand Master of Iowa), in command of the Union forces, interposed, and by making the house his headquarters, not only preserved the library but also the residence.

General Nelson A. Miles, Indian fighter, and for several years commander of the American army, and General Russel A. Alger, Secretary of War during the war with Spain, were members of the Masonic fraternity. General George M. Moulton, who commanded a brigade during the war with Spain, was afterwards Grand Master of Masons of Illinois. Many prominent officers of the army and navy, who took part in that short conflict, are Freemasons, and among them Theodore Roosevelt, President of the United States, and General William R. Shafter (recently deceased) and Admiral Schley, the former commanding the American land forces before Santiago and the latter the squadron which performed such brilliant service off the coast.

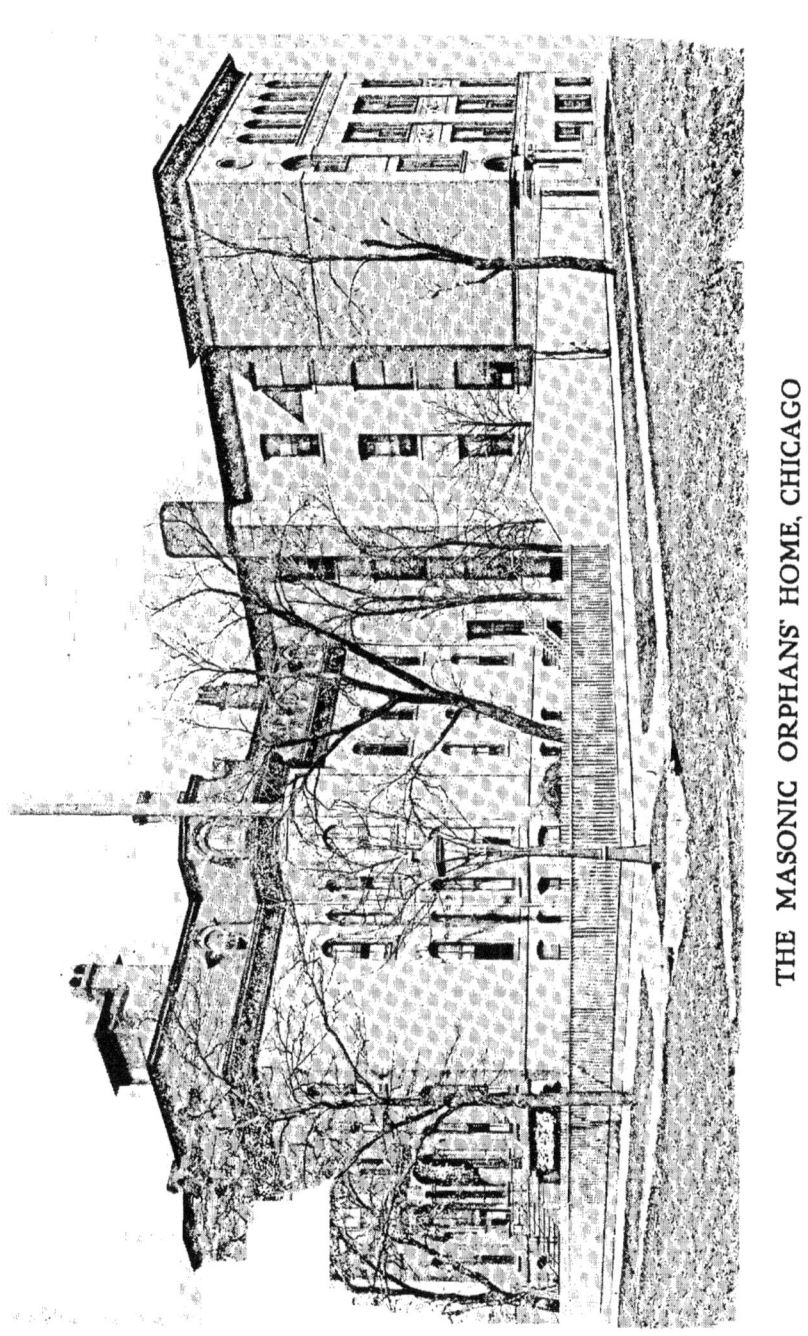

THE MASONIC ORPHANS' HOME, CHICAGO

In reviewing the roll of members of Occidental Lodge, No. 40, we point with pride to the long roll of patriotic brethren who responded to their country's call and offered their lives a sacrifice upon the battlefields of Mexico, the sunny South, Cuba, Porto Rico and the Phillipines.

> Like God's own voice, in after years,
> Resounds the warrior's fame,
> Whose soul his hopeless country cheers,
> Who is its noblest name.
> —ALBERT PIKE.

William Osman, the Masonic patriarch, and venerable editor of the Ottawa *Free Trader,* fought gallantly at the battle of Buena Vista in the war with Mexico.

General W. H. L. Wallace, Past Master of Occidental Lodge, commanded a company in Colonel Hardin's regiment in the war with Mexico. In 1861 he raised the Eleventh regiment Illinois infantry, and for gallantry at the battle of Fort Donelson was promoted Brigadier General. He was mortally wounded at the battle of Shiloh, and died April 8, 1862, with the rank of Major General.

Colonel Theophilus Lyle Dickey was a member of Occidental Lodge. In 1846 he commanded a company of infantry in Colonel Hardin's regiment in the Mexican war. He raised and commanded the Fourth regiment of cavalry during the Civil war and was a gallant and dashing cavalry leader. He was made chief of cavalry on General Grant's staff. At the close of the war he was elected one of the Judges of the Supreme Court of Illinois.

Colonel Daniel Fletcher Hitt, a member of Occidental Lodge, was the hero of three wars, the Black Hawk, Mexican and Civil, and distinguished himself for fearlessness and heroic achievements. He commanded the Fifty-third Illinois during the Civil war.

M

The three brothers, William L., Theodore C. and John Fletcher Gibson, were all in the Mexican war. Their father, John Gibson, was a Captain of Pennsylvania troops during the war of 1812. William L. was Lieutenant Colonel, and Theodore C. was Major of the Fifty-third during the Civil war. They were among the first to answer their country's call and raised companies for the Eleventh Illinois infantry.

John Morrill, E. C. Henshaw, David R. Gregg, O. C. Gray and Bradford C. Mitchell, father of our worthy brother Marshall B. Mitchell, fought Santa Anna at Buena Vista, and shared the glories of victory with others whom we have named in the war with Mexico.

> Still, still our glorious banner waves,
>   Unstained by flight or shame,
> And the Mexicans among their hills still
>   Tremble at our name.
> So honor unto those that stood!
> Disgrace to those that fled!
> And everlasting glory unto Buena Vista's dead!
>   —ALBERT PIKE.

Douglas Hapeman, a member of Occidental Lodge, was the beloved and gallant Colonel of the One Hundred Fourth regiment during the Civil war.

J. H. Widmer was Major of the same regiment. Colonel A. B. Moore was the first Colonel of the One Hundred Fourth. They, too, were members of Occidental Lodge.

John Morrill, a member of Occidental Lodge, was Colonel of the Sixty-fourth Illinois infantry, and for gallantry was brevetted Brigadier General. He was also in the war with Mexico.

Joanis O. Harris was Surgeon of the Fifty-third, and Reuben F. Dyer, Surgeon of the One Hundred Fourth during the Civil war.

Hubert A. McCaleb was Colonel of a regiment of infantry. He, too, was a member of Occidental Lodge.

Philo Lindley was Quartermaster of the Fifty-third Illinois during the Civil war, a Past Master of Occidental Lodge.

E. C. Henshaw and Charles Houghtaling were Captains of artillery.

Thomas C. Fullerton, Moses Osman, Frank G. King, Leman A. Rising, Patrick Ryan and E. H. Smith were Captains. Arthur L. Wagner and James Rolla Chapman, graduates of West Point, were distinguished officers in the regular army. W. H. Higby was Captain of Company A, Third Regiment, Illinois National Guard, and C. L. Gapen and W. E. W. MacKinlay were in Company C, Illinois National Guard, in the war with Spain in 1898. W. E. W. MacKinlay is now an officer in the regular army.

Other veterans of the Civil war who were members of Occidental Lodge were:

David Batcheller.	Edward L. Herrick.
Henry P. Brunker.	John Hilliard.
George J. Burgess.	Geo. W. Hyde.
Thomas I. Conger.	David Krouse.
David A. Cook.	J. F. Marriner.
Frank J. Crawford.	Henry Mayo.
James R. Cross.	Wm. McCombs.
Wm. G. Earl.	Wm. A. McCullom.
Frank C. Flora.	John L. Morrison.
Joseph Ford.	E. A. Nattinger.
George W. Fuchs.	Samuel S. Pearson.
Wm. P. Gregg.	Charles E. Pettit.
Sheldon B. Griswold.	Samuel W. Porter.
Wesley B. Hall.	Ira Potter.
S. I. Haney.	W. E. Prichard.

John M. Purrucker.   Wm. K. Stewart.
Thomas Reedy.   Willard S. Wheeler.
John H. Shepherd.   Charles J. Yockey.
J. B. Smith.

> In a few more years they will all be
> Under the sod and the dew,
>   Waiting the judgment day;
> Under the rose the blue,
>   Under the lilies the gray.

CHARITY.

Foot to foot, on mercy's errand,
　　When we hear a Mason cry,
Hungry, thirsty, naked, homeless,
　　Let us heed and let us fly.
And what'er his pain or grief,
　　Quick with bread to feed the hungry,
　　Quick with raiment for the naked,
　　Quick with shelter for the homeless,
　　Quick with God's own sympathy.

A reference to the records of Occidental Lodge will reveal the fact that Occidental Lodge, in a commendable degree, responded to the call of distress and all worthy Masonic charities.

Appeals for assistance from worthy sources always appeal to the charity of Occidental Lodge, and liberal amounts are contributed and charged up to the charity fund.

Occidental Lodge took an active part in the organization of the Illinois Masonic Orphans' Home in 1885. The author of this work, while Master in 1884, in his annual address to Occidental Lodge, laid special stress on the necessity of a home for the widows and orphans of Freemasons, and called the Lodge's attention to the wonderful accomplishment of the Masonic Orphan's Home of Kentucky, of which he was an annual contributor, and also of similar institutions in other Grand Masonic jurisdictions, including the Masonic Male and Female schools of England and Ireland.

A committee was appointed at this, the annual communication in 1884, to prepare and present a memorial to the Grand Lodge, praying that body to take the necessary steps to endow such an institution. It was not a new subject to present to the Grand Lodge for its favorable consideration, for it had been a live and engrossing topic among the craft for more than thirty years.

The committee appointed by Occidental Lodge never had an opportunity to present the memorial of Occidental Lodge to the Grand Lodge, because of the active work of the brethren of Chicago Lodges, who, on the 11th day of March, 1885, secured articles of incorporation from the Secretary of State, and proceeded to organize

The Illinois Masonic Orphans' Home.

On the 20th of April, 1885, a meeting of the promoters was held in the parlors of St. Bernard Commandery, No. 35, K. T., when a formal organization was effected. The author of this work, then Master of Occidental Lodge, was present, and pledged the support of Occidental Lodge, and was among the first to contribute toward the worthy project, and, in recognition thereof, holds life membership certificate number one.

At this meeting a code of by-laws was adopted and the following officers elected:

George M. Moulton, President.
Henry Turner, Vice-President.
Gil. W. Barnard, Secretary.
Wiley M. Egan, Treasurer.
George W. Warvell, Counsel.

Trustees: Henson Robinson, Chas. A. Moses, D. H. McDonald, Herschel W. Dryer, George M. Moulton, Thos. E. Miller, S. T. Gunderson, Geo. W. Warvell, John J. Badenoch, Gorman B. Coffin, John A. Crawford, Henry Turner.

Board of Visitation: Dr. W. A. Stevens, of Chicago, and P. W. Barclay, of Cairo, for one-year term. L. L. Munn, of Freeport, and James G. Elwood, of Joliet, for two-year term, and Norman T. Gassette, of Chicago, and W. L. Milligan, Ottawa, for the three-year term.

At the first annual meeting of the Illinois Masonic Orphans' Home, held in the Armory of Apollo Commandery, No. 1, K. T., March 9, 1886, in his annual report, delivered on this occasion, the president, brother George M. Moulton, had this to say about Occidental Lodge:

"You will notice that Occidental Lodge, No. 40, located at Ottawa, is the banner lodge, by a large majority, so far as membership in this Association is concerned, embracing as it does in its fold ninety-eight active members and four life members. The brethren of Occidental Lodge are no different from the craft elsewhere in the state. They are not any more wealthy or inclined to giving for charitable purposes. The gratifying result stated is simply the result of a worthy brother's persistent effort for a few weeks among the fraters. Brother W. L. Milligan, with the interest of the Association at heart, canvassed thoroughly his Lodge, and, as a result, we have an income from that Lodge of nearly $100.00 annually (this did not include the four life members, $200.00), sufficient for the entire support of one orphan. If there were in every Lodge in the state as earnest a worker as brother Milligan, our absolute unqualified success would not be a matter of conjecture."

The brethren who contributed $50.00 each and received certificates of life membership, were W. L. Milligan, Daniel F. Hitt, Asa Mann Hoffman and John D. Hammond. At this meeting, Alex T. Darrah, of Bloomington, then Grand Master, A. B. Ashley, Kewanee, Jacob Krohn, Freeport, and W. L. Milligan, of Ottawa, were elected as trustees for the three-year term. (W. L. Milligan was subsequently re-elected for a second three-year term.) A sum of $10,000.00 was appropriated for the purchase of a site for the home, should such purchase become necessary during the year.

A suitable property and buildings was subsequently purchased at the cornor of Sheldon and Carrol avenues, and was formerly dedicated by the Grand Lodge, October 7, 1886, and the Illinois Masonic Orphans' Home soon became a credit and an honor to the promoters, and yet the Grand Lodge had no connection with it whatever.

April 7, 1888, brother Robert A. Miller, a resident of Moultrie county, Illinois, executed a will, bequeathing to the Masonic Grand Lodge of the state of Illinois a tract of land of 264 acres, located one and three-quarters miles from the city of Sullivan, upon condition that said Grand Lodge shall cause to be erected and maintained thereon a suitable home for such widows and orphans of Masons, as said Grand Lodge may, from time to time, designate, reserving only a life estate for his wife. Brother Robert A. Miller died in 1891. Mrs. Miller died August 20, 1891, thus leaving the property free to come into possession of the Grand Lodge if it would accept it under the provisions of the will. Should the Grand Lodge refuse to accept the property it then would have become the property of Moultrie county.

Through the untiring efforts of brother George M. Moulton, Grand Master, the Grand Lodge accepted the property at the annual communication of the Grand Lodge in October, 1902, and erected thereon a Masonic Home, and on the Grand Lodge formally accepting this property, and building a Masonic Home thereon, the Illinois Masonic Orphans' Home of Chicago was transferred to the management of the Grand Lodge, under the following conditions:

"The Illinois Masonic Orphans' Home required as conditions precedent to the transfer of their property, and the rights of which it may be possessed, that the principal sum of the endowment fund, amounting to approximately $30,-000, be kept intact, and that only the interest accruing therefrom be expended in the accomplishment of the object for which said corporation was organized, also the further condition that the M. W. Grand Lodge will continuously maintain a home at or near the city of Chicago, for the orphan

MASONIC HOME AT SULLIVAN, ILLINOIS

children of deceased Master Masons of this jurisdiction, and that the M. W. Grand Lodge will pledge itself to continuously administer the trust now devolving upon the Illinois Masonic Orphans' Home, the equivalent in all respects as it has been heretofore administered."

The funds of the Illinois Masonic Home for the aged, approximately $9,000, were also transferred to the M. W. Grand Lodge, upon condition that the principal sum be kept intact as a permanent fund, and only the interest accruing therefrom be expended in the accomplishment of the object for which said Illinois Masonic Home for the aged was organized.

The reports to the Grand Lodge in October, 1906, showed that sixty-six children were being cared for and educated by the Illinois Masonic Orphans' at Chicago, and fifty-five old people were being cared for and made as comfortable as possible in their declining years in the Masonic Home at Sullivan, Illinois.

THE DEAD.

For I say that those who have lived well are still living,
rather than those are who lead ill lives.

—EURIPIDES.

He mourns the dead who lives as they desire.

—YOUNG.

In compiling the roll of our fraternal dead, for all of
whom we mourn, we found so many who were distinguished in military and civil life and Masonic standing that it
may seem invidious to make special mention of any, yet
there were some who were so conspicuous in military fame
and distinguished in the civil affairs of our country and active in Masonic circles, that in justice to their memory an
epitome of their biography, reciting their military prowess,
the glory of their intellectual worth, and the beauty of
moral merit that adorned their homes and sanctified their
Masonic and domestic relations, should be inscribed as a
tribute to their memory on the pages of the history of Occidental Lodge.

203

IN MEMORIAM.

[By Norman T. Gassette, Chicago, and Past Grand Commander,
K. T., Illinois.]

I.

Alas! When all is said which we can say,
Above the pallid, cold and silent clay,
When throbbing, sobbing dirge and funeral song
Their force have spent upon the morning throng;
When tone as well, from speaker's voice has sped,
Naught then is left but memories of our dead.

II.

Hush! Hear the wheel's loud rumble in the street,
The din of business and fast-stirring feet;
No thought is there, midst traffic's hardened strife,
Of death's fell work, with finite hope and life.

III.

Since man has lived to think, and toil, and die,
Some hope he's sought on which he might rely.
With hands outstretched, in potent voice of prayer,
He has invoked an answer everywhere.
Seraphic visions fill his mind at times,
And music sounds as if from far-off climes.

IV.

The war then from the earth comes rushing in
To draw his thoughts from God to earth's foul din;
And hence the sons of Egypt sought to find
Some solace for the worried, wearied mind.

V.

So, for their dead a sleeping place they made
In vaulted crypt, hid under earth's deep shade,
Above each crypt a Mastaba was found,
Where oft the beat of saddened hearts would sound.
Around, above and on the walls was spread
A record of the deeds of all their dead.

VI.

The rumble in the noisy street goes on.
They heed it not, in death's still Parthenon,
And kneeling down, they spake then of the soul,
In halo clothed, far off, from earth so cold.

VII.

We do not need to write upon the walls
The deeds of these, our dead. Where falls
A shadow on the floor, or roof above,
Is record made, a silhouette of love;
And deep within our hearts we seem to feel,
A spirit cause, to make us pause and kneel.

VIII.

Then let the wheels roll on, out in the street,
But let us oft, in this our chapel meet,
And here review the memories of the dead,
Then silently retire, with noiseless tread.

SHELBY DOOLITTLE.

Brother Doolittle was born in 1821, and was but 27 years old when he died. Brother Doolittle died at Princeton, Ill., after an illness of but thirty-six hours, on Sabbath morning, January 9, 1848.

Brother Shelby Doolittle was raised in Occidental Lodge in 1846, and his is the first death among the brethren of Occidental Lodge that we can find any record of. Brother Doolittle lived in Ottawa about three years, and by the excellence of his character and the kindness of his disposition had won many warm friends among the citizens of Ottawa. He was a man of firm principles, of high tone, generous feeling and warm and benevolent heart. His talents were of an order that promised usefulness in his profession, that of a lawyer. The news of his sudden and painful death was received with deep sorrow by his friends and brethren. Brother Doolittle was a bright and true Mason, who, in his intercourse with his brethren of the mystic tie, as well as with the world, ever regulated his conduct by the square. The death of brother Doolittle having been made known to the brethren of Occidental Lodge, the following resolutions were adopted:

Resolved, That the brethren of this Lodge, whilst they desire to bow with submission to the Divine will, cannot but express their deep sorrow at the early removal of so worthy a brother, whose kind and affable demeanor had endeared him to a large circle of friends, by whom, as well as the members of this Lodge, his loss will be deeply and severely felt.

Resolved, That the brethren of this Lodge tender their kindest sympathies to the relatives and friends of the deceased, with the assurance that the memory of their departed brother and friend will long be cherished in the kindly affections of the brethren with whom he was connected in the Masonic tie.

Resolved, That these resolutions be entered upon the records of this Lodge, and a copy of the same be forwarded to the relatives of the deceased, and also published in the Ottawa *Free Trader.*

His work was not done, yet his column is broken,
Mourn ye and weep, for ye cherished his worth,
Let every tear drop be sympathy's token,
Lost to the brotherhood, lost to the earth.

IN TIME TO COME.

The flowers are dead that made a summer splendor
  By wayside nooks and on the sunny hill,
And with regret, these hearts of ours grow tender,
  As sometimes all hearts will.

We loved the blossoms, for they helped to brighten
  The lives so dark with wearying toil and care,
As hopes and dreams forever help to lighten
  The heavy loads we bear.

How like the flowers, whose transient life is ended,
  The hopes and dreams are, that for one brief hour
Make the glad heart a garden bright and splendid
  About love's latticed bower.

One little hour of almost perfect pleasure,
  A foretaste of the happiness to come.
Then sudden frost—the garden yields its treasure,
  And stands in sorrow dumb.

Oh, listen, heart! The flower may lose its glory,
  Beneath the touch of frost, but does not die,
In spring it will repeat the old sweet story,
  Of God's dear by and by.

In heaven, if never here, the hopes we cherish,
  The flowers of human life we count as lost,
Will live again. Such beauty cannot perish,
  And heaven has no frost.

WILLIAM HENRY LAMB WALLACE

Worshipful Master 1848 and 1849

BRADFORD C. MITCHELL.

Brother Bradford C. Mitchell, father of brother M. B. Mitchell, came to Ottawa in 1836, and at the time of his death had been a resident of Ottawa more than twenty years. We quote from the Ottawa *Free Trader* of Sept. 25, 1858: "Mr. Mitchell has been a resident of Ottawa for over twenty years past, and being an industrious, kind and amiable man, had a very large circle of friends. He was also a member of the Masonic fraternity, the Odd Fellows society, of the Niagara fire company, and had been a soldier in Mexico (was in Capt. Dickey's La Salle county company. —Author). On this account, besides a very large number of citizens, his funeral on Sunday was attended by all the civic societies of which he had been a member, and by the military companies of our city, all together forming the finest and largest funeral procession ever witnessed in Ottawa. He was buried, in accordance with his expressed wish, by the Masonic fraternity, whose beautiful and impressive ceremonial on the occasion was witnessed by the vast concourse with deep awe and reverence."

Brothers Thomas J. Wade, Philo Lindley and Oliver C. Gray were appointed a committee to draft resolutions on the death of Brother Mitchell, which were presented to and adopted by Occidental Lodge, No. 40, A. F. & A. M., and are as follows:

It having pleased our Supreme Grand Master to call from labor below to everlasting refreshment above our beloved brother, Bradford C. Mitchell, and being deeply impressed with the loss thus sustained, be it

Resolved, That Occidental Lodge, No. 40, A. F. & A. M., in the death of our beloved brother, has lost one of its best and most faithful members, and though his place in the Lodge may never be filled, the memory of him and his truly

N

Masonic virtues, will ever remain a green spot within our hearts.

Resolved, That we deeply sympathize with the widow and orphans of our departed brother, and may "He who tempers the wind to the shorn lamb" take them in His fatherly protection, and aid us in our efforts to console them in their great bereavement.

Resolved, That the members of this Lodge wear the usual badge of mourning thirty days.

Resolved, That a copy of these resolutions be printed in the city papers, spread upon the records of this Lodge, and furnished the family of the deceased.

THE LAST FAREWELL.

How many a strong hand that grappled ours
      In truest faith;
How many a generous heart, with mercy filled,
      Lies low in death;
How many a beaming eye that caught the light
      From the better shore;
How many a tongue that thrilled our inmost chords
      Will speak no more;
How many a seat where sat the good and true
      Is vacant now;
How many a foot in mercy's quest that flew
      No more shall go;
How many a knee that bent with ours in prayer
      Or prayed alone;
Has vanished from our mystic brotherhood
      And gone—and gone
To the Celestial Lodge, and Land of Peace,
      And Light and Song,
Where war and bloodshed have no entering,
      Nor vice, nor wrong;
Where the Supreme Grand Master wise presides,
      · No blight, no curse,
And keeps in holy welcome, crowned and blest,
      A place for us.

W. H. L. WALLACE.

General W. H. L. Wallace was born at Urbana, Ohio, July 8, 1821, and came with his parents to Illinois in 1834, first locating in Deer Park, La Salle county, Illinois. In 1845 he came to Ottawa and entered as a student of law in the office of brother T. L. Dickey. At the opening of the Mexican war, in 1846, he enlisted as a private in a company raised by brother Dickey in Ottawa, and on the organization of the campaign was made orderly sergeant, but was soon promoted to third lieutenant, and finally to the position of adjutant of Colonel Hardin's regiment. He distinguished himself at the battle of Buena Vista by his bravery and heroism. At the close of the Mexican war brother Wallace resumed his studies in the office of brother Dickey, whose daughter he subsequently married. Of his career as an attorney, it is sufficient to say that it was eminently honorable and successful.

On the breaking out of the Rebellion he was invited to command the Eleventh regiment of Illinois volunteers. He cheerfully yielded to the call of his companions in arms and gave himself to his country.

For his bravery at Fort Donelson, he was commissioned Brigadier General, and for distinguished services he was advanced to act as Major General just before the battle of Pittsburg Landing. At this battle he bore himself nobly and safely through the perils of that unlooked for and overwhelming assault on Sunday till about 4 P. M. Finding his division liable to be flanked on either side, he had just given command to his brigade commanders "to fall back steadily," and while overseeing its execution the fatal messenger sealed his lips in silence. The ball passed from near the top of the left ear along the temple, taking in its exit the left eye. He disengaged his feet, as if to dismount, and fell to the ground. He was supposed to be dead. His brother-in-law, Lieutenant C. E. Dickey, and two men bore him tenderly after his retreating columns till the hard pressure of the foe obliged them to leave him on the field. The next day, our troops having recovered the field, found him unconscious, but alive, his pockets rifled and a blanket tossed over him. He was immediately transferred to Savannah to the care of his wife who had arrived the day previous on a visit, but as yet had not seen him. A slight return of consciousness, an occasional smiling recognition of his companion in sorrow, and at last a motion of his finger pointing her to the peaceful Heaven above, were his last acts. The very last acts, coupled with his solemn written resolve after his seemingly providential deliverance at Donelson, to this effect: "For this almost miraculous preservation of my life amid such dangers, I am resolved that henceforth all I am shall be the Lord's," leaves us the consolation in sorrow that he had found rest in Heaven.

General Wallace was universally respected, loved by many, naturally noble and generous, always courteous, his life in most respects far above that of ordinary men, was a model of manly dignity and honor, and yet of engaging simplicity and unaffected modesty.

The deceased had occupied a prominent position in La Salle county and held a high place in public esteem. His remains were brought to Ottawa and met at the Rock Island depot at four o'clock Monday morning, April 14th. The tolling of church bells announced the hour of arrival. An escort of Knights Templar and a delegation of citizens met the remains at the depot and accompanied them to his late residence, from whence, at two P. M., they were laid in state in the Supreme Court house, where they were viewed by thousands of citizens and strangers. Tuesday morning, attended by the Masonic fraternity, the body was carried to the Episcopal church, from which, after appropriate funeral services, it was taken for interment to the family burial ground of brother T. L. Dickey, near his residence on the north bluff, and deposited in its last resting place with the solemn and impressive ceremonies of the Masonic order.

Brother Wallace was raised in Occidental Lodge in 1846 and was Master of Occidental Lodge during the years 1848 and 1849.

> Too soon, too soon, alas, for earth and us,
> The Temple yet unfinished, he is gone.
> Weep, craftsmen, not for him—is not his fame
> Secure?—but for the stricken mourners left,
> Who, now, on tracing board, shall wisely draw
> The strange device that binds the finished work
> With the undone, making a perfect fane,
> By closing up in one the grand design.
> Fallen the stroke, the inexorable blow,
> Too soon, too soon, alas! for earth and us.

"If I die it is glory enough to die in such a cause, and furnish no reason for regret. Man must die some time and to die nobly is a boon granted to few."

—GEN. WALLACE'S LETTER TO HIS WIFE.

HIS BONES ARE DUST.

How often we see quoted the beautiful lines:

"His bones are dust,
His sword is rust, etc."

But how few know the author of them. This was the English poet Coleridge, and they occur as a part of a poem. Here is the connection:

Where is the grave of Sir Arthur O'Kellyn?
Where is the grave of that good man and true?
By the side of a spring in the breast of Helvellyn,
Under the boughs of a young birch tree.
The oak that in summer was sweet to hear,
And rustled its leaves in the fall of the year,
And whistled and roared in the winter alone,
Is gone, and the birch in its stead is grown.
    The knight's bones are dust,
    And his good sword rust,
    His soul is with the saints, I trust.

PHILO LINDLEY.

Brother Lindley had been Circuit Clerk and afterwards County Clerk of La Salle county for a number of years. He was a kind, noble hearted man, and as an officer had no superior. He was Adjutant of the Fifty-third Illinois regiment at the time of his death. His remains were brought to Ottawa on Monday, and laid in state in the court house, until 10 o'clock Tuesday, when they were borne to the Baptist church, and thence to the Illinois avenue cemetery, where they were consigned to mother earth by the solemn and impressive ceremonies of the Masonic fraternity of Occidental Lodge.

> "He slept an iron sleep,
> Slain in fighting for his country."

PHILO LINDLEY

Worshipful Master 1852 and 1856

THE BELLS OF LONDENDERRY.

I.
How sweetly rang the bells, when we chased the honey bee,
And loudly sang the lark, to you, love, and to me,
While winds of sunny April were whispering in glee;
Sing merry!
When childhood heard the bells of Londonderry.

II.
How softly rang the bells when we climbed the misty hill,
When we reached the pebbled cradle of the foamy mountain rill,
And pledged our love at noontide when every bird was still;
Sing merry!
So clearly rang the bells of Londonderry.

III.
And sprightly was the dancing beneath the flowered thorn,
When the little eastern moonlight, like plenty's golden horn,
Lit our way from stile to stile through the fields of whispering corn.
Sing merry!
So gayly rang the bells of Londonderry.

IV.
But now the mountain flowers have lost their rich perfume,
And the lark has now no rapture, the nodding rose no bloom,
Since they took you from the ocean to lay you in the tomb.
Never merry
Shall sound for me sweet bells of Londonderry.

V.
But merrily they'll sound when my heart has passed away,
To the fisher near his nets, and the hillman mowing hay,
To mothers at their doorsteps, and lovers in the May
Making merry,
Shall chime the silver bells of Londonderry.

GEORGE S. STEBBINS.

Brother George S. Stebbins was born at Springfield, Mass., in 1833, and was about 34 years of age at the time of his death. Brother Stebbins came to Ottawa in 1855, and entered the store of Cushman & Lindley as bookkeeper and clerk, and afterwards, for several years, as bookkeeper for Mr. Cushman, private banker. Thence he entered the office of County Treasurer, when Hon. S. R. Lewis was Treasurer, as bookkeeper and accountant, and at the close of Mr. Lewis' term he was for two successive terms elected County Treasurer, an office for which he was peculiarly fitted, and the duties of which he performed with singular fidelity and ability. On retiring from the Treasurer's office he became a partner of the firm of Colwell, Clark & Stebbins. Of him the Ottawa *Free Trader* said:

"We could dwell, did our space permit, fondly and eloquently on the many virtues of the deceased. He was a genial, kind hearted man, with a hand open as day to melting charity. No call in the way of voluntary contribution, whatever its object, if worthy, ever passed brother Stebbins without a liberal response. Modest and unassuming, almost to a fault, he was yet a ripe scholar, and enthusiastic student of the classics, and as a writer wielded perhaps the most graceful pen in Ottawa."

Brother Stebbins was a member of Ottawa Commandery, No. 10, K. T., Shabbona Chapter, No. 37, R. A. M., and Occidental Lodge, No. 40, A. F. & A. M. His funeral was one of the largest ever witnessed in Ottawa. It took place from the Episcopal church Sunday, December 1, 1867, and his remains were accompanied to the cemetery by Occidental Lodge and members of the Masonic fraternity from every Lodge in the county. Ottawa Commandery, No. 10, K. T., acted as escort, while at the grave, in accordance with the request of the deceased, the impressive service of the Masonic fraternity was observed.

The following resolutions were adopted by Occidental Lodge, No. 40, A. F. & A. M.:

WHEREAS, It has pleased the Supreme Architect of the universe to take from our number, by the hand of death, our beloved brother, George S. Stebbins; and,

WHEREAS, Brother Stebbins has for many years been an influential and prominent citizen as well as a member of the different Masonic organizations of this city; therefore,

Resolved, That, in his death, our order has lost a true and worthy member of our society, an active and pure minded citizen; a bereaved wife a devoted and kind husband, and his children a loving and affectionate parent.

Resolved, That we deeply sympathize with the widow of our deceased brother in her loss, and that we will mourn with those that mourn and weep with those that weep.

Resolved, That we will ever cherish the memory of our departed brother, and will ever imitate his virtues and bear witness to his high standing as a citizen, a close and true friend, a decisive, prompt and devoted Mason.

Resolved, That these resolutions be spread upon the records of this Lodge, and be published in the papers of this city, and a certified copy of the same be furnished to the family of the deceased.

> Dust to dust, the dark decree!
> Soul to God, the soul is free!
> Leave him with the lowly lain—
> Brother, we shall meet again.

THE GOLDEN DAYS DEPARTED.

I.

O voices still beneath the churchyard sod,
  Bright eyes that glistened behind long lashes,
Warm beauty early given back to God,
  Red lips that now are ashes!

II.

Ah, so it is!   All that hath ever been
  Experienced by the spirit is immortal;
Each hope and joy and grief is hid within
  The memory's sacred portal.

III.

And yet the soft glow of the midnight hour—
  A strain of haunting music, sweet and olden,
A dream, a bird, a bee, a leaf, a flower,
  A sunset rich and golden.

IV.

Can fling that portal open, and beyond
  Appears the record of each earlier feeling;
All hopes, all joys, all fears, all musing fond,
  In infinite revealing.

V.

Till all the present passes from the sight,
  Its cares and woes that make us weary-hearted,
And leave us basking in the holy light
  Of golden days departed.

J. C. AVERY.

Brother Julius Cæsar Avery died Tuesday morning, November 22, 1870. W. S. Easton, W. M., called a special communication of Occidental Lodge the evening of the same day. Brother Avery being held in such high esteem among the brethren, a large attendance was present. The Worshipful Master announced the death of brother Avery, and stated that it was the wish of his relatives that the funeral exercises should be of a strictly Masonic character, and should take place from the residence of George Avery, at 2 o'clock P. M., Wednesday, November 23, 1870. The committee on resolutions, consisting of brothers Thomas J. Wade, John F. Nash, Arthur Lockwood, Robert M. McArthur and Robert Henning, presented the following resolutions, which were unanimously adopted:

Loving hands have clothed the mortal remains of our beloved brother Julius Avery with the habiliments of the grave, and with saddened hearts have laid him gently down to sleep in the house appointed for all the living; the solemn words, "Dust to dust, ashes to ashes, earth to earth," have been uttered, and all that was mortal of our brother has passed from our sight forever.

It is eminently fit that this Lodge, of which he was so long a cherished member, should give expression to its feeling of sorrow and bereavement for its loss, and should say to the immediate relatives of our deceased brother, and to the world, that we loved him as a brother; that his memory is, and ever will be, dear to us, and while it is not our province to indulge in panegyric, we cannot refrain from saying that in the Lodge, he was in every sense a brother, and in the world a man.

Resolved, That these, our feelings and sentiments, be entered upon the records of this Lodge, a copy transmitted to the relatives of our deceased brother, and a copy furnished the press.

Resolved, That our Lodge be draped in mourning and its members wear the usual badge according to our custom.

The Worshipful Master appointed as pall-bearers brothers David P. Jones, J. B. Rice, J. H. Shepherd, Herman Silver, E. F. Bull, H. M. Godfrey, J. C. Hatheway and George Beatty, and brothers E. S. Hobert and Ed. H. Smith a committee on music. Brother Benjamin Padgett was appointed to carry the holy writings, and brother Frederick F. Crane, Marshal.

On November 23d, at 2 o'clock P. M., the Lodge met in special communication, with William S. Easton, Worshipful Master, and a large assembly of brothers of Occidental Lodge, also large delegations from sister Lodges. The usual ceremony was conducted in the lodge-room, after which, under the escort of Ottawa Commandery, No. 10, K. T., the Lodge proceeded to the residence of Mr. George Avery, brother of the deceased, where the usual Masonic services were held, after which the procession was formed and proceeded to the cemetery, where the remains were consigned to the grave under the impressive ceremonies of the order.

Julius C. Avery was born at New Milford, Susquehanna county, Pa., in 1831, and was therefore at the time of his death 39 years of age. Brother Avery was educated in the best schools in the vicinity of his birthplace, but being thrown upon his own resources, about 1850, he came West, located at Ottawa, and commenced the study of law in the office of Hon. M. E. Hollister, supporting himself at the same time by teaching school. About 1853 (in the meantime having been admitted to the bar and opened an office) he joined an elder brother, who had just returned from California, in the purchase of the newspaper office of the Ottawa *Free Trader,* of which he was editor about one year, when he sold his interest and returned to the practice of law. In this he rose rapidly, and in about 1856 became the second member of the law firm of Gray, Avery & Bushnell, and on the retiring of O. C. Gray, a few years afterwards, from the firm he became the law partner of the Hon. Washington Bushnell, remaining such until his death. Brother Avery had held the office of city clerk, city attorney and mayor of the city of Ottawa. In 1870 he was nominated for Congress on the Democratic ticket, and ran against the Hon. B. C. Cook. The county and district were overwhelmingly Republican, yet he carried La Salle county by 800 majority, and cut down the Republican majority in the district from 7,600 to 2,600.

As a Mason, he was true to its teachings. His character and worth as a public officer and private citizen were delineated so eloquently and lovingly in court proceedings that we regret we have not space to give the whole or even a part of the proceedings. His hand was "open as day to melting charity," he gave liberally to both public and private objects, but without ostentation. If ever a man observed the divine injunction, "Let not thy left hand know what thy right hand doeth," it was our friend and brother who is gone. His was not a charity trained in religious schools, as a matter of duty, it was spontaneous, the outgrowth of a generous nature. He could not withhold his hand or shut his heart against appeals to his benevolence. Of him, the Hon. E. F. Bull said, in the presence of the Circuit Court:

"The oldest member of the profession can study his character with profit; the youngest can find in his professional conduct an example for truthfulness, for honesty, for candor, for strict integrity and all other graces that should adorn our profession, worthy of close imitation."

As writ on walls in friendship's holy shrine,
  His sorrowing brother's tributes here are told;
This threshold space, I would the power were mine
  To gild with sunlight's pure, unshadowed gold

That those here passing, joyous minded, might
    In kindred spirit, read these lines aright.
For shadows never chilled the pleasant way,
    When access to his heart the poor would crave;
Across his path the sunlight quivering lay
    And halo-like, is radiant o'er his grave.
His generous heart illumined his whole career;
    Then why should shadows hold dominion here?
Some inward source his joyous nature knew,
    Some fountain-head, whose flower-like virtues grew,
Whose fragrance, incense wise, o'er honors breathed,
    Whose honors hallowed, now alas, bequeathed
To brothers, us who gave, who henceforth will
    Esteem them, prized before, more precious still.

JULIUS CAESAR AVERY

IN MEMORIAM.

TO OLIVER CROMWELL GRAY.

[Written by Juliette E. Prescott, Ottawa, Ill.]

As once, oh, truest friend, I placed a tiny rose,
    Blushing and sweet, upon thy silent breast,
So I this tribute bring at thy life's close,
    Hoping that thou wilt see it with the rest,
    And find it fair, though very frail, at best.
God had so many gifted souls, alas! could He
    Not leave me one,—almost my only one?
For I shall miss thy face; nor ever hope to see
    Thy like again till life and work are done,
    Till all is ended and my rest begun.
We covered all thy casket with fair flowers,
    Trying, O Death! to hide thy ghastliness;
Strewed them beneath thy bier that bitter hour,
    Thinking our tenderness to thus express,
    Striving in vain, to make our loss the less.
Only a fragrant bud to place upon thy stone,—
    Thy master hand hath reared the wonderous imagery
Thy busy brain hath wrought, until it now has grown
    Into a stately monument for thy bright memory.
    Far more imperishing than any shaft may be,
That, crumbling, stands in marble cities of the dead,
    Thy marvelous structure grandly looms aloft
In everlasting light, and whitely gleams instead,
    Where loving memories, shadow-like and soft,
    Play o'er it in the "Greenwood" of the soul—waft
With fragrance of past kisses, fresher, purer praise,
    Later homage to thy transfigured soul.
So mayst thou, in thy new far-off and hidden ways,
    Be kept in mind of those that are not whole.
    Lean somewhat from thy place of high control,
For we have need of thee—advisor, counselor,
    And dear, familiar friend! Oh, vanished years
Of sweet companionship! Oh, days of yore!
    Oh, tender heart! that never turned from tears,
    Coldly unheeding: how this thought endears
Thee to the souls that stand alone and dumb!
    Even thy mantle was not left behind

O

To comfort those who, desolate and numb,
    Do watch thy upward flight, the light to find,
    Leaving thy cross, upon thy brow to bind
The blessed crown of righteous deed and faithful words
    (For by their works shall they each one be known;
Who are, in truth, the just, and who the Lord's;
    We know that grapes are not of thistles born,
    And never gathered was a fig of thorn).
Dear friend, we shall retain thee in remembrance sweet,
And though in earthly paths we never more shall meet,
With tender, old-time greeting we shall stand
Together yet, in friendship's better land.

OLIVER CROMWELL GRAY.

Brother Oliver Cromwell Gray was born at Steubenville, Ohio, January 1, 1821, and descended from an old English family of the same name, of which Thomas Gray, poet and author of the "Elegy in a Country Churchyard," was a branch.

He was admitted to practice law in 1841 at Cleveland, Ohio, and continued in the practice until war was declared with Mexico. At this time, he was First Lieutenant of the Jefferson Grays, of Steubenville, Ohio, and left with that organization for the seat of war. During the continuance of the war with Mexico, he served as Adjutant of the Third Ohio regiment, commanded by Col. Samuel R. Curtis, afterwards Governor of Iowa, and, during the Civil war, Major-General of Volunteers.

Brother Gray came to Ottawa in 1853, and entered into a law partnership with Washington Bushnell, and later was senior member of the law firm of Gray, Avery & Bushnell, the strongest firm of practitioners that ever graced the bar of La Salle county. In 1868 brother Gray was nominated for Congress by the Democratic party, and ran against the Hon. B. C. Cook, and, although the district was strongly Republican, he was defeated by only a small majority.

A complete biographical sketch of O. C. Gray, reciting his student life in Ohio, his services in the Mexican war, his adventurous career in California in the early stages of the gold excitement, and then all his trials and triumphs as a leading lawyer at the local and Supreme Court bar of Illinois, would be of absorbing interest.

Of him, the Hon. Judge J. C. Champlin said, in part, in addressing the bar of La Salle county, on the death of brother Gray:

"The character of the great advocate was embellished by the singular varied and graceful accomplishments of the man. Artistic beauty, whether of material or of thought, sprang from the hours of his recreation, and we and nature remain his debtors for the graceful habiliments in which he has presented them. His imagination, cultivated simply as a feeder to his reasoning powers, and as a door for the escape of the emotions of his heart, showed the wide expanse and the profound depth he explored in his "Worship of the Woods," to find the source from which all that is divine in man had sprung; and his "Sea Coral's Dream" was the herald of his approach ever upward to the realm where Dante and Milton will hasten to welcome him as their well-loved neophyte, to become, perhaps their honored peer. Ever upward! His manly form and graceful mien, we shall see no more. He has ascended to meet his friends, whose voices, like his own, have resounded through these halls—Wallace, Avery, Arrington, White, Spring and Butterfield, Baker, Hoes and Purple, with whom they have been conversing tender also their greetings, and, opening their ranks, receive him as their peer. In this noble company, in a region where time, opportunity and space are infinite, he will complete the ascent, so worthily commenced before he departed from these halls forever.

"Brave, skillful antagonist! Powerful, yet genial and graceful associate! great reasoner, by the light of whose intelligence, judicial wisdom evolved its judgment! Honored citizen, generous friend, illustrious advocate,—we salute, and bid thee farewell!"

Oliver Cromwell Gray affiliated with Occidental Lodge in 1854, and was elected Master the same year.

Oliver Cromwell Gray departed this life on Monday evening, July 31, 1871. Worshipful Brother Robert Henning called a special communication of Occidental Lodge, No. 40, A. F. & A. M., Tuesday evening, August 1, 1871. A large number of the brethren were present. Worshipful brother Henning announced the death of brother O. C. Gray, and stated that the object of the meeting was to make the necessary arrangements for attending the funeral, it having been his request that this Lodge perform the last sad office of consigning his remains to Mother Earth. Brother L. A. Rising was appointed Marshal, and brothers J. B. Rice, James O'Donnell, David Batcheller and John Stout pall-bearers, and, on motion, Ottawa Lodge, No. 41, I. O. O. F., was requested to appoint four pall-bearers to act in conjunction with those appointed by Occidental Lodge. Brothers J. B. Rice, John Stout and W. S. Easton were appointed a committee on resolutions. (No resolutions on record.)

Occidental Lodge, No. 40, met in special communication August 2, 1871, at 2 o'clock P. M., when a procession was formed by brother L. A. Rising, Marshal, and proceeded to the residence of our late brother, O. C. Gray, where his remains were taken in charge and conveyed to the Episcopal church, where religious services were held, after which they were conveyed to the cemetery and consigned to the earth with the impressive ceremonies of our order.

> At last life's powers fail;
>   The silver cord is loosed, the wheel
> Of life, and golden bowl are broken;
>   The sunny days return no more;
> There comes through every avenue, the token
>   That Death is knocking at the door!
> The grinders cease; the eyes grow dim;
> Gray hairs are blossoming above;
> The ear no more receives the happy hymn,
>   The heart no more is kindled up with love;
> The ruffian, Death, his work completes,
>   The mourners go about the streets,
> Our souls with sympathy to move!
>   Beneath the green springs we entomb
> Him, the delight of the Mason's home!

LOTHROP PERKINS.

Brother Lothrop Perkins was born at Middleboro, Mass., in 1844. He came to Ottawa in 1864, and clerked for S. B. Gridley, who had a general store on Court street. He afterwards became a partner of Mr. Gridley. He also was bookkeeper for W. H. W. Cushman, and managed his affairs for some little time. At the time of his death he was superintendent of the Ottawa Gas Company.

Brother Perkins became one of the active, useful and public-spirited men whom the community get accumstomed to lean upon, and, being naturally large-hearted, full of geniality and popular to a degree, no doubt, had he lived, he would have been advanced to a most enviable place in the service of the people. He was a man, no less noted for his ability and efficiency in all he undertook, than for his wonderful magnetism, that seemed to bring every resource spontaneously to his aid.

His funeral was under the auspices of Occidental Lodge. Members of the Blue Lodges were present from every Lodge in La Salle county. Ottawa Commandery, No. 10, Knights Templar, acted as escort. Knights Templar were present from Peru, Mendota, Morris and Joliet, and the local members of Oriental Consistory, 32°, Valley of Chicago, were present.

The funeral cortage was the most imposing ever witnessed in Ottawa. It was headed by the police in full uniform, city council in carriages, fire department and members of the board of supervisors, of which he was a member, and which was in session when he died, the Knights Templar in full uniform, Occidental Lodge and brethren of the Blue Lodges, the officers and pall-bears in silk hats and Prince Albert coats, which, with their white gloves and aprons, made one of the most imposing and significant Masonic funerals ever held in Ottawa.

The beautiful and impressive Masonic burial service was most impressively rendered at the grave, when all that remained of our beloved friend and brother was consigned to his last resting place.

Brother Perkins was a member of Occidental Lodge, No. 40, A. F. & A. M., Shabbona Chapter, No. 37, R. A. M., Oriental Council, No. 63, R. & S. M., Ottawa Commandery, No. 10, K. T., Oriental Consistory, 32°, Valley of Chicago.

SONG.

When autumn's chilly winds complain,
  And red leaves withered fall,
We know that spring will laugh again,
  And leaf and flower recall.

But when love's saddening autumn wears
  The hues that death presage,
No spring in winter's lap prepares
  A second golden age.

So when life's autumn sadly sighs,
  Yet smiles its cold tears through,
No spring with warm and sunny skies,
  The soul's youth will renew.

Love blooms but once and dies for all,
  Life has no second spring,
The frost must come, the snow must fall,
  Loud as the lark may sing.

O Love! O Life! ye fade like flowers,
  That droop and die in June.
The present, ah! too short, is ours,
  And autumn comes too soon.
                    —ALBERT PIKE.

WASHINGTON BUSHNELL

WASHINGTON BUSHNELL.

One of the greatest orations ever delivered in Ottawa, Illinois, was delivered by Washington Bushnell on July 4, 1854. In closing, he said: *"Here is still my country, zealous though modest, innocent though free, patient of toil, serene amidst alarms, inflexible in faith, invincible in arms."*

Great truths from a wonderful man. It was my pleasure to know Washington Bushnell personally when I was a mere boy, and as I grew to manhood my admiration of the man became stronger and stronger. He was one of Illinois greatest men. He was a powerful advocate in jury trial, eloquent and convincing in his appeals to the people upon the political questions of the day, keen, analytical and persuasive in his parliamentary debates in the State Senate during the most exciting period in the history of our country.

Persons who were familiar with his impressive manner and towering form will appreciate his appeal to his hearers in closing his speech in the eventful debate in the State Senate of Illinois, in the winter of 1862 and 1863, on the resolution declaring the war a failure: "And now, I call upon you, young men, by all you are, or hope to be, by all that is virtuous and pure on earth, and by all that is sacred in Heaven, to stand by your country in its fearful struggle for the supremacy for humanity and for liberty, over injustice and oppression. I call upon you, mothers, by that which never fails in women, the love of your offspring, teach them as they climb upon you knees and lean upon your bosom the blessings of liberty. Swear them upon the altar of liberty to be true to their country and never forsake her. I call upon you, old men, for your prayers and benedictions, for the success of our country in this the hour of her extremity.   May not your last sun go down in the West upon a nation of slaves, but when you shall breathe out life in death, may your eyes behold the flag of our glorious Union, floating upon freedom's air, without one star missing or stripe erased, securing alike freedom to all; and may the same glorious scene be witnessed by your children's children, until the last knell of time shall be heard ringing out upon chaos, 'time was, but is not.' "

Washington Bushnell was a powerful man, both physically and mentally, being six feet three inches in height.   He was more than ordinarily commanding in appearance, and was conspicuous among men.   In disposition, he was gentle and lovable, charitable and human to an unusual degree. No appeal for Masonic aid ever passed him without a generous response.   He was devoted to his family, and furnished them one of the most delightful and commodious homes in Ottawa.

Brother Washington Bushnell was the youngest son of Stephen Bushnell, a descendant of the Puritans, who came over in the Mayflower.   His mother was Vincy Tuttle, the daughter of Joel Tuttle, who was a veteran of the Revolutionary war.

Washington Bushnell was born in Sullivan, Madison county, N. Y., September 30, 1825.   Graduated at the National Law School, Poughkeepsie, N. Y., 1853.   Was admitted to the bar and came to Ottawa the same year, and was a member of the law firm of Gray, Avery & Bushnell, the strongest firm of practitioners in Illinois.   He was elected to the State Senate in 1860, and re-elected in 1864. Was elected Attorney-General of the state in 1868.   Was State's Attorney of La Salle county from 1857 to 1861, inclusive.   He was also city attorney of Ottawa in 1853 and 1854.   In the administration of the office of State's Attorney he showed great ability.   He was impressive in debate, and wielded with effect the arts of oratory, of which he was master, and which, in after life, in the Senate, on the stump and before juries, brought him great fame.

Brother Bushnell was a member of the Constitutional Convention in 1861. The first statutory law in the United States, giving women equal property rights, was placed on the statute books of Illinois by a fifteen minutes speech by Washington Bushnell, before the State Senate of Illinois, while he was a member of that body.

Washington Bushnell was a personal friend of both Abraham Lincoln and Governor Yates during the stormy days of 1861-'65. He married Phœbe M. Charles, daughter of Christian H. Charles, who was a member of Ottawa Lodge, No. 114, Grand Lodge of Kentucky.

He was raised in Occidental Lodge, No. 40, December 12, 1864. He never held any Masonic office because of his many other duties occupying all of his time, but he was a zealous Mason from principle, and gave his aid and influence whenever called for.

He died June 30, 1885, and was buried with Masonic honors. He left surviving, his widow, Phœbe M. Bushnell, and Vincy T., Juliet C., Susan B., Sylvia A. and Phœbe, his daughters, and Theron B., his son.

How fast they fall—those we have known,
As leaves from autumn branches blown,
    So quickly sear!
Yes, one by one they drop away,
As withered leaves fall and stray
    And disappear.

LONG AGO.

I.

We wandered in a garden fair,
   When summer sun was shining,
And laden was the balmy air
With scent of roses rich and rare
   Around us intertwining.
There trilled the thrush his glorious song;
There thrilled the echoes all night long,
   The warbling nightingale.
You taught me all each songster said,
And in each floweret's heart you read,
   Some hidden tale.
You said their message I should know;
'Twas simple as an easy rhyme—
But that was once upon a time
      Long ago!

II.

We parted in a woodland glade
When autumn's woods were sighing,
In gold and russet bright arrayed
A glowing canopy displayed
   The summer leaves a-dying;
And, but the wind, no other sound
Than a leaf fluttered to the ground;
   And a far-off robin singing,
We heard. You guessed my thoughts and said:
"In spring, the swallows who have fled
   Will back be winging;
The trees a bright emerald show,
The rose a richer crimson glow
Than any gleamed in this year's prime."
All this was once upon a time,
      Long ago.

THOMAS JEFFERSON WADE.

Father Wade was born at Lunsbury, Mass., September 3, 1801, and had reached the ripe old age of eighty-five years at the time of his death, more than one-half of which was spent as a laborer in the Masonic vineyard. And of all the degrees, the author of this work has had con-- ferred on him, none were more impressive to him than that of the first degree, as conferred upon him by Father Wade on that April night in 1879. It was a gentle, yet forceful, tender and affectionate, eloquent and impressive exemplification of that most beautiful first step in Masonry. It made a deep and lasting impression on my mind, and now, twenty-eight years since, it is just as vivid as on that eventful night.

Father Wade was made a Mason in Joliet Lodge, No. 10, in 1841. (The charter of this Lodge was revoked in 1845, and a dispensation for Mt. Joliet Lodge granted by the Grand Master.) He was appointed one of the Deacons. On June 16, 1842, he was elected Senior Warden of Joliet Lodge, and on December 27th, of the same year, Secretary On November 20, 1843, was re-elected Secretary. On February 1, 1844, he was elected Master. The charter of this Lodge was revoked in 1845, and Father Wade affiliated with St. John's Lodge, No. 13, Peru, Ill., July 17, 1845. On June 4, 1846, he was elected Master, and on June 10, 1847, was re-elected Master.

On November 23, 1848, he affiliated with Mt. Joliet Lodge, No. 42, at Joliet, Ill., and on February 15, 1849, was elected Senior Warden, and was elected Master in 1850.

He affiliated with Occidental Lodge, No. 40, in 1854, and was Master during the years 1855, '57, '59.

Father Wade was a patriarch in Free Masonry, and, in addition to the offices above held, he served acceptably a number of years as Grand Lecturer, exemplifying the ritual known as the Preston and Barney lectures, and a Masonic Lodge in Bloomington is called the Wade-Barney Lodge, in honor of Father Wade and John Barney. He was also District Deputy Grand Master of the Ninth Masonic District for several years. He was also Grand King of the Grand Chapter of Royal Arch Masons.

In all the walks of life, Father Wade was an upright man and Mason, whose heart was filled with kindness, and

> Who never made a brow look dark,
> Nor caused a tear but when he died.

He was broad and catholic in his views, and to all to whom christianity holds out its promise of an existence continued somewhere, where the earthly virtues shall continue and grow, it is a matter of great exultation that a soul so pure and lofty has passed on, and without a stain to another stage of being where "That which is true life lives on."

Father Wade's life was not fragmentary and unfinished, but full-orbed and complete. Death was not an interruption, but a climax. His sun neither clouded nor eclipsed, but followed the appointed path to the western horizon.

The funeral services were conducted by Occidental Lodge, No. 40, and I, then Master of Occidental Lodge, pronounced the last farewell to the dear old friend and brother, whose command revealed to me the first "light" of Masonry.

THOMAS COXEY FULLERTON.

Brother Thomas C. Fullerton was born in lower Merion township, Montgomery county, Pa., August 21, 1839, and came to Illinois with his parents in October, 1855, settling on a farm in Freedom township, La Salle county. He enlisted in the army September 25, 1861, as a private in Company A, Sixty-fourth Illinois, "Yates Sharpshooters," and through meritorious services and deeds of bravery and heroism won promotions until April 1, 1864, when he was appointed Assistant Inspector on the staff of General Sprague. He also held the same position on the staff of General Dodge. He was aide-de-camp on the staff of General Ransom at the time of General Ransom's death. He was the last officer to speak to General McPherson a moment before he was killed. He was a favorite of General Dodge and a friend of General Ransom.

After the war closed he entered the office of Glover, Cook & Campbell, and began the study of law, and was admitted to the bar in January, 1866. He opened an office in Huntsville, Alabama, August 24, 1866, and was appointed Assistant United States District Attorney for the Northern District of Alabama. He was subsequently appointed registrar in bankruptcy, and served until January, 1871, when he resigned and removed to Washington, D. C., to practice before the various courts and commissions. He removed to Ottawa in November, 1881, and continued the practice of his profession. He was appointed Master-in-Chancery in 1888, which office he filled until his death.

Brother Fullerton was twice married. In 1861, at Freedom, La Salle county, Illinois, he married Almeda D. Dyer, who died while he lived in Washington, D. C. By this union he had one son, Wm. D. Fullerton, who is now one of the leading practitioners at the La Salle county bar, and one of our most distinguished Masons.

On July 15, 1886, he married Vincy, eldest daughter of brother Washington Bushnell. To them were born four children, Charles Bushnell, Theron, Almeda and Anne, who, as they are growing to manhood and womanhood, are the joy and pride of their mother.

Brother Fullerton died while a candidate for Congress, August 2, 1894, having received the Republican nomination for that office. His election was a foregone conclusion, and once a member of that body his future would certainly have been brilliant. His sudden death was a shock to his many friends and fellow citizens, by whom he was held in the highest esteem, as evidenced by the participation in the last sad rites by a host of men of fame and position from far and near.

In the private and social walks of life brother Thomas C. Fullerton enjoyed the esteem and confidence of a wide circle of friends, greater than usually fall to the lot of many others. He was in every sense a pure, upright, manly man, strong, yet unobtrusive, warm hearted and generous in his ways, tenacious in his friendships, and though tolerant of common human weaknesses, hated cringing meanness, dishonesty, hypocrisy and littleness. As a Mason, he was true to its teachings, as he was loyal to his country, devoted to his family and faithful to every trust reposed in him.

He was raised in Occidental Lodge, No. 40, February 25, 1864. Was elected Senior Warden in 1885, and was Senior Deacon in 1886. He was also a member of Shabbona Chapter, No. 37, Royal Arch Masons, and Ottawa Commandery, No. 10, Knights Templar.

> Night came,
> Releasing him from labor,
> When a hand, as from the darkness,
> Touched him, and he slept.

JOHN DEAN CATON

The first one raised in Occidental Lodge. Worshipful Master in
1846, 1850 and 1851.

JOHN DEAN CATON.

Brother John Dean Caton was born in Monroe, Orange county, New York, May 19, 1812. He was the son of Robert Caton, a man of small means. Brother Caton came west to Chicago in 1833, and was the second lawyer to open an office in what is now the great western metropolis. He practiced law in Chicago until 1839, when he moved to a farm he purchased in Will county, Illinois. He remained on the farm but three years. Came to Ottawa and resumed the practice of his profession, when he was appointed Associate Justice of the Supreme Court to succeed Justice Ford. He was later elected to the same office by the General Assembly, and afterwards, when the constitution was revised in 1848. was re-elected by the people. He was chosen Chief Justice by his associates in 1855, serving until the following June. He was re-elected in 1857, and served as Chief Justice from 1858 until 1864, when he resigned to take personal charge of his immense personal interests. It is proper to here state that being one of the first Justices of the Supreme Court in Illinois he had no precedents from which to base his decisions, and to this day many of the decisions of Judge Caton are the law of the land and form the groundwork, or foundations, of the decisions of the jurists of the present day. He was a man of immense brain power, and mind industry, most extensively traveled in this and foreign countries, and was the author of several valuable books on travel and natural history. He had an extensive acquaintance with prominent men in all parts of the world. He was among the first to be made a Mason in Occidental Lodge, while the Lodge was yet working under dispensation. John Barney, who introduced the Prestonian system of lectures in Illinois and the Mississippi valley, conferred the degrees on brother

P

Caton, December 11, 1845. Brother Caton was elected Master of Occidental Lodge June 23, 1846, and was installed into office as Worshipful Master when the Lodge was constituted under charter, October 10, 1846, and presided until June 18, 1847, when brother G. L. Thompson was elected Master. Brother Caton was also Master of Occidental Lodge in 1851, and took quite an active interest in the craft until the pressure of other affairs occupied all of his time.

He was of large physique, and a man that would attract attention wherever he went. Was social and affable in disposition. He built a beautiful home on the north bluff, and, in connection with it, maintained a beautiful park, stocked with elk, deer and antelope. He also had a beautiful home in Chicago, where he died July 30, 1895. His remains are buried in Ottawa avenue cemetery.

AUTUMN.

It is the evening of a pleasant day,
  In these old woods. The sun profusely flings
His golden light through every narrow way
    That winds among the trees: His spirit clings
    In orange mist around the snowy wings
Of many a patient cloud that now, since noon,
  Over the western mountain idly swings,
Waiting, when night-shades come, alas! too soon,
  To veil the timid blushes of the virgin noon.

The trees with crimson robes are garmented
    Clad with frail brilliancy by the twinkling frost
For the young leaves that spring with beauty fed
    Their greenness and luxuriance have lost,
    Gaining new beauty, at too dear a cost,—
Unnatural beauty, essence of decay.
    Too soon, upon the harsh winds wildly tossed,
Leaving the naked trees ghost-like and gray,
    These leaf-flocks, like vain hopes, will vanish quite away.

How does your sad, yet calm, contented guise,
    Ye melancholy Autumn solitudes!
With my own feelings softly harmonize;
    For though I love the hoar and solemn woods,
    In all their manifold and changing moods,
In gloom and sunshine, storm and quietness,
    By day, and when the dim night on them broods,
Their lightsome glades, their deep, dark mysteries,
    Yet a sad heart best loves a still, calm scene like this.

Soon will the year, like this sweet day, have fled,
    With swift feet speeding noiselessly and fast,
As a ghost speeds to join its kindred dead,
    In the dark realms of that mysterious Vast.
    The shadow peopled, vague and infinite Past.
Life's current downward flows, a rapid stream,
    With clouds and shadows often overcast,
Yet lighted by full many a sunny beam,
    Of happiness, like sweet thoughts in a gloomy dream.

Like the brown leaves, our loved ones drop away,
    One after one, into the dark abyss,

Of sleep and death; the frosts of trouble lay
    Their withering touch upon our happiness,
    Even as the boar-frosts of the Autumn kiss
The green life from the unoffending leaves;
    And Love, and Hope, and Youth's warm cheerfulness,
Flit from the heart;—Age lonely sits and grieves,
    Or sadly smiles, while youth his day-dream fondly weaves.

Day draweth to its close: Night cometh on:
    Death, a dim shape, stands on Life's western verge,
Casting his shadow on the startled sun,
    A deeper gloom that seemeth to emerge
    From endless night. Forward he bends to urge
His eyeless steeds, fleet as the tempest's blast;
    Hark! Hear we not Eternity's grave surge,
Thundering anear? At the dread sound aghast,
    Time, pale with frantic terror, hurries headlong past.

1842.   —ALBERT PIKE.

JAMES McMANUS.

Brother McManus was born March 17, 1836. He became a zealous worker in the Masonic vineyard, and was held in high esteem by the brethren of Occidental Lodge, and we, who were his co-workers in Masonry, reflect with fondness, his characteristics as a man and a Mason.

He was one of our very best ritualists, and possessed a wonderful faculty for committing and retaining the esoteric work, which he made his particular study. It was he who introduced the present standard work in Occidental Lodge. He was dignified in his actions and firm in his decisions as a presiding officer.

Brother McManus was an exemplary citizen, and faithful to every trust reposed in him. He was true to his friends, and, as a husband and father, loving and indulgent. But the family circle and the Lodge that once knew him shall know him no more on earth. His earthly work is finished, and we believe has stood the test of the overseer's square, and from the Supreme Grand Master has he received the welcome acclamation, "Well done, good and faithful servant."

Brother McManus affiliated with Occidental Lodge, No. 40, December 17, 1877. Was Senior Warden in 1880-'81; Worshipful Master in 1882-'83; Secretary 1897-'98, until his death, September 23, 1898.

> His life was gentle,
> And the elements so mixed him
> That nature might stand up and say
> To all the world: This was a man.

DANIEL FLETCHER HITT.

Daniel Fletcher Hitt was born in Bourbon county, Ky., June 13, 1810. He was a man of marked ability and of more than ordinary intelligence. He was a man of honor and integrity, which to him was more precious than the riches of the world. He was of fine physique, six feet two inches in height, and as erect and straight as an Indian. His features were of the truly Grecian type, and he had an eye like an eagle. To once see him was to ever remember him. His personal appearance, his generous impulses, his native dignity, and his superb manliness, these all conspired to make him one of God's true noblemen. His "religious experience" was the joy of doing good; his confession the sublime but silent testimony of a noble life; his creed, the golden rule.

By profession, he was a civil engineer. He completed his literary education in Oxford, Ohio, and came as a civil engineer to Illinois in the employment of the Government in the preliminary survey for the construction of the Illinois and Michigan canal in 1830, and located at Ottawa. He also spent much of his time at Galena, Ill., while surveying the wild prairies of northern Illinois preparatory for the staking of claims by the settlers who were then moving to Illinois.

He saw active service in the Blackhawk war, and was at that time attached to Gov. Stephenson's rangers. He also saw service in the Mexican war and was Colonel of the Fifty-third Illinois during the Civil war. But upon receiving injuries, from being thrown from his horse at the battle of La Grange, he was compelled to resign January 2, 1863. He participated in the battles of Shiloh, Gravel Ridge, the Russell House, Corinth and La Grange. He was made a Mason in Alexandria-Washington Lodge, No. 22, A. F. & A. M., Alexandria, Va., and affiliated with Far West Lodge, No. 29, Galena, Ill., working under the jurisdiction of the Grand Lodge of Missouri, July 31, 1841. He affiliated with Occi-dental Lodge in 1854. Demitted in 1857; became a charter member of Cement Lodge, at Utica, Ill., 1859. Re-affiliated with Occidental Lodge in 1882. He assisted in and encouraged the organization of Ottawa Lodge, which obtained its charter from the Grand Lodge of Kentucky in 1839, and, in his zeal for the fraternity, advanced the price to obtain the charter. There is no record that he affiliated with Ottawa Lodge. Thus, in his early manhood, he joined the mystic order and stood loyal by its banners, exemplifying its teachings throughout his life. He was made a Royal Arch Mason in Fredericksburg Chapter, Va., and was knighted in Ottawa Commandery, No. 10. Passed the circle of perfection in Oriental Council, No. 63, R. & S. M., and constituted a sublime Prince of the Royal Secret, 32°, in Oriental Consistory, Valley of Chicago.

He was laid to rest in the Ottawa avenue cemetery May 13, 1899. A large cortege accompanied his remains to their last resting place in the valley he loved so well. Oriental Consistory, Valley of Chicago, of which he was an esteemed frater, was represented by Gil. W. Barnard, 33°, Chicago, and W. L. Milligan, 33°, D. Hapeman, 32°, and Theo. C. Gibson, 32°, Ottawa.

His casket was surrounded by many beautiful floral tributes, among which was a beautiful Masonic tribute from Oriental Consistory, on which was the motto, in purple immortelles, *"Deus Meumque Jus,"* God is Just. A good man and true. Farewell! A last, long, fond farewell! Dear friend and brother. Peace to your ashes.

LOVE'S HARVESTING.

Nay, do not quarrel with the seasons, dear,
Nor make an enemy of friendly time.
The fruit and foliage of the falling year
Rival the buds and blossoms of its prime.
Is not the harvest moon as round and bright
As that to which the nightingales did sing?
And thou, that call'st thyself my satellite,
Wilt seem in autumn all thou art in spring.
When steadfast sunshine follows fitful rain,
And gleams the sickle, where once passed the plow,
Since tended green hath grown to mellow grain
Love then will gather what it scattereth now,
And, like contented reaper, rest its head
Upon the sheaves itself hath harvested.

—ALFRED AUSTIN.

DANIEL FLETCHER HITT

SOLOMON DEGEN.

While we profess to love the living, we cannot but mourn the dead, and it is my privilege, knowing brother Solomon Degen as I knew him, to indulge the thought that the beautiful and sublime virtues of Masonry cheered his fainting heart as he passed into the great unknown. And while we tearfully note the fact that upon his venerable head glistened the frosts of nearly three-quarters of a century, and that he was not exempt from the trials of our common humanity, let us dry our eyes in the genial warmth of that radiance which has produced the blessings of each succeeding season, and let us discern in the sweet memories by which his name is enwreathed the fragrance which imperceptibly distils upon the willing and obedient of all God's creations.

Brother Solomon Degen was born in Shinsheim, Germany, January 11, 1831. He came to America and to Ottawa in 1855, where he entered the store of Lipman Raugh, clothier, as clerk. In 1857, in partnership with his brother, Isaac, he opened a meat market at the corner of Columbus and Madison streets, where is now located brother Charles Campbell's livery barn, which they conducted until 1859, when he went to Colorado, where he remained for one year, and returned to Ottawa, where he embarked in business with his brothers, Isaac and Jacob, under the firm name of Degen Bros., buyers, shippers and importers of live stock, until 1894, when he retired.

His Masonic record began in 1858, when he was raised to the sublime degree of Master Mason in Occidental Lodge, No. 40, since which time, and up to the time of his death, he had been an active and consistent worker in the quarries, and it is not in disparagement of any of the Past Masters of Occidental Lodge to make the assertion, broad as it may

seem, that to brother Solomon Degen is Occidental Lodge,
No. 40, indebted for its existence on the roll of Lodges
owing allegiance to the Grand Lodge of Illinois, to-day.
There are but few of the veterans of Occidental Lodge on
our roll of membership to-day. Those ante-dating brother
Degen in membership are brother Wm. Osman, raised in
Occidental Lodge, June 13, 1846, brother John F. Nash,
raised 1851, brother Theodore C. Gibson, raised 1856, and
brother William K. Stewart, raised 1857. A loyal brotherhood of men, who bore the burden and heat of the day,
and stood for Occidental Lodge during the stormy days
after the destruction of the Masonic hall and opera house
block by fire, December 27, 1874.

Well, do I remember when he was Master, how, when
there was no money in the treasury to pay necessary expenses of the Lodge, or appeals of charity, brother Degen
would intercept the brethren, as he met them on the street,
and demand a contribution to charity or for necessary expenses of the Lodge, and he would never take "No" for an
answer. Charity was one of his distinguishing characteristics, and no brother appealed to him in vain, nor was there
a petition for aid ever refused by Occidental Lodge during
his presence. His was the true Masonic charity, and we recall with affection his frank disposition, his active charity,
his honesty of purpose, the sincerity of his covenant, the
gentleness of his love, and the strength of his attachments.
To our latest day, the memory of brother Solomon Degen
will be to us a pleasant savor, endeavoring, as we shall, to
remember him not with the upturned face and pallid lips of
the dead, but in his best estate, when his presence was an
inspiration and his hearty sincere greeting an event to stir
the blood of a stoic. He will live in the memory of his
countless friends for his manly qualities and his unfailing
devotion to principle. His was a big, noble, generous heart.

Brother Degen was an active worker and held several important offices in Shabbona Chapter, No. 37, R. A. M., and in Oriental Council, No. 63, R. & S. M. In domestic life he was without reproach, and left surviving three sons and one daughter, who were the joy and pride of his fireside. He lived an upright and honorable life, and when the pale reaper came to put in his sickle, he so gently and imperceptibly drew around our brother the mantle of dreamless slumber, that the golden gleam of an endless morning glanced upon the ripened and garnered grain, while yet the midnight stars were reflected in the tears of those gathering in somber silence about the cast-off earthly husk.

THE DAY STAR IN THE EAST.

I.

Each morning, in the eastern skies, I see
  The star that morning dares to call its own.
  Night's myriads it has outwatched, outshone,
Full radiant dawn pales not its majesty;
Peer of the sun, his herald fit and free.
  Sudden from earth, dark heavy mists are blown,
  The city's grimy smoke to pillars grown,
Climbs up the sky, and hides the star from me.
Strange that a film of smoke can blot a star!
  On comes, with blinding glare, the breathless day;
  The star is gone. The noon doth surer lay
Than midnight gloom, athwart its light, a bar,
But steadfast as God's angels, planets are.
  To-morrow's dawn will show its changeless ray.

II.

The centuries are God's days: within his hand,
  Held in the hollow, as a balance swings,
  Less than its dust are all our temporal things.
Long are His nights, when darkness steeps the land;
Thousands of years fill one slow dawn's demand;
  The human calendar its measure brings,
  Feeble and vain, to lift the soul that clings
To hope for light, and seeks to understand.
  The centuries are God's days; the greatest least,
  In His esteem. We have no glass to sweep
His universe. A hand's breadth distance dies
  To our poor ears, the strain whose echoes keep
  All heaven glad. We do not grope and creep.
There always is a Day-star in the skies.

DOUGLAS HAPEMAN.

Born January 15, 1839. Came to La Salle county with his parents in 1845, and located on a farm in Earl township. At the age of thirteen he began to provide for his own support as an apprentice in the office of the Ottawa *Free Trader,* of which, after the close of the Civil war, he became associate editor with William Osman. Brother Hapeman's patriotic spirit was aroused at the firing on Fort Sumpter in 1861, and he immediately answered his country's call by enlisting in Company H, Eleventh Illinois infantry. This was one of the best regiments that went to the field of battle from Illinois, and was commanded by General W. H. L. Wallace, Past Master of Occidental Lodge. Brother Hapeman was chosen Second Lieutenant of his company. He soon won distinction and recognition for bravery, and the skill with which he commanded his company at Fort Donelson. He won special mention from the War Department for bravery on the field of Shiloh.

In August, 1862, he was tendered the command of the One Hundred Fourth Illinois regiment, which he accepted. In command of this regiment, he made a splendid record, by reason of his military prowess and skill, his splendid discipline, and the care he took of his men, as evidenced by the love and esteem ever after entertained for him by the officers and men who served under him.

Brother Hapeman was a man of refinement, modest and unostentatious. He was a progressive citizen and active business man until within three years of his death, when owing to failing health he retired from active participation in business affairs. We were always pleased to meet brother Hapeman, as he always had a heart, warm and well wish greeting for everyone. He was raised in Occidental Lodge, No. 40, in 1861, and continued his membership until his death, June 3, 1905.

> The veteran sinks to rest,
> Lay it upon my breast,
> And let it crumble with my heart to dust,
> Its leaves a lesson true
> Their verdure teacheth well
> The everlasting greenness of my trust.

WHEN THE BOATS COME HOME.

There's light upon the sea to-day,
   And gladness on the strand;
Ah! well ye know that hearts are gay
   When sails draw nigh the land!
We follow them with thoughts and tears,
   Far, far across the foam;
Dear Lord, it seems a thousand years
   Until the boats come home!

We tend the children, live our life,
   And toil, and mend the nets;
But is there ever maid or wife
   Whose faithful heart forgets?
We know what cruel dangers lie
   Beneath the shining foam,
And watch the changes in the sky
   Until the boats come home.

There's glory on the seas to-day,
   The sunset bold is bright;
Me thought I heard a grand-sire say,
   "At eve it shall be light!"
O'er waves of crystal touched with fire,
   And flakes of pearly foam,
We gaze—and see our heart's desire—
   The boats are coming home.

               —SARAH DOUDNEY.

DAVID A. COOK.

David A. Cook was born in Freeport, Ohio, May 18, 1840. Came to Mendota, Ill., in 1855, and since that time resided in La Salle county. He attended the Northwestern University in Evanston in 1859-'60-'61. In July, 1861, he enlisted in the Twelfth Illinois infantry, and took part in the campaigns of the regiment, until the battle of Shiloh, April 6, 1862. In this engagement he was very severely wounded, and was not able to return to active duty until September of the same year. On October 3, 1862, he was again wounded at the battle of Corinth. He again reported for duty on January 10, 1863, but was unable to do duty, and resigned his commission as Lieutenant January 2, 1863. He was mentioned in general orders for gallant service at Fort Donelson and Corinth. In this battle, by reason of the death of the Captain and First Lieutenant, he acted as Captain of his company. He returned to Mendota and took up the study of law with Judge Gilman, and was admitted to the bar in 1865. He practiced his profession in Mendota eleven years, and in 1876 moved to Ottawa, Ill., and became a member of the law firm of Bushnell, Gilman and Cook. He continued the practice of law until 1890, when President Harrison appointed him bank examiner. In this position, he gave the most satisfactory reports, and was the most popular and successful examiner in the employment of the government, as evidenced by his being continued through the Democratic administration of Grover Cleveland, and continued until his death, which occurred September 21, 1905.

Brother Cook was a member of the Seth C. Earl Post, G. A. R., and of the Military Order of the Loyal Legion of America.

He was made a Mason in Mendota Lodge, No. 176, Mendota, Ill., in 1864. Was Master during the years 1871-'74. Demitted from Mendota Lodge and affiliated with Occidental Lodge, No. 40, January 1, 1878.

He adorned every station which he held with marked ability. In person, he was compactly built, with a fine, manly countenance and dignified bearing, and easy and precise in all his movements. In readiness, grace and accuracy, he had no superiors. He enjoyed to the fullest degree the confidence of all who knew him. He was a lover of fine works of art, and took delight in decorating his home with rare artistic works.

As a husband, he was devoted, and as a father, loving, patient and tender.

Let his virtues be remembered and imitated and his memory be cherished. Farewell, brother!

> Yet being dead, we live! If ever once
> In genial mood, we dropped the generous word
> Or penned the loving precept; if in prayer
> We sought the common father, and besought
> His aid to save the sorely tempted soul.
> If from the scanty hoard, we drew a mite
> To help the poor and sorrowing, then, dear friend,
> We have not lived in vain; we, being dead,
> Shall live forever in the life of God.

Q

IN MEMORIAM.

I.

I have no welcome for thee, smiling Spring!
Thy smile is not for me; so let me go:
   We once were friends, and may be friends again:
   Thou canst not charm away my present pain:
Alas, my wounded heart! Too well we know
The grief the living suffer from Death's sting.

II.

Now, while I find me out some leafless tree,
Standing all smitten, 'midst the verdurous wood;
   And couching on the wither'd leaves it wore—
   The leaves so joyously it whilom wore—
Maybe, I'll ease me of my mournful mood,
When nature thus shall sympathize with me.

III.

The melancholy message of the morn,
The answering echo of the aching eve,
   And all the tracery of the sunny shade—
   The writing by the leafy sunshine made,
Remind me only of my cause to grieve,
Pass by, ye Days! Ye make me more forlorn.

IV.

Yet, then thy voice the same sad story brings
In muffled repetition, shrouded Night!
   Hush! Whispering winds come from yon sacred ground:
   Night's starry eyes gaze on that new made mound:
And thinking, thinking on the piteous sight,
I would for me were spread the peace-bird's slumbrous wings!

IN MEMORIAM.

THIS PAGE IS DEDICATED TO THE MEMORY OF

Shelby Doolittle, died January 9, 1848.
Jacob B. Rich, died December 23, 1849.
William K. Brown, died August 16, 1850.
John Palmer, died July 22, 1852.
Wm. P. Thomas (or Thompson), died August 16, 1855.
W. W. Cavarly, died August, 1855.
Henry G. Cotton, Sr., died November, 1856.
Alson Woodruff, died 1856.
Bradford C. Mitchell, died September 18, 1858.
James Russ Murphy, died 1859.

> How cold would be the tomb,
> How desolate its gloom,
> Were there no faithful tears to fall above.
> Oh, who could bear to die,
> Did not we know some sigh
> Will move some spirits in memorial love?

IN MEMORIAM.

THIS PAGE IS DEDICATED TO THE MEMORY OF

Theodore Hay, died September 26, 1860.
William Henry Lamb Wallace, died April 10, 1862.
Jared B. Ford, died November 9, 1862.
Chauncey U. Wade, died February 15, 1863.
Francis C. Flora, died 1863.
Charles Turk, died 1863.
Philo Lindley, died June 25, 1864.
J. B. Smith, E. A., died April, 1864.
Samuel I. Haney, died 1864.
Thomas I. Conger, died 1864.

> In each cold bed a mortal sleeps—
> The silent lodge is here!
> Pale death an awful vigil keeps,
> Through all the changing year.

IN MEMORIAM.

THIS PAGE IS DEDICATED TO THE MEMORY OF

S. M. Pettingill, died January, 1865.
Alexander Magill, died July 9, 1867.
George S. Stebbins, died November 29, 1867.
Samuel C. Walker, died October 23, 1869.
Frank P. Brower, died April 8, 1870.
Julius Cæsar Avery, died Nevember 22, 1870.
Charles Henry Nattinger, died December 9, 1870.
Champlain P. Chester, died February 26, 1871.
Oliver Cromwell Gray, died July 31, 1871.
Henry P. Brunker, died February 20, 1872.

> What tears have wet these grassy mounds,
> What sighs these winds have heard!
> Oh, God, have not the piteous sounds,
> Thy pitying bosom stirred?

███████████

IN MEMORIAM.

THIS PAGE IS DEDICATED TO THE MEMORY OF

George Schneider, died April 11, 1872.
John H. Shepherd, died June 27, 1872.
Simon Alschuler, died February 13, 1873.
Fernando C. Prescott, died February 22, 1874.
Amasa C. Childs, died May 18, 1874.
Octavius R. Hanbury, died 1875.
Edward L. Herrick, died April 11, 1876.
James N. Colwell, died October 10, 1876.
Henry F. Clark, died January 10, 1877.
Daniel D. Thompson, died May 31, 1877.

> Shall man thus die and pass away,
> And no fond hope be left?
> Is there no sweet, confiding way
> For bosoms all bereft?

███████████

IN MEMORIAM.

THIS PAGE IS DEDICATED TO THE MEMORY OF

Thomas Ryburn, died 1877.
Hubert A. McCaleb, died March 24, 1878.
Absalom B. Moore, died July 7, 1879.
Allen Jordan, Jr., died July 12, 1879.
Patrick Ryan, died January 3, 1881.
Samuel Eyster, died June 29, 1881.
Lorenzo Leland, died August 26, 1881.
Charles W. Cook, died January 10, 1882.
John Powe, died May 26, 1882.
William Stadden, died June 5, 1883.

> From each cold bed a form shall rise
> When the great hour shall come!
> The trump shall shake the upper skies,
> And wake the lower tomb.

IN MEMORIAM.

THIS PAGE IS DEDICATED TO THE MEMORY OF

Lothrop Perkins, died September 16, 1884.
David P. Jones, died November 7, 1884.
Washington Bushnell, died June 30, 1885.
Robert Henning, died September 27, 1885.
Milton H. Swift, died May 14, 1886.
Robert McKim McArthur, died August 12, 1886.
Thomas Jefferson Wade, died September 6, 1886.
Asa Mann Hoffman, died May 4, 1887.
Ross C. Mitchell, died October 6, 1887.
Justus Harris, died November 27, 1888.

No weeping there, no tear, nor groan,
For these around us spread,
A shout shall reach the very throne
From the long silenced dead.

IN MEMORIAM.

THIS PAGE IS DEDICATED TO THE MEMORY OF

Eliphalet Follett Bull, died December 4, 1888.
Thomas Reedy, died March 4, 1889.
Henry M. Godfrey, died June 9, 1889.
Charles Snow, died September 9, 1889.
Nathaniel McDougall, died March 5, 1890.
Byron F. Maxon, died June 22, 1890.
William H. Carey, died September 1, 1890.
Frederick W. Gay, died May 6, 1892.
John Stewart Ryburn, died September 21, 1892.
Benjamin Beach Fellows, died March 3, 1893.
Henry Edgar Gedney, died January 31, 1894.

> Then hush our hearts, be dry each tear,
> Wake, oh, desponding faith!
> And when our Saviour shall appear,
> We, too, shall conquer death.

IN MEMORIAM.

THIS PAGE IS DEDICATED TO THE MEMORY OF

William E. Bell, died February 12, 1894.
Thomas C. Fullerton, died August 2, 1894.
Simon Zimmerman, died October 8, 1894.
William Stormont, died October 12, 1894.
David Robbins Gregg, died March 23, 1895.
John Dean Caton, died July 20, 1895.
Gilbert L. Thompson, died October 26, 1895.
John Brooks Rice, died February 24, 1896.
Reuben F. Dyer, died January 25, 1896.
George Beatty, died February 25, 1896.

> On these blest graves let sunbeams pour
> Their balmiest influence;
> On them let each reviving shower
> Its gracious pearls dispense.

IN MEMORIAM.

THIS PAGE IS DEDICATED TO THE MEMORY OF

John A. Gray, died September 29, 1896.
Arthur Lockwood, died November 18, 1896.
David LaFayette Grove, died December 14, 1896.
David Batcheller, died December 28, 1896.
William C. Weise, died February 6, 1897.
James McManus, died September 23, 1898.
Daniel Fletcher Hitt, died May 11, 1899.
Adelbert J. Newell, died April 9, 1899.
Benjamin Padgett, died September 28, 1899.
Willis Herbert Ward, died May 27, 1900.

O'er these blest graves each gentle breeze
Its heavenly whispers breathe
O'er them the foliage of the trees
A crown of verdure wreathe.

IN MEMORIAM.

THIS PAGE IS DEDICATED TO THE MEMORY OF

Clarence Edward Tryon, died June 20, 1900.
Joseph Cushman Hatheway, died January 21, 1901.
Samuel Degen, died April 24, 1901.
Peleg A. Hall, died June 28, 1901.
Isaac Reed, died November 11, 1901.
Royal D. McDonald, died January 11, 1902.
Charles J. Yockey, died December 27, 1902.
Solomon Degen, died January 4, 1903.
Calvin D. Phillips, died August 7, 1903.
Edward A. Nattinger, died September 1, 1903.

Round these blest graves at dead of night,
May angel bands combine,
And from their Mansions ever bright,
Bring something all Divine.

IN MEMORIAM.

THIS PAGE IS DEDICATED TO THE MEMORY OF

John Haws, died January 8, 1904.
William W. Hardin, died September 7, 1904.
Joanis O. Harris, died January 10, 1905.
Daniel Charles Mills, died May 2, 1905.
Douglas Hapeman, died June 3, 1905.
David A. Cook, died September 21, 1905.
Frank G. King, died October 30, 1905.
John Fletcher Gibson, died February 24, 1906.
Clark Braden Provins, died June 4, 1906.
Samuel Richolson, died June 24, 1906.

> From these blest graves may hope revive;
> May Judah's Lion tell
> That we shall meet these dead alive
> For, oh, we loved them well!

THE OLD TYLER'S GRAVE.

While wandering through Ottawa avenue cemetery one beautiful Sunday afternoon, I beheld a broken marble monument. The upper half having been broken off and set up, leaning against the base. Upon it, I beheld a square and compass. Knowing it marked the last resting place of a deceased brother, I walked over to it and read:

"William K. Brown, died August 16, 1850."

It was the grave of the long lost Tyler of Occidental Lodge, who was Tyler in 1847, '48 and '49, and of Ottawa Lodge, No. 114, Grand Lodge of Kentucy, in 1840, and whose Masonic record I had been unable to trace later than 1849.

The mute evidence of his death was there engraved on that broken monument of white marble. Peace to his ashes.

God bless the old Tyler! How long he has trudged,
  Through sunshine and storm, with his "summonses due!"
No pain nor fatigue the old Tyler has grudged
  To serve the great order, Freemasons, and you.

God bless the old Tyler! How oft he has led
  The funeral procession from Lodge door to grave!
How grandly his weapon has guarded the dead
  To their last quiet home where the acacia boughs wave.

God bless the old Tyler! How oft he has knocked,
  When vigilant strangers craved welcome and rest.
How widely your portals, though guarded and locked,
  Have swung to the signal the Tyler knows best!

There is a Lodge where the door is not guarded nor tyled,
  There's a land without graves, without mourners, or sin,
There's a Master most gracious, paternal and mild,
  And he waits the old Tyler, and bids him come in!

And there the old Tyler, no longer outside,
  No longer with weapon of war in his hand,
A glorified spirit shall grandly abide
  And close by the Master, high honored shall stand.

—ROB MORRIS.

FUNERAL DIRGE.

I.

Solemn strikes the funeral chime,
Notes of our departing time,
As we journey here below,
Through a pilgrimage of woe.

II.

Mortals, now indulge a tear,
For mortality is here!
See how wide her trophies wave
O'er the slumbers of the grave!

III.

Here another guest we bring,
Seraphs of celestial wing.
To our funeral altar come,
Waft a friend and brother home.

IV.

For beyond the grave there lie
Brighter mansions in the sky!
Where, enthroned, the Deity
Gives man immortality.

V.

There, enlarged, his soul shall see
What was veiled in mystery.
Heavenly glories fill the place
Show his Maker face to face.

VI.

God of life's eternal day!
Guide us, lest from Thee we stray,
By a false, delusive light,
To the shades of endless night.

VII.

Calm, the good man meets his fate,
Guards celestial round him wait;
See! he bursts these mortal chains,
And o'er death the victory gains.

VIII.

Lord of all, below, above,
Fill our souls with truth and love;
As dissolves our earthly tie,
Take us to Thy Lodge on high.

David Vinton, the author of the above beautiful dirge, was a distinguished lecturer on Masonry, and teacher of the ritual in the Southern States during the first quarter of the nineteenth century. He was expelled by the Grand Lodge of North Carolina for making manuscript notes of Masonry. Brother Robert Morris thought he was imprudent but did not deserve so severe a rebuke. He died in great poverty in Russellville, Ky.

Dr. Mackey says: "To Vinton's poetic genius we are indebted for that beautiful dirge commencing, 'Solemn strikes the funeral chime,' which has now become in almost all the Lodges of the United States a part of the ritualistic ceremonies of the third degree, and has been sung over the graves of thousands of departed brethren. This contribution should preserve the name of Vinton among the craft, and in some measure atone for his faults, whatever they may have been."

OLIVER CROMWELL GRAY

Worshipful Master 1854

CHAPTER IV.

POEMS.

[Written by Oliver Cromwell Gray, Past Master of Occidental
Lodge, No. 40, A. F. & A. M.]

One who knew brother Gray, in a finely-written review, under the head of "Gossip with the Poets," thus spoke of him:

"We need not confine ourselves to standard works to find the ring of the true metal. What may be called a perfect verse is haunting our memory now, from the Song of the Cable, by Gray, of Ottawa,

> Drop me down in the deep while the tide is asleep,
> And a spell is upon the wave!

"The same writer says in the 'Sea Coral's Dream:'

> Upward build through sea-green portals,
> Lost Atlantis—home for mortals—
> Occidental elfin island, such as loomed on Plato's sight;
> An august domain for races—
> Tenants on life's hid oases;
> Let the base be laid in silence, let the summit rest in light!

"We could wish this sedate man would bend oftener to the lyre, when such strains flow from his touch.'

Brother Theophilus Lyle Dickey, Judge of the Supreme Court, in his remarks before the bar of La Salle county, on the death of brother Gray, said of the "Worship of the Woods":

"When I read that little poem entitled 'The Worship of the Woods,' I discovered that he was a man of deep sympathy and poetic thought, and that he was capable of sentiments of the most lofty, and at the same time of the most refined character. The thought of that poem is one that will never be forgotten by me. The suggestion is made

R—273

there that in the works of nature we are brought to appreciate the existence of God; the great Creator is brought to our minds by the manifestation of the grandeur of nature. He suggests that when we stand upon the border of the broad ocean and see the deep waves rolling, we are profoundly impressed that they are the work of God; but that poem suggests that it presents the Diety away in the distance and gives us the idea of his grandeur, but it is far off. So, he says, when we come upon the broad prairies of the Northwest, their immensity and their grandeur present to us very forcibly the idea of existence, action and controlling presence in this world of a great Creator—of Diety, with all his grandeur and infinite powers—but they still present to us the idea of a God away off in the distance. But when we come into the woods where the little leaflets and the flowers are at our feet, it makes us feel that God is near to us, and 'The Worship of the Woods' has more to do with the heart, with the sympathies, and the affections than those thoughts suggested by the broad ocean and the grand prairie. It struck me as one of the most beautiful, sound, sentimental thoughts that I have ever found in the writings of any poet in the world."

THE WORSHIP OF THE WOODS.

I.

In the boundless and billowy splendor
  Of the green-waving prairie we stand,
And fancy we see the creation,
  And hear the omnific command:

II.

"Thus far shalt thou go and no farther,
  And here let thy proud waves be stayed!"
And the ocean, transmuted to prairie,
  Stands in emerald glory arrayed.

III.

How it welcomes us all to its triumph,
  As it sways its broad pennant of green!
But God seems retreating, retreating,
  With each surge of the shadow and sheen.

IV.

Though the prairies are proud in their grandeur,
  And joyous as sea-waves at play,
Still, no holiness steals o'er our spirit,
  And God seems so far, far away,—

V.

Far away in his forest cathedral,
  In the deep and dim solitude, where
The solemn trees ever are bending,
  Like green-hooded hermits at prayer;

VI.

Where the boughs are all burdened with blessings,
  And the air o'erflows us with bliss,
As the breath of the morning impresses
  Its mystical virginal kiss;

VII.

Where the umbrage so sacred hangs idly,
  Like a holiday banner unfurled,
And the leaves fling their benisons downward,
  In dewdrops with beauty impearled;

VIII.

Where the incense falls, sprinkled from censers
　　Swung aloft by the hand of some sprite,
Baptizing us all in aroma
　　Distilled in the chalice of night;

IX.

Where the zephyrs but whisper their vespers,
　　As they halt by their shrines in the grove,
And the fount falters faintly its ave,
　　As it glides through the temple of Jove.

X.

Lo! the azure stained glass in the window,
　　In the rift of the ceiling above,
Where a sad star drops down, in the twilight,
　　Its marvelous message of love.

XI.

So the woods keep the Sabbath forever,
　　Though no chimes the awed echoes upstart,
Yet the stillness responds to our feelings,
　　As oracles answer the heart.

XII.

For the spot is too holy for voices,
　　And no sandaled foot here ever trod;
But the silence seems petrified music,
　　Enfolding the presence of God.

XIII.

And He lingers beneath the oak's shadow,
　　Outstretched, as the cherubim's wings,
And calls us beneath his pavilion,
　　To whisper us rapturous things.

XIV.

The Tree-spirit touches an organ,
　　And the waves of a diapase roll
Down the aisles of the forest a pæan
　　That melts in the aisles of the soul.

Ottawa, July 17, 1869.

THE SONG OF THE ATLANTIC CABLE.

I.

Drop me down in the deep, while the sea is asleep,
   And a spell is upon the tide,
    For the Tempest King now poises his wing,
    Like an eaglet in his pride;
Now the vaulting waves are fettered slaves,
   And aloft is a drowsy sky,
And the sea-nymphs woo the boundless blue,
   And the rainbow rides on high.
Down with Astreas, in brilliant bowers,
Festooned with clusters of living flowers,
Where the sea anemone veils its bloom,
And the sea-star lightens the spectral gloom,
Where the snowy star-coral buds and blows,
Is the lonely abode where I seek repose.
In the silent heart of the secret sea,
The Atlantic Cable's home should be;
Through his gemmed arcades I shall thread along,
And click, click, click, is my only song.

II.

How the sea upbraids whosoever invades
   The realm of his marvelous home,
As he dashes his wrath across the path
   To his palace beneath the foam!
How the siren raves as she rouses the waves,
   And musters the white-plumed band,
While forward they urge the serried surge,
   Till it halts on the treacherous strand!
But the spiry sea-urchin ceases his rout,
And the cuttle-fish twines its arms about,
And a myriad mermaids around me clamber,
Bury me deep in odorous amber.
And the Nereids crouch, as the winds unfold
Their fleeting tresses of green and gold,
And Triton hushes his boisterous gong,
Charmed by the "click" of my wizard song;
For the ocean monarch divides with me
The azure throne of the moaning sea.

III.

Strange nectar I sip from the Orient's lip,
  While the morning is at her mass;
There's a tremulous chime from the sentries of time,
  As the Pyramids' pomp I pass.
And I never blanch at the avalanche,
  And I mock at the cataract's roar,
While the glaciers gaze, in their mute amaze,
  As my march to the murmuring shore.
And I hug the hemispheres in my grasp;
I bridge the continents with my clasp;
The New World's hope and the Old World's toil
I wrap in the folds of my lightning coil;
I girdle the globe as it whirls aghast,
Prometheus is unbound at last,
And bears his magical spark for me
Through the lustrous depths of the conquered sea,
Bearing his burden of love along,
Cheered by the "click" of the cable's song.

IV.

I have shaken hands with the golden lands,
  I have kissed the emerald plain;
And my thunders speak from Laramie's peak,
  To their kindred across the main.
Where the sun meets the hilltops I hurry along,
  With my music I startle the Oread throng,
And I dream, as I play with the pearly sway,
  That the goldfishes past me glide,—
'Tis the voice of the sea that arouses me,
  Tempting me thus with a bribe:
"As age unto age my memory links,
I will tell how the Nummulite builded the Sphinx;
You shall hurl the dart of the Belemnite
At the lily flower-fish, Encrinite;
You shall see where the Tribolite troop was born;
You shall hear how the Ammonite wound his horn;
And your highway for thought shall be ever free,
If you whisper your secrets all to me.

V.

"Lost races rest in my desolate breast,
  While the centuries ebb and flow;
At my terrible beck the waif and the wreck,
  Like my vassals, come and go.

How I gracefully roll to some far-off goal,
    When fancying I am free,
But I writhe like a snake when my eyes awake,
    And the beach imprisons me!
Yet no triumphs of man on my bosom abide;
I hide with a bubble his baubles of pride.
My choristers chant him a requiem meet,
And the white waves weave him a winding-sheet.
No knells ever knoll, no bells ever toll,
No priest of the deep sings a psalm for his soul,
And no marble column or trysting-tree
Ever marks his grave in the scornful sea.
But my realms you shall rule with my trident strong,
If you'll tell me the theme of your mystic song."

VI.

"Proud braggart, hold! They will never be told
    To your ear, O flattering sea!
No flash will impart to your rapturous heart
    What mortals have whispered to me;
Then shroud me in mist, let the surf be whist
    On its silvery couch no more,
Lest some gossiping shell my secrets shall tell
    To the tattling, echoing shore.
Rest, reveling sea! No longer carouse!
Bring coy Amphitrite, your timorous spouse.
The lightning has left its cloud-built home
To dwell in our palace beneath the foam;
And we will abide with your beautiful bride
In our halls of wonder under the tide.
Thus ever through life some mystical thing
Enters and heralds itself our king,—
Unfathomed, but felt wherever we be,
A hidden cable under our sea."

—O. C. GRAY, OF OTTAWA.

THE SEA-CORAL'S DREAM.

I.

Deep in Neptune's nether empire,
Sceptred sat the coral grandsire,
While the myriad of his children danced with every ocean sprite;
Weary feet anon beat firmer
To the sea-shell's mimic murmur,
Reveling with the imps of Eblis, dreaming never of the light.

II.

Thus in gloom they gamboled ever,
Morning flushed their pallor never,
Pearls imperial would glimmer, but no starry bloom of night;
Smile-girt sky would not caress them,
Nor would rainbow banner bless them,
For they reared no altar to the Oriental God of Light.

III.

Then the revel was upbroken
By the monarch's voice outspoken,
And the white-clad myriads surceased dallying with Naiads bright:
"Work forever! 'Tis our duty,—
Overtop the wave with beauty;
We must build upon the darkness and so reach the realm of light,

IV.

"Upward build, through sea-green portals,
Lost Atlantis,—home for mortals,—
Occidental elfin-island, such as loomed on Plato's sight;
An august domain for races,
Tenants on life's hid oases,
Let the base be laid in silence; let the summit rest in light.

V.

"Work is worship! never tire!
Pile your magic fabric higher!"
Like a mystic band masonic, working, aye, with voiceless rite,—
With the compass and the bevel,
Tiny trowel, square and level,
They upbuild their towering temple, longing for the land of light.

VI.

Long they dreamed of misty mountain,
Played in Undine's fairy fountain,
Hearkened to the wild-wood warble, charming sylvan nymphs from
flight;
Saw the forest-shadows quiver
On the listless, wanton river,
Creeping to the bland embraces of an ocean broad and bright.

VII.

Watched the nautilus careering,
'Mid the unfettered tempests veering,
Saw the surf to breakers bowing, doffing countless turbans white;
Billows languid chasing billows,
Couching on Lethean pillows,
On their careworn mother's bosom, with the spectre stars of night.

VIII.

Dreamed of summer's roses sleeping,
Dreamed of auburn autumn weeping,
Spring's young zephyrs laughing, wafting odors to the blossoms
bright;
Fancied phantoms most appalling,
Winter's tears to snowflakes falling!
While the crystal icebergs glitter, waltzing on a sea of light.

IX.

Tempted were they without mercy,
By enchanters worse than Circe;
Sirens lured with maddening music, coldly folding them with fright.
Lulled and listening, as they linger,
Touch of coral-angel's finger,
Warns and woos them, while it whispers, "Onward, upward, to the
light!"

X.

Evermore they heed this motto,
Dying in their gorgeous grotto,
And entombed in stately order, robed in royal shrouds of white;
Sea-dirge sung or bones left bleaching,
These mute martyrs still keep preaching,
From the charnel leap the living; from the darkness dawns the light.

XI.

Laid in catacombs of glory,
They embalm earth's primal story,

Older than the bliss of Eden, budding ere the demon's blight;
 Carving hieroglyphic pages,
 They adorn the aisles of ages,
Some are moulding for Columbus continental visions bright.

XII.

 Cycles glided past the spoiler;
 Perished many a patient toiler;
But the ranks were closed and crowded with recruits in mail bedight;
 Hopeful that some coral brother,
 In some distant age or other,
Would, above the foam-crest peering, sit enthroned amid the light.

XIII.

 Faithful coral sons and daughters,
 You have reached the radiant waters,
And have heard the petrel prophet, ere the storm-king rules in
  might;
 Hymns of halcyons, without number,
 Rock the top surge into slumber;
Fascination floats around you, in the gleaming land of light.

XIV.

 They have triumphed o'er all danger,—
 Sunlight clasps each sea-born stranger,—
Glad Aurora kisses this unsullied host with fond delight;
 Twilight with her glamour greets them,
 Far-off Alcyone meets them;
Coral dreamers! Island builders! Welcome to the land of light.

XV.

 And their dream is yet unbroken,
 Yet they hear words spirit spoken:
"Strive now for the empyrean! Climb to its effulgent height!
 Beaconed by the heavenly Pharos,
 Mount where dauntless seraphs dare us,
Wonder-workers! stand united, like a phalanx armed for fight!"

XVI.

 They will never faint nor falter
 Till they rear a star-lit altar,
And a lofty, dazzling temple, in the chosen cherub's sight;
 With such aim some still are building,
 All their toil with glory gilding,
Dreaming nevermore of darkness,—ever of celestial light.

XVII.

Will they reach that lustrous haven
With their fame in halos graven?
"Surely, down Time's shoreless vista," echoes Faith, with fervid
    plight,
    "They have bravely borne the burden,
    And will win a golden guerdon,
When the Coral's dream is ended,—ended in the holy light."
    1865.   —O. C. GRAY.

MASONIC ORATION.

[Delivered by Oliver Cromwell Gray, Past Master of Occidental
Lodge, at Princeton, Illinois, on June 24, 1859.]

FRIENDS AND BROTHERS:

On my first visit to your beautiful village, I am heart-
ily glad to meet you, one and all, on the natal day of the
patron saint of our order, St. John the Evangelist—a name
alike consecrated to Freemasonry and our holy religion.

To-night we come from the Holy Lodge of the St.
Johns at Jerusalem to greet you; but I regret extremely
that the partiality of my brethren should have selected me
as the mouthpiece for our ancient and honorable institution—an institution more ancient than the Golden Fleece or
Roman Eagle, and more honorable than the Star and Garter, the crowns of kings and diadems of princes—ancient,
as having existed from time whereof the memory of man
runneth not to the contrary, and honorable, as tending in
every particular so to render all men who will conform to
its precepts.

In presenting the claims of the fellowship, I feel very
much like the silly Athenian, who, having a splendid mansion for sale, carried around with him a single brick as a
sample. The dry details of the law profession are well cal-
culated to chill poetic ardor, and turn into the dullest prose
imaginable even a eulogy upon one of the most beautiful
institutions of the times. Although we have nectar as sparkling as Hebe's hand ever bore, and ambrosia sweet as celestial lip ever tasted in the fabled days, yet to such a banquet I cannot invite you.

A mere neophyte myself, just passed the charmed threshold—enamored of the gorgeous splendors of the vestibule,

and astonished at the magnificent array of symbolic tracery upon the walls, which crowd upon the eye at each advancing step, instead of attempting to describe them, I feel more like craving information, and uttering the dying wish of the immortal Goethe, "Give me more light, Lord; give me more light."

High as St. John the Evangelist stands upon the calendar of the church, Freemasonry has assigned him a still higher position.

From the building of the temple to the Crusade, Masonic Lodges were dedicated to Solomon, King of Israel, our first Grand Master.

Among the various orders of knighthood that were found upholding the flowery banner of the cross in those chivalric wars, none were more conspicuous than the noble and magnanimous order of the Knights of St. John. So great was the esteem in which they were held that Hallam, in his "Middle Ages," records that Don Alphonso, King of Castile and Aragon, on his death-bed, being childless, by his will bequeathed his crown and kingdom to the order of the Knights Templar, and every Pope, from St. Peter down to Pope Clement V., in the fourteenth century, patronized our noble order. Their valor in battle and their wisdom in council had never been questioned, and their standard fluttered proudly in the breeze as the Christian hosts lay encamped before the walls of the Holy City.

Our brethren of the ancient craft, or symbolic Masonry, went forth also to aid in redeeming the sepulchre of our Saviour from the hands of the infidel. Between these and the Knights of St. John there existed a reciprocal feeling of kindness and brotherly love, strengthened by long association and continued struggles in their sacred mission. On the plains of Jerusalem they entered into a solemn compact, and it was mutually agreed between them that from thenceforward all Lodges whose members acknowledged the divinity of Christ should be dedicated to St. John the Baptist and St. John the Evangelist, reserving to our Jewish brethren the right of dedicating their Lodges still to King Solomon; and to commemorate that distinguished event, there has since been represented in every regular and well-governed Lodge a point within the circle, etc.

We have borrowed his birthday from the Scandinavian mythology. It was the magnificent Gothic festival which was celebrated in honor of Thor, the Scandinavian Jupiter, and was astronomical in its origin and references. It commenced at the winter solstice, and was commemorative of the creation; for, being the longest night in the year, they assigned to it the formation of the world from primeval darkness, and called it Mother Night; and as the nights began to shorten and the days to increase, as the sun acquired strength in his journey to the north, so they hailed with festivities this time of increasing light and coming comfort. When Christianity was first promulgated to the northern nations of Europe, the people were unwilling to relinquish their annual rejoicing, and thus the Yule-Feast of the Goths was applied to the nativity of Christ, and became Christmas. The Scandinavians in like manner celebrated the summer solstice—the shortest night and the longest day—in honor of Odin, their god of battles. Freemasonry, borrowing both these splendid myths, has made the summer solstice, on the 24th of June, the birthday of John the Baptist, and the winter solstice was assigned as the birthday of St. John the Evangelist, just as the vernal equinox, when the days and nights are equal, was assigned as the birthday of St. Patrick, the patron saint of Ireland.

We therefore celebrate this day, and set it apart as a day of Thanksgiving. For years continued blessings have been showered upon our country and our brotherhood. To-day plenty fills all the borders of our extended empire—

> . . . . "And Peace
> Pipes on her pastoral hillock a languid note,
> And watches her harvests ripen, her herds increase,
> And the cannon-bullet rusts on the slothful shore.
> And the cobweb woven across the cannon's throat,
> Shakes its threaded tear in the winds forevermore."

To-day the star of empire, in its circuit from the east to the west, halts in the mid-heavens and stoops down from its home on high to bless us. To-day thousands throughout our fair Union have met, as we have met, to feed the perpetual fires that burn upon our holy altar like the vestal virgins of Rome.

> "Chaste as the icicle that curdled by the frosts from purest snow.
> And hangs on Diana's Temple."

We have met to offer up to the great I Am the incense of thankful hearts, more acceptable a sacrifice than the blood of victims, and to drink together once more at "Siloa's brook that flows fast by the oracle of God."

To-day our brethren come from the Aroostook and the Rio Grande to offer their oblations at this shrine. They come from the granite hills of New England, with hearts as firm and true as their emblem rock on which the sure foundations of the earth are laid. They come from the palmetto groves of the Carolinas, and from the Everglades of Florida, laden with perfume from their orange homes. They come from the wilds of the Columbia,

> "Where rolls the Oregon and hears no sound,
> Save its own dashing."

They come from mountain glens of the great Sierra Nevada, from that far-off gold land, where on hillside above blooms an endless flora, and in the valleys beneath, rivers freighted with the glitter of gold, roll ever on to the calm western sea.

And the brotherhood from the broad prairies of our own state send their joyous greeting to the mystic tie in every land. Yes, everywhere songs of praise from happy hearts cheer the welkin, and hail this festive gala day of our fraternity.

Freemasonry has descended as a boon from former generations. Our fraternity stands to-day in the pride of old age, hoary with the weight of years, like a pyramid in the solitude of time, around whose base the waves of bygone ages have washed without wasting, and upon whose summit sits a halo of refulgent glory. She carries the mind back to the Crusades of the Middle Ages, when the Knights Templar struggled for the sepulchre of our Saviour, stretching back to the end of the Babylonish captivity, when Zerrubbabel, prince of Judah, rebuilt the house of the Lord; back to the time when the wise king of Israel deposited the Ark of the Covenant in the Holy of Holies, when the great Temple was finished; back to the time when Bezaleel and Aholiab built the Tabernacle by divine command; back to the time when Jehovah revealed his name, and delivered the law to Moses at the burning bush, as he kept the flocks of Jethro, priest of Midian; back to the time when, at Padanaram, in the visions of the night Jacob saw the mystic ladder reaching from earth to heaven, upon which the angels ascended and descended, bearing messages of mercy from God to fallen man; back to the time when the patriarch Abraham in his open tent received the blessing, and the promise that his progeny should be as the stars of heaven for multitudes; back to the times when Enoch, in anticipation of the deluge, buried in the bowels of Mount Moriah the sacred pillars on which he chiseled the arts and sciences of his day.

Freemasonry was great and respected before the wolf that suckled Romulus and Remus howled upon the banks of the Tiber, and

"The Niobe of nations! there she stands,
Childless and crownless in her voiceless woe,
The Goth, the Christian, time, war, flood and fire,
Have dealt upon the seven-hilled city's pride."

Freemasonry

"Saw her glories star by star expire,"

and

"She who was named eternal, and arrayed
Her warriors but to conquer—she who veiled
Earth with her haughty shadow, and displayed
Until the o'er-canopied horizon failed,"

has passed away, but Freemasonry remains.

Freemasonry was great and respected before the smoke of sacrifice rose from the Pantheon, and before ever a gladiator stood in the Flavian amphitheatre.

The Papacy of Rome is ancient, but the long line of Supreme Pontiffs is as a thing of yesterday, when compared with our venerable institution.

The monarchy of Great Britain is ancient, but Freemasonry was great and respected ages before the Saxson first set foot upon her shores; and to-night, in England, the encampment of Baldwin, which was established at Bristol by Richard the Lion-hearted and the Templars who returned with him from Palastine, hold their regular meeting in high festival, in honor of our patron saint.

Freemasonry was great and respected before the Republic of Venice was founded; before Grecian eloquence was heard in the Areopagus; before an oracle was ever consulted at Delphos; before the philosophy of Plato and Aristotle were taught in the shades of the Lyceum or the groves of the Academy; before a pilgrimage was ever made to the shrine at Mecca; before Homer wrote the Iliad. The

S

Republic of Venice is gone, as if it never had been, but Freemasonry remains. The hush of centuries is on the lips of the orators of Athens, but Freemasonry still survives. For ages the oracle of Apollo has given back no answer, and the proud philosophy of Greece has bowed in humility to the irresistible spirit of the times, and, after having wooed and won the world's memory, yielded at last to the philosophy of Bacon, and the reveries of these ancient masters live only in the wild dream of the scholar as he brushes the cobwebs from his library. Thousands of years have passed away, and the land of Priam lives only in song. Thousands of years have passed away since the conquering Achilles bore the vanquished Hector in triumph round the Walls of Troy, and the deeds of the descendants of the ancient Teucer are pensioners upon the pen of the blind old man of Scio, deeds that "ought not to wither though the earth forgot her empire, with a just decay."

But Freemasonry still survives. She stands to-day a beacon of light and a proud memorial of truth, and the attentive ear still receives the mystic word from the instructive tongue, and the mysteries of our order are safely lodged in the repository of faithful breasts.

While these brilliant circumstances grace her annals and render her venerable, Freemasonry still presents herself in the vigor of youth, with no wrinkles upon her brow, no stain upon her escutcheon, she links the modern with the ancient civilization, she stands upon the ruins of the bowers of Eden, vindicating her claims to existence upon the fallen condition and helpless dependency of humanity, and hopes at last to aid in restoring the race to its first estate, and man to the throne of the Grand Master of the universe. For years she has, with an open hand, dispensed her blessings broadcast; like the dew of heaven, is shed in the quiet watches of the night, unseen indeed, but ever felt in the freshness and verdure it contributes to produce. Like the magic dew which falls from the moon upon the pestilential airs of Egypt, after the overflowing of the Nile, whose virtue is said to be so balmy and so healing that when the first drop descends even contagion dies, and loveliness invigorates and re-animates the earth.

Years of trial and persecution find our order to-day more flourishing than at any former period. Like the cinnamon tree, which, when bruised by the axe of the relentless woodsman, only fills the air with increased odor, so persecution has only rendered our fellowship more ennobling and sublime. Masonry has had her hours of darkness and trouble, but they have been so brief as almost to be imperceptible. They have been like night in the summer of the polar clime. The dawn of the succeeding morning breaks and reddens in the east before the last ray of the preceding arctic sunset has faded from the western horizon. Happily for the world, the once very general antipathy to secret societies has diminished in exact ratio as the principles of the order have been diffused, and the benefits bestowed have been realized. Happily for mankind, all opposition is now confined to the feeble assaults of superstitious bigots and arrant Pharisees, which soon will have

"Gone glimmering through the things that were—
A school-boy's tale, the wonder of an hour."

As Antæus, the fabled giant, renewed his strength every time he touched mother earth from which he sprang, so we have met to renew our vows and rejuvenate our vigor by recurring to those first principles upon which our fraternity is founded. Whole ages of glory lie in the bright track over which we have traveled; all of our past has been prosperity, all of our present is pregnant with blessings, all our future augurs of hope and triumph.

To the fabled heavens of the ancient heathen poets, a

new star was added every century, but every year a new star appears in our mystic firmament. As new and manifold duties press upon us, our institution seems to acquire new strength and beauty adequate to the occasion which requires its exercise, as the arch of the sky at midnight, when all the heavens twinkle with crystalline delight, bears its burden of starry beauty with the same ease as when, in the dimness of twilight, evening's one blue star hangs in throbbing gleam above the horizon.

A defense of secret societies at this late day would seem to be a work of supererogation. Masonry, in imitation of the secret and inscrutable ways of God, and copying the workings of all nature in obedience to divine law, lays her plans in secrecy and silence; and only when all the discordant elements with which works are harmonized in the Lodge, does she go forth into the world to practice those divine precepts, taught there only to the initiated, which raise the virtues, animate the bliss, and sweeten all the toils of human life. For in the mute land of silence, where ear hath not heard, and in the mystic deeps of secrecy, where eye hath not seen, forever dwells and forever works the still and invisible spirit of God: and only when the work is done comes there from the fathomless darkness the fiat, let there be light. Silence and secrecy are the harbingers of all revelation and all good work. As it was in the beginning, so now and ever, out of darkness comes light, and out of secrecy comes all great results.

The bee will not show his temple-craft to the open eye of day, but he builds ever in the silence and secrecy of darkness, whilst his fellow-laborers go out in the first light of the morniing, to touch the blossoms which opens to its kiss, and to beg the honey dew-drop, which the darkness of night has distilled with mystic alchemy, in the bright cup of the flower. The spirit of beauty will not form the pearl amid the auroral radiance of earth. She collects not her materials from the sparkling top foam of the wavecrest, where the storm-king rides and rules with noise and tempest the upper sea. No, but far down in the deep ocean, in darkness where the light-bearer never visits, and in silence, where the tempests bear no rule or mastery, the pearl is moulded and cradled in its shell, and worn by mortals as a glowing witness that light and beauty ever spring from darkness and silence. It is in the bud that the rose, the oldest emblem of secrecy, steals its color from the sky. While a bud, it borrows its blushes from the silent night, and there it folds them up in secrecy, until all is ready, bursting into bloom only to show its beauty to the gaze of day. Birds do not carol in the meridian hour, or amid the city's tumult, but in the woody depths and primeval solitudes, in the dimness of dawn and twilight, pour forth their melodious roundelays; and the nightingale, the sweetest of them all, sings only to the silent and secret ear of night. The glad summer note of the swallow is twittered from his nest in the cottage wall. But the wild scream of the eaglet is only heard from the precipice top, where silence reigns and makes all else her slaves. It is there that

> "He clasps the crag with hooked hands,
> Close by the sun, in lonely lands,
> Ringed with the azure world he stands.
> The wrinkled sea beneath him crawls,
> He watcheth from his mountain walls,
> Then like a thunder-bolt he falls."

Yes, the fierce emblem bird of our native land, born in his lonely eyrie, cradled and fledged in the silent cloud, with an aspiration ever for light, mounts up to meet the sun at his coming, feeds in his noontide beam, and screams in pride his war-note only to the tempest and the storm.

What a beautiful illustration, and sanction of silence and

secrecy was the building of Solomon's Temple! The plan
was given by Jehovah to Moses alone, apart from all the
hosts of Israel, amidst the thunders of Horeb, so that no
ear but his should hear it, or his holy name. The site was
selected by God himself, and hallowed by the most brilliant scenes in all Bible history. It was on Moriah, the
mount of vision, on the threshing-floor of Ornan, the
Jebusite. It was the spot where God had proved the faith
of the patriarch Abraham, when he commanded him to
offer up Isaac, his only son, as an atonement, alone and absent from kith or kindred, and from the mortal eye. It was
the spot where David met and appeased the destroying angel. It was the spot where, in after-time, the great sacrifice was made, in silence, as when the lamb is dumb before
the slaughter, and in the darkness of the frowning heavens.
God would not permit David to touch the work, for war
and tumult had been his calling. It was reserved for Solomon, a quiet man of peace and secret counsels. Prophecy,
ages before, had enjoined that the habitation of God should
not be polluted in the building by the sound of any metal
tool. The stone were all hewed, squared, and numbered in
the quarries of Zeradatha, where they were raised; the
brazen work was all cast upon the clay grounds of Succoth,
on the banks of Jordan; the timbers were all felled and prepared in the forests of Lebanon, and the whole was set up
by wooden mallets prepared for the purpose; and when the
building was completed, its several parts fitted with
such exact nicety that it had more the appearance of the
handiwork of the Supreme Architect of the universe than
of human hands. How eminently fitting that all discord
should be confined to the mountains, the quarries and the
plains.

How noiseless and how secret was the reign of love,
when the light-fiat burst on the rude and benighted void,

and how silently did the sceptre glide from the genius of darkness! Alone in the illimitable gloom, the Universal Love-Spirit echoed its own though unto itself, "Let there be light, and there was light." As yet there was no human thought to wonder at the grand design, no human knee to bend in adoration and in awe before the high Designer, no human heart to be the shrine, where alone in spirit and in truth, there could be worship to the veiled unknown. No cherubim or seraphim existed to harp Him honor in the Temple of Infinity, nor had the voiceless chant of Holy, Holy, Holy, yet rung from angelic lips.

How secret was the charge given to the starry host, when marshaled at the will of Love, the morning stars, singing together for joy, were taught their work to blaze and bless throughout all coming time. How silent was the bright procession, when orb after orb, and sphere after sphere, passed in pageant and review before the Omniscient Eye, rolling ever on through the boundless labyrinth of space, without a track or footprint, but guided ever in their fantastic mission alone by the spirit-finger of God, without a clash that silent brotherhood making ever, as they move along in harmony, music which delights the ear of Jove!

Such are the evidences of nature in favor of secret concert of action, and revelation equally gives its seal of approbation to the same sublime teaching. From the mount comes the divine voice, "When thou doest alms, let not thy left hand know what thy right hand doeth, that thine alms may be secret." "When thou prayest, enter into thy closet, and when thou hast shut thy door, pray to thy Father," which is in secret; and singular, yet true, there is no instance on record where our Saviour prayed in public. When He touched the eyes of the two blind men, their sight was straightway restored, and He charged them, saying, "See that no man know it."

He did not take with Him to the mountain his twelve disciples to see the transfiguration, when Moses and Elias appeared and talked with Him, and the bright cloud which overshadowed Him was only seen, and the voice of the cloud, saying, "That is my beloved son, in whom I am well pleased," was only heard by Peter and James and John, and He charged them, saying, "Tell this vision to no man."

So poetic, so sublime, and so godlike is silence that we find it deified in all the ancient mythology. The Egyptians worshiped Harpocrates, the son of Isis, as the God of Silence. He was represented as a perpetual youth, crowned with a mitre, holding in his left hand the cornucopia, while a finger of the right hand crossed the lips. In Rome, the image of Tacita, or the Goddess of Silence, was placed upon the altar of Volupta, or Pleasure, with its mouth sealed, because those who endure their cares in silence, and their sorrows with patience, do thereby obtain the greatest pleasure. The selection of a woman by the Romans to represent this divine virtue, what a rebuke on those who say that women cannot keep secrets!

Secret association finds a sufficient defense in its object, which is to induce unity of action, for order is Heaven's first law.

How divine is unity. She is the Halcyon, who sings the sea into stillness, and calms the billows, and well might the illustrious Hooker exclaim, "Her seat is in the bosom of God, and her voice is the harmony of the world."

No wonder that the ancients gave the harp to Apollo, as the symbol of his rule in heaven. No wonder that they fabled that Orpheus, by the power of music, tamed wild beasts, stayed the course of rivers, and caused whole woods to follow him. Descending into hell, with no protection but his talismanic harp, he so charmed Pluto himself, by the sweetness of his harmony, that he restored Eurydice to life, and permitted her to return with her husband, Orpheus, to earth again. No wonder that they fancied that the statute of Memnon issued strains of melody when touched by the rays of the rising sun. No wonder that they feigned that Amphion built the wall of Thebes, the city of the hundred gates, each stone moving to its place in order at the sound of his lyre. No wonder that they thought that Arion, shipwrecked at sea, holding on to his harp, was taken up by a dolphin, who was charmed by his music, and carried him safely on his back into Corinth. Extravagant as these myths seem to be, they are fully justified by the fact. Yes, "Behold, how good and how pleasant it is for brethren to dwell together in unity! It is like the precious ointment upon the head, that ran down upon the beard, even Aaron's beard, that went down to the skirts of his garment; as the dew of Hermon, and as the dew that descended upon the mountains of Zion, for there the Lord commanded his blessing, even life forevermore."

The mission of Freemasonry in the world is no less than to elevate the intellectual, moral and social condition of the whole human family, and no brother doubts but that the sublime tenets of our profession, if practiced, are fully competent to the accomplishment of the noble task. Thus, the aim of our order is high and holy.

Like Alcestes in Virgil, we set our target in the Empyrean, and shoot at the very stars, confident always, that though the arrow may deflect and fall below our aim, yet it will strike and make its mark far above the object at which the cold world aims. Man is a microcosm, or little world, in himself, and although there is a divinity which shapes our ends, rough-hew them as we may, yet, to a great extent, man is the artificer of his own fortune, and it is for him to make himself a Pantheon full of gods, or a Pandemonium full of demons.

The Lodge is a miniature universe, and furnishes a perfect model of political as well as social government, holding out the isolated patriarchal household as the most perfect model of society, suggesting that that government is the best in which to injure the humblest individual were to insult the whole community. Longfellow's youth, who bore upward ever amidst the snow and glaciers of Mont Blanc that banner with the strange device, "Excelsior," is but an apt emblem of the innate aspiration we all have for something higher and nobler. The law of progression and improvement is stamped upon all created things. Audible through long centuries comes to this age the low whispered prayer of the first radiata for a higher form of life. Every fossil on the stone-page was a prophet of the next better type which would succeed him, and every meanest atomlet of matter has been waiting since the nebular era with patience to be made into thought and mind by this alchemical process of progression, and then perish to be translated still higher. Each created thing holds in solution all the types below it, still dropping the lower, one by one, as they become useless, and thus man possesses still many faculties and qualities of inferior animals, which must be eradicated. Yes, progression is a law of being from the monad to the seraph. To advance that standard in the direction of social improvement, is the grand aim our order has in view. United by the cement of brotherly love and affection into a sacred band of brothers, among them no contention should exist but that noble contention, or rather emulation, of who can best work and best agree; we learn from our fellowship to subdue the passions, do unto others as we would wish them to do unto us, keep a tongue of good report, maintain secrecy, and practice charity. Like a young Argus, her hundred eyes are watching ever over the wants of our fellows. Like a young Briareus, she stretches her thousand arms around the globe in loving embrace. The fondest hope she has is the ultimate establishment of an universal brotherhood, founded on perfect equality. The ancients fabled that the monster Sphinx sat at the roadside and propounded her riddle to every passer-by; and whoever failed to answer it she devoured. Masonry, too, sits and propounds her riddle to every man. It is, "Where is thy brother?" Whoever returns the heartless answer of Cain, "Am I my brother's keeper?" is not worthy of society, and, like Cain, should be driven from it as an outcast. We teach that in the common attributes of manhood all the race are peers, all stand upon one common level, all tend to one common destiny; to that undiscovered country from whose bourne no traveler returns. "God hath made of one blood all nations of men to dwell upon the face of the earth." Deny this revelation as we may, yet the universe itself is but one vast pictorial and illuminated page, whereon the same sublime truth is infinitely multiplied by God's own marvelous autograph.

> "All are but parts of one stupendous whole,
> Whose body nature is, and God the soul."

The diamond must be taught its close fraternity to coal, as the coal already owns the plant as its brother; for carbon is the basis of them all, and a small change in combination produces the great apparent difference. God is love, and the kingdom of heaven is within us. Worship is bringing the love within us in contact and association with the love to God. Our only method to love and serve God is to love and serve our fellow-men, and the only evidence of our loyalty to Heaven is our love to humanity. This is the keynote to the tune after which orbs and angels march. Our fraternity adopts the sublime and august sentiment of Novalis, the German mystic, "There is but one Temple in the world, and that, the body of man." Nothing is holier than this high form. "Bending before men is a reverence done to this revelation in the flesh, and we touch heaven when we shake hands with a human being, in hearty recognition of his equal manhood." Masonry repudiates with contempt the aristocracy of blood, as well as the aristocracy of the dollar, while she bows with reverence to the aristocracy of merit, based upon higher intellect and better heart.

> "Rank is but the guinea's stamp,
> The man's the gold for a' that."

To the lawyer who inquired of our Saviour, "Master, which is the great commandment in the law?" he replied, "Thou shalt love the Lord, thy God, with all thy heart, and with all thy soul, and with all thy mind. This is the first and great commandment, and the second is like unto it : thou shalt love thy neighbor as thyself." This, my friends, is the arcanum—the great secret of our order.

There are four great cardinal duties to the performance of which the Mason is bound by indissoluble ties: to God, to his country, to his neighbor and to himself. Discarding all sectarian creeds, our order is still so far interwoven with religion as to lay us under obligation to pay that rational homage to Deity which constitutes at once our duty and our happiness. We are bound never to mention the name of God but with that reverential awe which is due from a creature to the Creator. We are to implore his aid in all our laudable undertakings, and to esteem Him as our chief good.

The claims of our country upon us we must at all times fully recognize. We must be true to her. We must be obedient to her laws as long as they last, and faithful to her flag so long as it floats, whether in mockery of peace it droops in glory on the lazy air, or whether, with its rainbow beauties outspread, it waves in triumph over the din of battle. With the hero in the lay of the Last Minstrel, we must say,

> "Breathes there the man with soul so dead
> Who never to himself hath said,
> This is my own, my native land!"

We must never forget that other patriotic sentiment:

> "One land there is, the land of every pride,
> Beloved by Heaven o'er all the earth beside."

To the brotherhood and to the race we owe manifold duties. We must relieve their wants, soothe them in distress, and sympathize with them in their misfortunes. Our heart and our hand must be forever joined in promoting mutual prosperity, rejoicing at each other's weal, and weeping at each other's woe. At the touch of adversity, heart should open to heart, like the touch of the magic spear with which the genius of Milton, in Paradise Lost, armed the angel Ithuriel. "Be to a brother's virtues ever kind, and to his failings ever blind." We should ever be near and ready to succor each other in time of need, near and ready to raise and save a falling brother, warn him of approaching peril, whisper in his ear good and wholesome counsel, aid in his reformation, never forgetting that we must judge him with candor, admonish him of his errors with friendship, and reprehend him with justice. If in prison, we should visit him, and if we can do no more, let us at least act like the heroine in the Corsair did to the captive

> "She pressed his fettered finger to her heart
> And bowed her head and turned her to depart,
> And lovely as a noiseless dream is gone—
> And was she here, and is he now alone?"

> "What gem hath dropped and sparkles on his chain?
> The tear most sacred shed for other's pain,
> That starts at once bright, pure from Pity's mine,
> Already polished by the Hand Divine."

When a brother is sick, we must watch over him, and

dispense with a liberal hand the corn of nourishment, the wine of refreshment, and the oil of joy. When a brother dies, we throw our last green gifts into his grave, to remind us that we have an immortal part within us which shall survive the tomb, and which shall never, never, never die; and as we give earth to earth, dust to dust, and ashes to ashes, we cover over his foibles and his memory with the broad mantle of Masonic charity. But love's duties extend beyond the brother's tomb. We must educate the orphan, and with a gentle hand "temper the wind to the shorn lamb." Samaritan-like, we must bind up the wounded spirit of the widow, and not "suffer the winds of heaven even to visit her too roughly."

To himself, to his wife and to his children, the true Mason owes obligations, which he must also discharge. He must learn to subdue his passions, and to be temperate in all things, in his desires as well as in his affection. He must limit his desires in every station in life, and in the severe school of discipline learn to be content at every turn of the wheel of fortune, rising to eminence by merit, so that he may live respected and die regretted. Remember the moral of the fable, where Bacchus, desirous of rewarding Midas, King of Phrygia, for some service he had rendered him, promised to grant Midas whatever power he most wished. The King of Phrygia, in his folly, desired that whatsoever he touched should turn into gold. The wish was granted, but the gift was fatal and proved his ruin. To temperance we must add fortitude, justice and prudence, and to prudence we must never forget to add patience, and when thus blended, like the hues of the rainbow, they form the pure, white light, which is a symbol of the glory around the apocalyptic throne. Let no difficulty discourage the true Mason, but let each successive failure only stimulate him to renewed effort. Life, at best, is but an Olympic game, and Eternal

Fame stands, bearing in her trembling hand the diadem, ready to crown the victor. The first snowflake which falls on the naked rock near the summit of the Alps, melts in a moment; a thousand others melt as they fall. Presently one solitary flake obtains a foothold, a million others close around it, and a little snow-pile drifted in the rocky cleft, warmed by the sun, glides gently from where it fell, rolls gathering ever down the height; the chamois bounds wildly from the glacier at its approach, and in a moment the peasantry in the valley are buried beneath the mighty avalanche; and the patience of the first snowflake has accomplished a mighty wonder. You have heard how Cuba, like a vast coral gem, sits on the bosom of the Gulf, blooming like an Eden on the wave. You have heard how beautiful is the island-city of Havana, and how it looms like a floating oasis on the desert and storm-rocked waters, as if Circe herself, by the mystic charm of her enchanted wand, had thither wooed and won all the found beauties of sea and sky, in order to embody to our actual eye, and thereby realize the wild dream of Plato, when in a philosophic vision, and through the dim vista of centuries, he saw arise toward the sunset sea his fair Atlantic isle, where humanity had reached the bright ultimate of perfection. If the realization was gorgeous, more gorgeous and mysterious still was the conception and progress of the work. It leads the spell-bound fancy through the charmed mazes of mystery away back to the geological ages, long enough before the birth of human history, or even of human thought. Then one solitary coral insect, moved by the divine impulse, which taught him to do his duty and die, first laid, in the silence of the fathomless depths, the corner stone of this coral isle. Full well he knew that his destined home was not in the darkness of the deep, for he felt an aspiration for the land of light, and prompted by the still, small voice of God, which ever whispered to him, "Higher, higher," he built, and built evermore, higher and even higher, to the surface of the sea, where the floods of light sit throned on the ocean-wave, and blush o'er the dome of the island temple of the surge. Full well he knew that age would roll into age, that the silent centuries and the voiceless cycles would come and go, and still his toil remain undone, and still his work be incomplete. Full well he knew that these silent ages, millions of his co-workers were doomed to die amidst their labor. So they did; but as these voiceless martys to patience, these mute apostles of fidelity, preached ever, "Be faithful and patient to the end," the ranks were filled and the handicraft was plied busy and busier still; for they believed that the day would come when the light would be reached, and that some coral-brother, in the dim and uncertain future, would sit above the wave, and work in light and joy upon the summit of that coral home, whose base was laid in darkness. Yes, long-suffering patience, like harmony, is divine.

Faith, Hope and Charity are the principal tenets of our profession. Faith is the corner-stone upon which our mystic edifice is erected; Hope crowns the archway where our good genius enters and presides; and Charity, spread over our magic Temple, like a canopy envelops it in purity for-ever. This triple chain links human heart to human heart, and binds us all to the throne of God.

Masonry repudiates with high disdain that sentiment of Goldsmith's hermit:

> "What is friendship but a name,
> A charm that lulls to sleep,
> A shade that follows wealth and fame,
> And leaves the wretch to weep,"

and turns in triumph, and points to the past, which is full of illustrious examples. At the siege of Troy, after the victorious Greeks gave permission to Aeneas to carry off whatever was dearest to him, as a Trojan and a man, he left behind him the Palladium, which the whole nation regarded as the safeguard of Troy, and bore off upon his shoulders from the flames of the burning city the old Anchises, his hoary-bearded sire. The Greeks, astonished at this eminent example of filial tenderness and affection, permitted him also to carry away his household gods; and the genius of Virgil paints Aeneas at Carthage, a captive to the admiration of Dido, when requested by the queen, at the banquet, to relate the glories of his past career, selecting this act as his favorite theme.

What heart has not thrilled at the story of that Grecian daughter, who, when Cymon, her aged father, was imprisoned and condemned to die of hunger, gained access to his cell and nourished him? The Greeks, struck dumb at the devotion of the daughter, reversed the sentence, and returned the old man to light and liberty.

Who can forget the history of the Syracusan friends? When Dionysius, the tyrant of Syracuse, sentenced Pythias to die, he begged permission to return once more to his home to take a farewell of his wife and child. The tyrant-king, intending to deny this last request, granted it upon a condition which he thought would be impossible for Pythias to perform. It was that he should procure some one to remain as security for his return, under equal forfeiture of his life, in case he failed. His friend Damon heard the condition, accepting it without solicitation, and Pythias obtained his temporary freedom, and they parted, and in

"Parting, they seemed to tread upon the air,
Twin-roses by the zephyr blown apart,
Only to meet again more close, and share
The fragrance of each other's heart."

The hour of execution came, and Pythias, prevented by adverse winds, had not yet returned. The king and his courtiers were present, and Damon calmly mounted the scaffold of execution. The royal mandate, "Executioner, do your duty," had been given. A distant voice was heard; the crowd gave way, and in a moment Pythias was on the scaffold, and in the arms of Damon, his benefactor. The heart of Dionysius was melted; the tyrant even wept. Leaving his throne, and ascending the scaffold, he exclaimed, "Live, live, ye incomparable pair! You have borne undoubted testimony to the existence of virtue, which equally evinces the existence of a God to reward it. Live happily, live renowned, and form me by your precepts, as you have instructed me by your example, to be worthy to participate in so sacred a friendship." How beautiful in life and in death was the love of Jonathan and David! Well might the prophet celebrate so sublime an instance of attachment, and exclaim that the son of Saul loved the Hebrew shepherd as he loved his own soul, and that their souls were knit together; and well might the Psalmist sing, "Thy love to me was wonderful, surpassing even the love of woman." Nobly did David repay his friendship when he restored to Mephibosheth, the lame son of Jonathan, the lands of his father, and commanded him to eat continually at the royal table even with Solomon, his son.

The genius of Sterne, in Tristam Shandy, has thrown around the character of Uncle Toby, a splendor which dwarfs even the fame of conquerors. "Go," said he one day to an overgrown fly which had buzzed about his nose and tormented him all dinner-time, and which after infinite attempts he had caught at last, as it flew by him. "Go, I will not hurt a hair of thy head." Rising from his chair, crossing the room, he raised the window, and opening his hand as he spoke, to let it escape. "Go," said he, "why should I hurt thee? This world is surely wide enough to hold both thee and me."

Who does not feel better by having read the story of Lefevre, the poor lieutenant? "Thou hast left this matter short," said Uncle Toby to Corporal Trim, "and I will tell thee in what." "When thou madest an offer of my services to Lefevre, as sickness and traveling are both expensive, and thou knowest he was but a poor lieutenant, with a son to subsist as well as himself out of his pay, that thou didst not make an offer to him of my purse; because, had he stood in need, thou knowest, Trim, he had been as welcome to it as myself." "Your Honor knows," replied the corporal, "I had no orders." "True," said Uncle Toby, "thou didst very right, Trim, as a soldier, but certainly very wrong as a man. And when thou offered'st him whatever was in my house, thou shouldst have offered him my house, too. If we had him with us, we could tend and look to him, and in a fort-night he might march." "He will never march in this world," said the corporal. "He shall march," replied Uncle Toby. "He will never march but to his grave," said the Corporal. "He shall march to his regiment," replied Uncle Toby. "He will die, poor soul," said the corporal, "and what will become of his boy?" Cried Uncle Toby, "He shall not die, by —— !" And the accusing spirit which flew to heaven's chancery with the oath, blushed as he gave it in, and the recording angel, as he wrote it down, dropped a tear upon the word, and blotted it out forever. Let us, my brethren, imitate these illustrious examples of virtue.

Freemasonry, by the most impressive rites, instructs her devotees that the response of Zerubbabel to Darius the king was emphatically correct. The Persian monarch, at his feast, inquired of his courtiers which was the most power-ful, wine, woman or the king. When the prince of Judah was asked, he replied, "Neither. Truth is more powerful than them all." Struck by the opinion of Zerubbabel, king and courtiers, of one accord, exclaimed, "Truth is mighty and will prevail." And it has ever since been the motto of one of the orders of chivalry. Without truth we are all like Theseus, and grope through the world, a labyrinth far wider and darker than that of the ancient Cretan king. With truth on our side, we have the silken clue of Ariadne, by the aid of which we can make good our escape.

Such are the aims and teachings of our order, which she impresses upon the minds of her votaries by the most magnificent emblems.

First, the All-Seeing Eye, surrounded by rays of light. Among the Egyptians it was the emblem of Osiris, who was represented by a sceptre in which was placed an eye. It was the symbol of the sun, who represented God, whose eye sees, and whose sceptre governs all things. It reminds the Mason of that superintending Providence, who knows the most secret thoughts of our heart, and will reward us according to our works.

The Beehive is an emblem of industry and sociality, and recommends the practice of those virtues to all rational creatures. It teaches us that as we came into the world intelligent beings, so should we always be industrious ones, never sitting down contented and at our ease while our fellow-creatures around us are in want, when it is in our power to relieve them. It reminds us constantly that God could have made man independent of all other beings; but as dependence is one of the stringent bonds of society, mankind were made dependent on each other for mutual protection and security, as they thereby enjoy better opportunities of fulfilling the reciprocal duties of love and friendship to one another.

The Coffin and the Cassia are striking emblems of mortality, and admonish us of the state to which we are all hastening with a rapidity which is symbolized by the Hour-glass. Time will not permit me to go further.

Such are the purposes and principles of Freemasonry. Friends, they are worthy of your favor. Brethren, they are worthy of preservation in their purity at your hands.

To those of you who have never entered our portals, we have but one request to make. Never assail an institution whose objects and principles may tend to increase the sum of human happiness, because you do not comprehend their bearings nor mode of operation. Leave such work to ignorance and superstition.

One word to the fairer and better sex. I appeal to you, uninitiated matrons and maidens. To the matrons by that which never fails to find an answer in a woman's heart—the love of her children; and to the maiden by that which is equally as strong—always to foster by your kindly countenance an institution to which you owe a lasting debt of obligation. True, indeed, you are excluded from our Lodge, but it is not because we deem you unworthy of our secrets, or unfit co-workers with angels, much less with us, in all good causes; but if I must confess it, it is a consciousness of our own frailty. Love might enter the Lodge with you, jealousy might rankle in the breasts of brethren, and fraternal affection be distorted into bitter rivalry. Woman needs not the aid of mystic ceremonials to prompt her to deeds of benevolence, or "the sweet, small courtesies of life," nor the use of symbols to point her to the pathway of rectitude. Woman's heart is the true lodge where virtue reigns, and her warm and generous sympathies are the only incentives requisite for its practice. Let it not be supposed, however, that Freemasonry overlooks the claims of woman on our order for support and protection; nor that we are wholly apathetic to the sentiment that

> "The world was sad! the garden was a wild!
> And man the hermit sighed, till woman smiled!"

Yes, Freemasonry builds around the matron a wall of

fire, to preserve unsullied the sanctity of the domestic circle; and as the cherubim guarded the tree of life and knowledge in the midst of the Eden of bliss with a flaming word that burned every day; as the sleepless dragon, breathing fire perpetually, watched the golden fleece of Jason, and the golden apples in the garden of the daughters of Hesperus; so Freemasonry guards the maiden from the approach of the serpent, that allures but to ruin, with a shield broader, stronger and surer than that of Achilles.

The influence of woman in the formation of character is universally acknowledged. History is replete with brilliant examples. Coriolanus, banished unjustly from Rome, formed an alliance with her enemy, and with a victorious army returned to the gates of the capital, and threatened to level even the foundation of the city of the seven hills. The Roman women carried their jewels to him, and implored him to abandon his design. They failed. His own wife next entreated him to spare the city. Coriolanus turned to her a deaf ear; and when all had failed, Volumnia, his mother, melted the heart of the hero, and Rome was saved.

If the aphorism of the ancient sage was true, "Give me the making of the poems of a nation, and you may make the laws," how much more important is the sphere of the mothers of our race, who, by moulding the minds of its sons and daughters, are intrusted with the lofty charge of moulding the character of a nation and shaping its destiny! She can impart that impulse which a Lacedæmonian mother conceived to be the glory of her house, the love of battle and the clangor of arms, or, like gentle Hannah of the olden time, can dedicate the infant Samuel to be a priest of the most High God. The clay is in the hands of the potter, and you are answerable for the model. The softened wax and the sealing stamp are both in the maternal hand, and we hold you responsible for the impression. The sheet of blank paper is committed to your guardianship, and we charge you to look well to what shall be written upon it. While Free-masonry acknowledges a kindred duty with the mother, and her proud boast is that she aims at the formation of charac-ter, we are too conscious of our partial failure without your hearty co-operation. If the mothers will only pledge them-selves to do their duty to the youth while they remain under the parental roof, we will be responsible that your lessons of wisdom shall not be wholly lost upon them in manhood. We will be the oak if you will be the ivy. We will be the Doric pillar of strength to receive the buffetings of the storm, if you will only stand by our side, the Corinthian col-umn of beauty, to embellish the mystic temple which we raise to the genius of universal benevolence and philan-thropy. Cling to our cause as Ruth clung to Naomi, con-stant in your attachments, and not like Orpah, who gave the idle kiss and then deserted her. for the idols of Moab.

And now, my brethren of the order, our anniversary is ending, and we must part. When the next festival shall come, and brethren meet around our mystic shrine as we have met to-night, how sadly will our ranks be thinned. Then let us see to it, and so regulate our lives, that when we shall be called hence we may all be found ready. Death on every side of us is sounding his dread alarum in the outer courts of our tabernacle, and summoning us to his silent and spectral court, alike from the Lodge, the Chapter and the Encampment, each of which he invades without the cere-mony of initiation. One by one the pillars of our mystic brotherhood are falling around us, and our costliest gems are dropping continually from our charmed circle. Three pil-lars will alone survive—Faith, Hope and Charity—teaching Faith in God, Hope in immortality and Charity to all man-kind. Yesterday, Hope sat like a siren, filling our life with fascination and bewitching rapture, gilding our future with its fairy splendor, and intoxicating us with the subtle sweets of her chalice as we sipped. To-day, the fondest idol we can cherish and adore totters from its pedestal in the heart, and the pillar of our Hope is broken, and the cold lip almost moulders at the last long kiss of love, like the fruit which grows upon the shores of the Dead Sea, which turns to ashes, it is said, on the lip that touches it, and then there is a burden on our bosoms, and we have nothing left us to love but the dust, and the memory of the farewell wish. We, too, soon must follow. Soon the long, long sleep will be upon us, and there will be a hush in all our households, and a spell upon our loved ones who linger after us. Unseen voices are whispering to us that

"We are such stuff as dreams are made of,
And our little life is rounded with a sleep."

Even now, Death may have shot his warning arrow.

"Art is long, and time is fleeting,
And our hearts, though stout and brave,
Still, like muffled drums, are beating
Funeral marches to the grave."

One after another the stars in which we most delight, though tempting us on every side, are flickering and fading from our sky, reminding us that we have pitched our tents upon this planet but for a single night. Life is nomadic, and "we fold our tents like the Arab and as silently steal away." There is but

"One step to the white death-bed
One to the bier,
One to the charnal of the dead,
And one, oh! where?"

The King of Terrors has already bidden us, and is now beckoning us to his pale feast, where his gaze, like the Gorgon's will turn us into nothingness. All around us Nature is heard in sympathy, singing:

"Leaves have their time to fall,
And flowers to wither at the north wind's' breath,
　　And stars to set—but all,
Thou hast all seasons for thine own, O Death.

　　We know when moons shall wane,
When summer-birds from far shall cross the sea,
　　When autumn's hue shall tinge the golden grain—
But who shall teach us when to look for thee?

　　Is it when spring's first gale
Comes forth to whisper where the violets lie?
　　Is it when roses in our paths grow pale?
They have one season—all are ours to die!

　　Thou art where billows foam,
Thou art where music melts upon the air;
　　Thou art around us in our peaceful home,
And the world calls us forth—and thou are there."

But, my brethren, go on, go on, and still go on, though our path be full of peril and illusion. Let not our footsteps falter, nor our hearts be daunted, nor our high mission thwarted, for Heaven smiles upon order, and the good deeds of the Mason should ever be, like the flower of the cemetery, which grows more lovely and luxuriant in the close vicinity of Death, or like the century plant, which blooms only when it dies. Let our hearts always be open, and with the same liberality as the Roman candidates threw largesses to the electors, let us strew our gifts from that horn of plenty which Providence keeps ever full of choicest blessings. Then like the dove of the deluge, hovering over the waste waters of life, with the olive branch of peace, we will at last return from our errands of mercy to that divine ark, which will safely waft us over this tempestuous sea of trouble; for to the eye of faith already overhead, the rainbow, bursting through the scattering clouds, unfurled like a banner from the battlement above, shines spanning the dark sea of life, resting its farthermost base on the distant ocean of eternity, while all within its arch seems brighter and more resplendent than that without, betokening to us a promise and a covenant of higher and better things. So may each brother live and act his part, that when our labor of love is ended in the Lodge below, we can present at the celestial Lodge above, a long record of our welcome gifts of charity, so that when its portals of light open to receive us, may a mighty band of Masons, which cannot be numbered, be able, as they enter in, to chant the glad song of the Peri in Paradise:

"Joy, joy forever! Our task is done,
The gates are passed, and Heaven is won!"

FREEMASONRY.

[Written in 1875 by Rev. M. Magill, of Marseilles, Ill., after being present at a Masonic festival.]

I.

Hail, Masonry! Hail, noble art sublime!
Long may thy sons with purest lustre shine!
May the sacred principles of old
Be evermore retained with firm hold.

II.

Thy laws are good, thy precepts just and wise,
Thy secret teachings sanctioned in the skies;
In every clime, where human kind hath been,
Thy pure benevolence may be seen.

III.

Thy charity extends to earth's fair bounds,
By praise throughout the universe resounds,
The widow's cry, the orphan's bitter tear,
Has ever found thee ready to give cheer.

IV.

Thy sons, wide-spread, are found in every land,
A firm, united, faithful, trusty band;
Though clime or color mark them far apart,
Yet when they meet together, have one heart.

V.

Hail, Masonry! I love thy sons to see
Stand forth in ancient costume true and free.
I love to see thy banners wide unfurled,
I long to see thee spread throughout the world.

VI.

The wise, the good, the great of every land
Are proud to have a place and with us stand.
They prize the honor Masonry confers,
And pity each who ignorantly errs.

VII.

Let growling bigots spend their bitter spleen,
And "Ante's" rave and fret from morn till e'en;
Their futile hate is labor spent in vain;
Freemasonry will live and favor gain.

ESOTERIC WORK.

The esoteric or secret ritualistic work of Freemasonry is communicated by oral teaching and constitutes a very important part of a Masonic education, and many "bright Masons," as they are technically styled, can claim no other foundation for their Masonic reputation. But as Dr. Mackey aptly said, some share of learning more difficult to attain, and more sublime in its character, than anything to be found in these oral catechisms, is now considered necessary to form a Masonic scholar. However, since the best commentary on the ritual observances is to be found in the lectures, and since they also furnish the secret mode of recognition, which has always been the boast of the institution, a knowledge of them is absolutely necessary to every practical Mason, and a history of the introduction of these lectures and the changes they have from time to time been subjected to, we feel confident, will be of interest to the brethren at the present time.

In comparison to the age of the institution of Freemasonry, the present system of lodge lectures is of modern origin. Examinations of a technical nature to test the claims of the person requesting the privileges of the fraternity existed at a very early period. Such examinations were in vogue until at least the middle of the eighteenth century.

Previous to that time, brief extemporary addresses and charges in addition to the test catechisms were used by the Masters, which varied in excellence, according to the attainments and talents of the Master exemplifying the work. The charges and covenants contained no instructions on the symbolism and ceremonies, as at the present time, but were confined to an explanation of the duties of Masons toward each other.

The earliest authorized lectures, says Dr. Oliver, were those of Drs. Anderson and Desaulier, promulgated in 1720, perhaps at the same time they were compiling the charges and regulations from the ancient constitutions. They were written in the same catechetical form, as in use at the present time, but a great many changes have been made since those primitive lectures were introduced, especially in the United States; but, after all, there is a general feature of similarity which shows that the one derived its parentage from the other.

The production of the Anderson and Desaulier lectures was the Alpha of Masonic lectures. They were imperfect and to a certain extent unsatisfactory, and so much dissatisfaction was manifested because of the development of Masonic science and the increased intelligence of the brethren that it became necessary to prepare an improved system.

In 1732, Martin Clare, A. M., was commissioned by the Grand Lodge of England to prepare a new system of lectures which would be "adapted to the existing state of the Order, without infringing on the ancient landmarks."

Martin Clare was first mentioned in Masonic history as one of the Grand Stewards of the Grand Lodge of England in 1735. He was a man of learning and of literary habits and was recorded as a Master of Arts, and a Fellow of the Royal Society. He was appointed Junior Grand Warden by the Earl of Morton in 1741. Dr. Oliver says, that his version of the lectures was so judiciously drawn up that its practice was enjoined on all the lodges.

In the Clare lectures the symbol of the point within the circle was mentioned for the first time, and the numbers *three, five* and *seven* were introduced, and referred to the

Christian Trinity, the human senses and the institution of the Sabbath. Subsequently, these references were changed to prevent the cosmopolitan character of the institution of Freemasonry from being impaired by any sectarian references to religion.

A few years found the Clare lectures too short and not sufficiently elevated for the increasing demands of Masonic progress.

About the year 1770, Thomas Dunckerley, Esq., was authorized by the Grand Lodge of England to prepare a new series of lectures to take the place of those prepared by Martin Clare. Dr. Oliver says that Dunckerley was the Oracle of the Grand Lodge and the accredited interpreter of its constitutions. He held the office of Provincial Grand Master, and for his eminent Masonic services had been honored by the Grand Lodge with the rank of Senior Grand Warden. His lectures are said to have been very similar to those of Clare. It was Dunckerley who adapted the "lines parallel" as symbolic of the two Saints John, and to him is also ascribed the introduction of the theological ladder, with its three principal rounds, which beautiful and instructive symbol has been retained to the present day.

But the most important change made by Dunckerley was in respect to the Master's word. While in pursuit of his Masonic studies he frequently visited the Ancient, or Athol, Lodges, whose greatest point of difference from the moderns was the disserving of the third degree and establishing a portion of it as the fourth, or royal arch. He was pleased with this arrangement and in imitation of it reconstructed Dermott's royal arch, and introduced it into the legal Grand Lodge. This led to transferring the word formerly used in the third to the fourth degree and confining the former to the substitute. This is the origin of our "substitute" word used at the present day.

William Hutchinson was the Master of Bernard Castle Lodge, in the county of Durham, in the north of England. While Dunckerley was establishing his course of lectures in the London and adjacent Lodges, Hutchinson had prepared and was using a system of his own, which was adopted by many Lodges in his vicinity. He introduced a scientific element into Masonic lectures which was unknown to those compiled by Clare and Dunckerley. Hutchinson restored the ancient symbolism of the third degree, showing that in all times past its legend was typical of a resurrection from the grave.

William Preston prepared a system of lectures which superseded all those that had been in use. It is supposed that Preston and Hutchinson united in this undertaking, and that the Prestonian lectures, which were afterward universally adopted, were the results of the combined labor of the two. The Prestonian lectures continued to be used in England until the union of the two Grand Lodges in 1813, and it is said they are not yet entirely abandoned in that country.

In 1813, the two Grand Lodges of England, the "Ancients" and the "Moderns," were united, and it was then determined to revise the system of lectures. The Rev. Dr. Hemming, Senior Grand Warden, was instructed to perform this task, and the result was the Union or Hemming lectures, which are now the authoritative standard work of English Masonry. I have a copy of these lectures in my possession.

There is no such power in the United States to enforce a uniform ritual for every state in the union, with fifty Grand Lodges, each supreme in its own sphere, each claiming to have ample "light" in Masonry to regulate all its own concerns to the best ends; each believing itself capable of detecting the "true old work."

In the year 1800, a Mason came to this country from England, who had acquired the ritual in general use there from William Preston. He satisfied the Boston brethren as to his character and correctness as to his claims. He communicated the Preston Lectures to Thomas Smith Webb, who was publisher of a *Freemasons' Monitor*. Webb was a man of considerable talent, and devoted more attention to Masonry and knew more about it than any man in this country at that time. Webb communicated the Preston lectures to Henry Fowle, a highly distinguished Mason. And Snow, of Rhode Island, was indebted to Webb for his knowledge of the Prestonian lectures, which, by this time, he had changed slightly by reducing the number of sections, and, in the second edition of his *Freemasons' Monitor*, prepared the monitorial part in a practical and masterly manner to accompany them.

The celebrated lecturer, Benjamin Gleason, of Massachusetts, also acquired them from Webb, whose pupil he was, and greatly distinguished himself among the craft by his polished and classical manner of imparting them. Gleason was a graduate of Brown University in 1802. He became a public lecturer on geography and astronomy, belonged to Mt. Lebanon Lodge in 1807, and died at Concord, Mass., in 1847.

John Barney, who lies buried in Peoria, Illinois, brought the Preston lectures to Illinois and to the Mississippi Valley about the year 1819. He acquired them at Boston, Mass., from Webb himself, in 1816 or 1817. He communicated them to brother T. J. Wade, who afterward became one of the Grand Lecturers of Illinois. Brother Wade was Past Master of Occidental Lodge. Brother Barney also exemplified the Preston lectures in Occidental Lodge when he conferred the degrees of Freemasonry on John Dean Caton and Milton H. Swift, December 11, 1845, and on

THOMAS JEFFERSON WADE

Worshipful Master 1855, 1857 and 1859

Lorenzo Leland, November 29th, of the same year. Brother T. J. Wade was so strongly attached to the Prestonian lectures, as communicated to him by his friend and brother, John Barney, that when the Grand Lodge revised the work or lectures of this grand jurisdiction in 1869, he refused to abandon the old Prestonian system, and, as a result, was refused a commission as Grand Lecturer for Illinois. The Prestonian system was worked in Occidental Lodge at the time the compiler of this work was raised, and was used until about 1882, when brother James McManus, who had received from brother Chamberlain, president of the Board of Grand Examiners, the present standard work of this state, which even since that time has been revised several times, but the proceedings of the Grand Lodge fails to show by what authority such revision was made. One feature in particular was eliminated in 1882, while a school of instruction was exemplifying the third degree in Occidental Lodge on an actual candidate. This elimination was done then and there, and was never again used in the lecture of the third degree. It was a beautiful paragraph, in explanation of the g—s, and was eliminated from the ritualistic work for the same reason that the references to the numbers, three, five and seven, were changed in the Clare lectures in the 18th century.

Harmon G. Reynolds was Grand Master of the Grand Lodge of Illinois in 1869. In his address to the Grand Lodge at the opening session, he spoke of work and lectures as follows:

"In 1843, a convention of the most intelligent Masons from every part of the United States met at Baltimore, and harmonized all discrepancies in work. The manner of opening and closing Lodges, and the work and lectures of the symbolic degrees were distinctly agreed upon. John Barney was a member of that convention. He exemplified it in

U

this state, and it was adopted by the Grand Lodge in 1845, and has been the only authorized work in this jurisdiction since that time. John Barney taught that work and those lectures to R. W. Bro. James Fenton, Grand Secretary of Michigan, and to William A. Dickey, of this city (Springfield). I learned the entire lectures from brother Dickey in 1848, at Rock Island. In January, 1863, the Grand Lodge of Michigan appointed a committee on work, before whom, in April following, by invitation from them, I compared the entire work and lectures, including the opening and closing ceremonies, and they were found to be identical with those taught to brother Fenton.

"In 1865, I visited the Grand Lodge of Wisconsin, and in open session, compared the lectures with R. W. Bro. Melvin R. Young, then State Grand Lecturer, since Grand Master, and they were again found identical. They are the same that have been taught by R. W. Bros. Wade, Fisher, Chamberlain, our present inspectors and lecturers generally, I saw the same work wrought in Oriental, William B. Warren, Dearborn, Chicago, and Thomas J. Turner Lodges in Chicago, in September, 1866. Notwithstanding all this, the opinion was widespread that there were serious discrepancies and disagreements. To remedy this, Past Grand Master Gorin recommended the appointment of a committee to harmonize and restore the lectures to their original language. Upon comparison, it was found that the discrepancies were few, immaterial, and such as could easily be rectified.

"But while the Grand Lodge has not changed or modified the work, nor authorized the same to be done, another impression has gone forth that this Grand Lodge has abandoned its work, and that it actually has none. No impression could be more unfounded.

"To place this matter beyond all cavil, I appointed R. W. Brothers Fisher, Chamberlain, Prickett and Burr a committee of lecturers on discrepancies, myself acting as the umpire. The result of all these labors will be laid before you by the committee raised upon your order, and I urgently recommend that efficient measures be ordered to disseminate the work and lectures among the Lodges in this juris-diction."

Grand Master Gorin, in 1867, recommended that a com-mittee be appointed to revise the work and lectures of this Grand Jurisdiction, which was approved by the Grand Lodge, and said committee made its report at the annual communication of the Grand Lodge in 1869. It appears from the above extract from the address of Grand Master Reynolds that he was opposed to any revision. However, the committee at the annual communication of the Grand Lodge in 1869, made the following report:

"To the Most Worshipful Grand Lodge of Illinois, A. F. & A. M.:

"Your committee, appointed in pursuance of the order of the Grand Lodge, at the annual communication of 1867, for the purpose of revising the work of this jurisdiction, re-spectfully report that they have carefully considered the subject matter before them, have revised the work and are prepared to exemplify the same at the pleasure of this Grand Lodge."

Moved by W. Brother T. J. Heirs that the report be ac-cepted, which motion was lost.

Moved by R. W. Brother Joseph Robbins, G. O., that the report be received and the committee discharged, which motion was laid on the table.

On motion of Brother ———, ordered that the report be received and the work be exemplified at 7 o'clock, P. M.

Seven o'clock P. M., Tuesday, Oct. 5, 1869.

The M. W. Grand Master, officers, members and repre-sentatives present as in the morning.

Labor on the third and second degrees of Masonry was dispensed with, and resumed on the first.

The committee on work assumed the following stations:

R. W. Bro. John W. Clyde (33) as Worshipful Master.

R. W. Bro. George E. Lounsberry (290) as Senior War-den.

R. W. Bro. Joseph O. Cunningham (157) as Junior Warden.

R. W. Bro. Harrison Dills (1) as Treasurer.

R. W. Bro. Milo D. Chamberlain (97) as Secretary.

R. W. Bro. Thomas J. Prickett (241) as Senior Deacon.

R. W. Bro. Royal L. Munn (381) as Junior Deacon.

The opening ceremonies of the first degree were rehearsed.

Mr. Charles J. Heuston, having been duly elected by Springfield Lodge, No. 4, and at the request and by permission of said Lodge, and having answered the usual interrogatories in a satisfactory manner, was duly prepared, introduced and initiated an Entered Apprentice Mason.

Brother Heuston, having retired, labor on the first degree was dispensed with, and resumed on the third.

Upon motion duly seconded, the work as exemplified was re-affirmed as the work of the Grand Lodge of Illinois.

The Grand Lodge was called from labor to refreshment until Wednesday morning at eight o'clock.

Thus was the present standard work adopted by the Grand Lodge of Illinois, but, as heretofore stated, it was not universally worked by the Lodges for several years after the adoption, because the Preston, or so-called Wade-Barney work, had been the recognized work for so many years that it was hard for the Masonic workers to drop it and learn orally the new work.

Brother James McManus was the first to introduce the new work in Occidental Lodge when he was Master in 1881. He obtained it from R. W. Brother M. D. Chamberlain, and the compiler of this work received it from brother McManus.

Occidental Lodge was never more proficient in the standard work than at the present time, and to no one is she under greater obligations for such proficiency than to Brother A. J. Newell (who has long since received his reward in that house not made with hands, eternal in the heavens) and to

R. W. Brother W. D. Fullerton, the present efficient District Deputy Grand Master of the Ninth Masonic District.

Occidental Lodge is now honored by having three Grand Lecturers among its members, viz: R. W. Brothers Samuel B. Bradford, Herman S. Blanchard and Richard D. Mills, all of whom passed a most creditable examination and now hold commissions from the Grand Lodge of Illinois as Grand Lecturers.

THE WHITE APRON.

"It is an emblem of innocence and the badge of a Mason; more ancient than the Golden Fleece or Roman Eagle; more honorable than the Star and Garter, or any other order that can be conferred upon you at this or any future period, by King, Prince, Potentate or any other person, except he be a Mason."

Dr. Mackey says: "There is no one of the symbols of speculative Masonry more important in its teachings, or more interesting in its history, than the lambskin, or white leather apron. Commencing its lesson at an early period in the Mason's progress, it is impressed upon his memory as the first gift which he receives, the first symbol which is explained to him, and the first tangible evidence which he possesses of his admission into the Fraternity.

"Whatever may be his future advancement in the 'royal art,' into whatsoever deeper arcana his devotion to the mystic institution or his thirst for knowledge may subsequently lead him, with the lambskin apron, his first investure—he never parts.

"Changing perhaps its form and its decorations, and conveying, at each step, some new but still beautiful allusion, its substance is still there, and it continues to claim the honored title by which it was first made known to him on the night of his initiation, as 'the badge of a Mason.'

"If in less important portions of our ritual there are abundant allusions to the manners and customs of the ancient world, it is not to be supposed that the Masonic rite of *investure*—the ceremony of clothing the newly initiated candidate with this distinctive badge of his profession—is without its archetype in the times and practices long passed away. It would, indeed, be strange, while all else in Masonry is covered with the veil of antiquity, that the apron alone, its most significant symbol, should be indebted for its existence to the invention of a modern mind.

"On the contrary, we shall find the most satisfactory evidence that the use of the apron, or some equivalent mode of investure, as a mystic symbol, was common to all the nations of the earth from the earliest periods.

"Among the Israelites, the girdle formed a part of the investure of the priesthood. In the mysteries of Mithras, in Persia, the candidate was invested with a white apron. In the initiations practiced in Hindoostan, the ceremony of investure was preserved, but a sash, called the sacred zennar, was substituted for the apron. The Jewish sect of the Essenes clothed their novices with a white robe. The celebrated traveller, Kæmpfer, informs us that the Japanese, who practice certain rites of initiation, invest their candidates with a white apron, bound round the loins with a zone or girdle. In the Scandinavian rites, the military genius of the people caused them to substitute a white shield, but its presentation was accompanied by an emblematic instruction not unlike that which is connected with the Mason's apron."

Dr. Oliver, one of the most distinguished and learned of English Masons of the nineteenth century, says: "The apron appears to have been in ancient times an honorary badge of distinction. In the Jewish economy, none but the superior orders of the priesthood were permitted to adorn themselves with ornamented girdles, which were made of blue, purple and crimson, decorated with gold, upon a ground of fine white linen, while the inferior priests wore only plain white.

"The Indian, the Persian, the Jewish, the Ethiopian, and the Egyptian aprons, though equally superb, all bore a character distinct from each other. Some were plain white ones, others striped with blue, purple and crimson; some were of wrought gold, others adorned and decorated with superb tassels and fringes.

"In a word, though, the principal honor of the apron may consist in innocence of conduct and purity of heart, yet it certainly appears through all ages to have been a most exalted badge of distinction.

"In primitive times, it was rather an ecclesiastical than civil decoration, although in some cases the apron was elevated to great superiority as a national trophy. The royal standard of Persia was originally an apron in form and dimensions. At this day it is connected with ecclesiastical honors; for the chief dignitaries of the Christian church, wherever a legitimate establishment, with the necessary degree of rank and subordination is formed, are invested with aprons as a pecular badge of distinction, which is a collateral proof of the fact that Masonry was originally incorporated with the various systems of divine worship used by every people in the ancient world. Masonry retains the symbol or shadow; it cannot have renounced the reality or substance."

The color of the Masonic apron should be pure, unspotted white, which color has in all ages and countries been esteemed an emblem of innocence and purity. It should be made of lambskin, and in dimensions, 14 to 16 inches wide and 12 to 14 inches deep, with a fall, or bib, 3 to 4 inches deep.

THE MASTER'S HAT.

The Master wears his hat while presiding over a Lodge of Masons because it is an emblem of authority. It had its origin during the Middle Ages. Gothic justices always wore a cap or head-dress when presiding in court, as an emblem of their authority, and the people wore their hats while attending the tribunal as symbols of personal liberty. Gessler's well known emblem of subjection and superiority was a hat placed on a pole, as is well known to any schoolboy who has read the story of William Tell and the apple. Ancient Germans also regarded the wearing of the hat as a type of freedom, or as a release from servitude. And thus, while Mediæval Masons worked with their heads covered as a sign of freedom, the exceptional feature of the Master's hat contains the secret symbolism of authority at the present day.

THE GAVEL.

"The common gavel is an instrument made use of by operative masons to break off the corners of rough stones, the better to fit them for the builder's use, but we, as Free and Accepted Masons, are taught to make use of it for the more noble and glorious purpose of divesting our hearts and consciences of all the vices and superfluities of life; thereby fitting our minds, as living stones for that spiritual building, that house not made with hands eternal in the beavens."

It has been clearly demonstrated by learned mythologists that the Master's gavel has descended to modern Freemasonry with the symbolism of Thor's hammer. It is typical of absolutism and authority, and, when wielded with skill and energy, the Freemason within hearing of its knocks will humbly bow to the emblem of might with the same alacrity that the Norseman trembled at Thor's hammer. It convenes a Lodge of Masons as it convenes a court of justice, by a blow which notifies those within its sound that the Master has assumed the symbol of authority and calls, by virtue of the gavel, to order and submission.

LIGHTS.

A Lodge has three symbolic lights, situated E., W. and S. There is none in the N. * * * * * *

In a Masonic Lodge no light appears on the north side.

The north was especially symbolized in the judicial procedures of the Middle Ages. Below the judges, on the right, stood the accuser, on the left was the accused. The former in the south facing the north, and the latter in the north looking to the south.

In the center of the court, directly before the judge, stood an altar upon which rested an open Bible. South of the altar was deemed honorable and worthy for the plaintiff, but the north was typical of a frightful darkness.

When a person was put on trial in grievous criminal accusations, and made a solemn oath of purgation, his face turned toward the north, and in other cases, less aggravated, he faced the east.

The executioner, in executing the extreme penalty of the law, faced the convict toward the north, as a symbolism of eternal darkness.

BLUE LODGE.

The most solemn oath known to the ancient Teuton was sworn on a blue stone. This is undoubtedly the source from whence Masonic Altars covered with blue emanated.

The Druids also accorded equal reverence to this color. The conception involved in this symbolism has survived to modern Freemasonry, for we designate our places of meeting by the name of "Blue Lodge," typical of that unalterable constancy and zeal expressed by the ancient emblem. Hence the upholstering of the furniture in a Symbolic Lodge should be in blue.

ODE TO ILLINOIS.

I.

Oh, Illinois! What a Paradise blest,
    A garden of Eden, the pride of the west,
The home of the great, the proud and the free,
    States of the west! 'tis true I love thee.
Your rivers and creeks and your beautiful trees
    Are nursed by the sun and rocked by the breeze.
Your rippling brooks and your murmuring rills
    A requiem sing to your towering hills.
Your wide rolling plains and your mineral wealth,—
    God's fairest of lands, all blooming in health:

II.

The Father of Waters rolls swift by your side,
    Drifting away to old Mexico's tide;
The Great Lakes of the north triumphantly boast,
    That Michigan strands on your northern coast;
The Ohio and Wabash join in the throng,
    While on your southeast they murmur along.
The blue Illinois sings a mournful tune
    At the base of Starved Rock, an Indian tomb,
Where the brave Illini, our Indian tribe,
    Besieged by the Iroquois, fought, bled and died.
And Buffalo Rock stands proud in the vale
    To touch for the truth a historical tale.
And Ottawa, too, at the mouth of the Fox,
    A magnificent city built on the rocks,
Kissed by the sunbeams' reddening glow
    When the sun rises and when setting low;
The old fort on the hill—aboriginal strife,—
    The pioneer's home when fleeing for life.
Nature's own scenery, grand and sublime,—
    Beautiful city, grandeur is thine!
The smoke and the steam and the loud whistles shriek,
    The neighing of steeds and the jamming of streets,
The pulling and hawing and geeing about,
    Of teams coming in and teams going out,
Reminds me of home in my childhood's days,
    When wending from school with the sun's setting rays.
What fond recollections, my memory instills
    Of that home in the valley, environed by hills!

III.

Oh, proud Illinois!   The home of the true
    Defenders of right, the Red, White and Blue.
When cruel rebellion endangered the life
    Of our glorious nation, you rushed to the strife,
Your Wallace and Irwin and Lindley and Earle
    The Star Spangled Banner in Dixie unfurled.
On Donelson Heights, an Irwin you gave
    The fame of your arms the nation to save.
On Shiloh's dread field of carnage and strife
    There Wallace in battle gave up his life.
And Lindley, while home a recorder of deeds,
    At Altoona was slain by fell rebel creeds.
The brave Fifty-third at Jackson was bled;
    While charging the rebels by Earle they were led.
While flaming artillery was sounding the knell
    The heroic Earle exaltingly fell.

IV.

Oh! Goddess of Liberty, be proud of our State,
    We gave you a Lincoln, a President great.
With prospects of peace, while exulting with joy,
    Wilkes Booth, the assassin, did Lincoln destroy.
Entombed in our state in peace may he rest
    When war wages fiercely in doubtful contest.

1872.   —W. L. MILLIGAN.

ST. JOHN'S LODGE, No. 13,

Of Peru, Ill., was organized at Vermillionville, La Salle county, Ill., August 7, 1841, under dispensation granted by the M. W. Grand Lodge. The petitioners met in convocation in their lodge room in the village of Vermillionville, Saturday, August 7, 1841, and proceeded to open and organize a Lodge of Free and Accepted Masons, under the style and name of St. John's Lodge. Present:

Brother Luther Woodward, Worshipful Master.

Brother Andrew Kirkpatrick, Senior Warden.

Brother Mathias J. Ross, Junior Warden.

Brother Asa Holdridge, M. M., brother Samuel Norton, M. M., brother Angus McMillen, E. P.

A committee was appointed to draft and report a code of by-laws for the government of this Lodge, consisting of brothers Woodward, Kirkpatrick, Ross and Potter.

Both Kirkpatrick and Holdridge were appointed a committee to procure jewels and furniture for this Lodge.

Lodge adjourned to meet again on Saturday, two weeks from this day, at four o'clock P. M.

But one brother was raised in this Lodge during the year 1842—Steven W. Pain, March 31st.

January 30th, brother M. J. Ross, who died January 28th, was buried with the honors of Masonry. Brother Ross was one of the founders of the Lodge.

September 22d, the Lodge resolved to apply to the Grand Lodge for a charter, and passed the following resolution:

Also voted, That on account of the retired situation of Vermillionville, and by the advice of a number of brethren of Peru, we, after mature consideration, think it for the interest of the institution to remove this Lodge to that place, and ask the Grand Lodge to grant a charter for this Lodge at that place.

At the meeting of October 13th, the name of Warren Brown appears among the members. This is the same brother Warren Brown that was Secretary of Western Star Lodge, No. 107, the first Lodge organized within the present limits of the state of Illinois.

December 15th officers, as follows, were elected:

L. Woodward, Worshipful Master.

Harmer Whitehead, Senior Warden.

Samuel Norton, Junior Warden.

Dr. T. W. Hennessey, Treasurer.

Ambrose O'Connor, Secretary.

Warren Brown, Senior Deacon.

A. Kirkpatrick, Junior Deacon.

A. Holdridge, Tyler.

At the annual communication of the Grand Lodge of Illinois, convened at the city of Jacksonville, October 3, 1842, the committee on returns and work reported at the evening communication of the Grand Lodge recommending the granting of a charter to St. John's Lodge as No. 13, and its removal from Vermillionville to Peru, which was accordingly done.

This Lodge is still in existence and one of the most active and historic Lodges of Freemasons in Illinois. The writer's esteemed friend and Right Worshipful Brother, Frederick E. Hoberg, is its present efficient secretary. Luther Woodward, Andrew Kirkpatrick and Asa Holdridge were members of Ottawa Lodge, No. 114, under the jurisdiction of the Grand Lodge of Kentucky, in 1839 and 1840, and demitted in 1841 to organize St. John's Lodge, No. 13.

STARVED ROCK

One of the Historic Places in the Valley of the Illinois

STARVED ROCK.

[A reverie written by John D. Hammond, suggested by a visit to
Starved Rock, about 1882.]

I.

Where the sunlit prairies glisten
  By the sparkling Illinois;
And the bluffs in picturesgue grandeur,
  Tower towards the sky,
Lies a spot so rich in beauty,
  That the heart at nature's shrine
Bows and feels the inspiration
  Of those wondrous scenes sublime.

II.

'Tis not grand nor lofty mountains
  In this region that so please,
But a beauty in the landscape,
  And the verdure of the trees;
Mossy dells, where ferns lie hidden,
  In their tangled beds of green,
Wooded heights, where dew-drops glisten,
  In the summer's golden sheen.

III.

Far away the Illinois
  Rolls, a line of sliver light,
'Till in ribbon like dimensions
  It disappears from sight;
Flowing on by wooded hill-tops,
  Craggy peaks, the rocky glens;
Deep ravines and wondrous canyons,
  And the busy haunts of men.

IV.

What historic memories gather
  As we view this lonely spot!
We think of O-ma-wa-quah
  And the legends of Starved Rock;
Of that noble tribe of warriors—
  The once famous Illini—
Sent from here by slow starvation,
  To their hunting grounds on high.

V

V.

Like a gleam of flitting sunshine,
    All the past drops into view—
All its horrors, dreads and tortures,
    Pass before us in review.
Long we muse in thoughtful silence,
    Every passing scene a shock,
'Till the wild bird's joyous singing,
    From our reverie calls us back.

VI.

In a moment 'tis forgotten,
    All the horrors flit from view;
While the glorious panorama
    Lights the vision up anew.
Here we gaze on sunny landscapes
    Which in time may fade away,
But this monument of ages
    Will forever hold its sway.

HUMBOLDT LODGE, No. 555.

A resume of the history of Humboldt Lodge, No. 555, the only daughter of Occidental Lodge, No. 40, A. F. & A. M.:

On the first day of April, 1867, M. W. Jerome R. Gorin, Grand Master of the Grand Lodge, A. F. & A. M., of Illinois, on the petition of Joseph Gondolf, and the requisite number of brethren, issued a dispensation to form and open a new Lodge at Ottawa, Illinois, to be called Humboldt Lodge, and designated Joseph Gondolf as Worshipful Master.

At the annual communication of the Grand Lodge, held in Springfield, October 1, 1867, the committee on Lodges U. D., after examining the returns of Humboldt Lodge, U. D., recommended that a charter be granted to Humboldt Lodge as No. 555, which report was approved by the Grand Lodge, and Humboldt Lodge was soon after constituted, and is now, with a membership of one hundred and six, one of the most hospitable and charitable Masonic Lodges in Illinois.

Appeals for worthy charities were never known to have been refused by this Lodge, and the writer can personally testify to the degree of unanimity with which the brethren of Humboldt Lodge responded to the call for funds with which to found the Illinois Masonic Orphans' Home in 1885. Every member of Humboldt Lodge contributed liberally and cheerfully toward this worthy project.

Occidental Lodge is proud of the record her only daughter, Humboldt, has made since constituted forty years ago. The personnel of Humboldt Lodge is equal to any Masonic Lodge in this grand jurisdiction, and numbers

among its members many of the most successful professional and business men, and men of the highest social standing in our community.

Forty years ago Occidental Lodge had a membership
consisting of many of the best German speaking people in
Ottawa, and, because of this fact, and there being many
highly respectable Germans who maintained a favorable
opinion of Freemasonry and were desirous of becoming
members of a Masonic Lodge, but were deterred from so
doing because of their inability to understand the English
language, Joseph Gondolf, and other Germans who belonged to Occidental Lodge, petitioned the Grand Master
for a new Lodge in which they could exemplify the work
in their mother tongue.

The work was exemplified in the German language for
a number of years in Humboldt Lodge, and the early records were also written in German, but as the years wore
along, brethren of the English speaking language began to
knock at their outer door for admission, until, at the present
time, the proportion of German membership is not much
greater than that of Occidental Lodge, and the work long
ago ceased to be exemplified in German, and the records
are now written in English.

Members of Humboldt Lodge have filled important Masonic offices and presided over Shabbona Chapter, No. 37,
R. A. M., and Ottawa Commandery, No. 10, Knights Templar, and Brother Albert F. Schoch, Past Master of Humboldt Lodge, is now Grand Commander of the Grand Commandery of Knights Templar of Illinois.

Mention has heretofore been made as to ceremonials,
such as laying corner stones, celebrating St. John's Day
and other Masonic functions participated in by Humboldt

Lodge in that part of this work pertaining to the mother Lodge—Occidental.

During the past few years, St. John's Day has been most fittingly celebrated by Occidental and Humboldt Lodges jointly, and the brethren and their families have become accustomed to look forward to the festival and picnic of St. John's Day, June 24th, with a considerable enthusiasm.

The charter members of Humboldt Lodge were Joseph Gondolf, Henry Gondolf, Herman Alschuler, Adolphus Baedecker, Christian Forster, George W. Fuchs, Christian G. Irion, Charles G. Lutz, Mathias Maierhofer, George W. Ravens, Charles Theodore Rohde, Jacob Schmid, Herman Silver, Anton H. Strobel and Herman Warlick.

Of the above charter members, George W. Fuchs was raised in Occidental Lodge in 1856; Henry Gondolf and Herman Alschuler in 1859; Anton H. Strobel in 1861; Christian G. Irion, November 17, 1862; Joseph Gondolf June 1, 1863; Charles G. Lutz July 18, 1864; Herman Warlick, August 1, 1864; Jacob Schmid, November 20, 1865; Henry Koch, November 19, 1866, and were demitted from Occidental Lodge by law of affiliation as charter members of Humboldt Lodge, November 18, 1867.

THE MASTERS OF HUMBOLDT LODGE.

Joseph Gondolf, 1867 and 1868.

Henry Koch, 1869 to 1873, inclusive.

George W. Ravens, 1874 and 1881.

George W. Fuchs, 1875 to 1877, inclusive.

Henry Gondolf, 1878 to 1880.

Isaac Weil, 1882 to 1884.

Otto J. Gondolf, 1885 to 1887.

Al. F. Schoch, 1888, '89, '90 and 1896.

Charles Geiger, 1891 and 1892.

George H. Pruett, 1893.

Phillip Leiner, 1894 and 1895.
Henry Bestman, 1897 and 1898.
George H. Haight, 1899 to 1901, inclusive.
Fred A. Hatheway, 1902 to 1904, inclusive.
R. A. Nickerson, 1905.
Phillip J. Wendel, 1906.

ADIEU! A HEART WARM FOND ADIEU!

Adieu! a heart warm fond adieu!
　　Dear brothers of the mystic tie!
Ye favoured, ye enlightened few,
　　Companians of my social joy!
Though I to foreign lands must hie,
　　Pursuing Fortune's sliddry ba',
With melting heart, and brimful eye,
　　I'll mind you still, though far awa'.

Oft have I met your social band,
　　And spent the cheerful festive night,
Oft honoured with supreme command,
　　Presided o'er the sons of light;
And by that hieroglyphic bright,
　　Which none but craftsman ever saw!
Strong memory on my heart shall write,
　　Those happy scenes when far awa'.

May freedom, harmony and love,
　　Unite you in the grand design,
Beneath the Omniscient Eye above,
　　The glorious architect divine!
That you may keep the unerring line,
　　Still rising by the plummet's law,
Till order bright completely shine,
　　Shall be my prayer when far awa'.

And you farewell, whose merits claim,
　　Justly that highest badge to wear!
Heaven bless your honour'd noble name,
　　To Masonry and Scotia dear!
A last request permit me here,
　　When yearly ye assemble a',
One round, I ask it with a tear,
　　To him, the bard, that's far awa'.

The above poem was written by Robert Burns as a sort of farewell to the Masonic companions of his youth, when he was on the point of leaving Scotland for Jamaica, 1786. Robert Burns was made a Mason during the summer of 1783, when he was twenty-three years of age. He died July 21, 1796.

ADDENDA.

Mention is made on page 35 of the appointment on February 6, 1846, of brothers C. V. Kelley, J. D. Caton, T. Lyle Dickey and M. H. Swift, a committee on the resolution of Harmony Lodge, No. 3, Jacksonville, Ill., which Lodge had complained to the Grand Lodge regarding negroes being admitted into Masonic Lodges in Chicago.

At a communication of Occidental Lodge, February 20, 1846, this committee was instructed to report at the next regular communication.

John G. Reynolds says in his "History of Masonry in Illinois" (records read) :

"At this communication, the committee appointed to report on the subject of the Chicago circular, made their report in the words following, to-wit, which report being accepted was ordered to be printed, and the Secretary instructed to forward copies of the same to the Grand Lodge and the several Lodges in the state, with as little delay as possible."—*March 6, 1846.*

Reynolds says: "On the opposite page is the remark, 'Here follows the report.' If the report was ever recorded, it has long since faded, for the page is as guiltless of ink as it was the day it left the mill where it was manufactured."

Since going to press, through the kindness of R. W. Bro. Fred E. Hoberg, Secretary of St. John's Lodge, No. 13, Peru, Ill., I am able to herewith produce the report of the above committee, a certified copy of which he fortunately found among the old records and files in the archives of St. John's Lodge:

At a meeting of Occidental Lodge, held at Mason's hall, in Ottawa, La Salle county, Ill., March the 6th, 5846,—

The committee to whom was referred the Circular from

three Lodges in Chicago in reply to the Circular from Harmony Lodge, No. 3, Jacksonville, Ill., made their report, which was unanimously adopted, and is as follows:

The Committee to whom was referred the Circular from the Lodges in Chicago, as, also, that from St. John's Lodge, No. 13, Peru, and another from Harmony Lodge, No. 3, Jacksonville, Ill., respectfully offer the following report:

Your Committee have had the whole matter, as far as communicated to them, under consideration, and regret exceedingly that such hastiness of action had been pursued by H. L., in respect to the allegations contained in their Circular against certain practices said to be followed in one of the Lodges in Chicago, over which the M. W. G. M. presides.

Your Committee, however, are of the opinion that it was not the intention of H. L. to create any discord amongst the fraternity, or injure the character and standing of the M. W. G. M.; but that their proceedings, however hasty, arose from an over-anxiety and zeal for the preservation of the order and beauty of our ancient and honorable institution.

Your Committee would further state, that the circular from the three Lodges in Chicago, as well as the letter therein from the M. W. G. M., is, and is hereby acknowledged to be, a full and unequivocal refutation of the charges contained in the circular from H. L., proving to the full satisfaction of your committee their falsity, and exciting both surprise and regret, that any Lodge of Free and Accepted Masons should accuse a sister Lodge of unmasonic conduct without first making inquiry as to the truth of such a charge.

Your Committee would further express disapprobation of the conduct of the brother who made these statements, so injurious to that harmony which is the strength and beauty of our ancient and honorable institution, and sincerely hope that he will repent of his error, acknowledge his fault, and make amends to those whom he would have injured.

Resolved, That, in the opinion of this Lodge, the report from the Lodges in Chicago, and the letter of the M. W.

G. M., are a complete and entire refutation of the charges made by H. L. on the Lodges in Chicago, as well as on the standing of the M. W. G. M.

Resolved, That a copy of this report and resolutions be sent to the M. W. G. M., Grand Lodge of Illinois, and to the several Lodges in the state, and that the Secretary is hereby ordered to transmit the same with as little delay as possible.

CHARLES V. KELLY,
JOHN D. CATON,
T. L. DICKEY,
M. H. SWIFT,
L. LELAND,
Committee.

I certify that the above is a true copy of the report presented and unanimously adopted at a regular communication of Occidental Lodge, held March 6, 5846.

M. H. SWIFT, Secretary.

NEGRO LODGES.

Since this subject has been approached in the history of Occidental Lodge, we believe it of interest to the brethren to recite, in condensed form, the history of Negro Lodges, and their relation to legally constituted Lodges.

I have in my possession the history of negro Masonry and its introduction into America, which agrees with that given by Dr. Mackay in his Encyclopedia of Freemasonry.

On September 20, 1784, a charter for a Master's Lodge was granted, although not received until 1787, to Prince Hall and others, all colored men, under the authority of the Grand Lodge of England. The Lodge bore the name of "African Lodge, No. 429," (see note) and was situated in the city of Boston. This Lodge ceased its connection with the Grand Lodge of England for many years, and about the beginning of the present century (19th) its registration was stricken from the rolls of that Grand Lodge, its legal existence, in the meantime, never having been recognized by the Grand Lodge of Massachusetts, to which body it had always refused to acknowledge allegiance.

After the death of Hall and his colleagues, to whom the charter had been granted, the Lodge, for want of some one to conduct its affairs, fell into abeyance, or to use the technical phrase, become dormant. After some years it was revived, but by whom, or under what process of Masonic law, is not stated, and information of the revival given to the Grand Lodge of England, but no reply or recognition was received from that body.

After some hesitation as to what would be the proper course to pursue, they came to the conclusion, as they have themselves stated, "that with what knowledge they possessed of Masonry, and as people of color by themselves, they

were, and ought by right to be, free and independent of
other Lodges." Accordingly, on the 18th of June, 1827,
they issued a protocol, in which they said:

"We publicly declare ourselves free and independent of
any Lodge from this day, and we will not be tributary or
governed by any Lodge but that of our own." They soon
after assumed the name of the "Prince Hall Grand Lodge,"
and issued charters for the constitution of subordinates, and
from it have proceeded all the Lodges of colored persons
now existing in the United States.

Dr. Mackey says further: "Admitting even the legality
of the English charter of 1784, which, however, is question-
able, as there was already a Masonic authority in Massachusetts upon whose prerogatives of jurisdiction such charter
was an invasion; it cannot be denied that the unrecognized
self-revival of 1827, and the subsequent assumption of
Grand Lodge powers, were illegal, and rendered both the
Prince Hall Grand Lodge and all the Lodges which emanated from it clandestine. And this has been the unanimous
opinion of all Masonic jurists in this country."

(NOTE.—Dr. Mackey is in error as to the number being "429." I have a list published in London of the names
and numbers of all the Lodges granted warrants by the
Grand Lodge of England from and including the year 1721
to and including the year 1813, and among the list I find
chartered in 1784, No. 459, African Lodge, Boston, New
England. No. 459, and not No. 429, as Dr. Mackey has
it, was the number this Lodge was known under in the list
1781-1791, and as No. 370, list 1792-1813.—Author.)

POLITICAL AND CIVIL OFFICES.

Among the political and civil offices held by members of Occidental Lodge (pages 183 to 186, inclusive) the names of brother Lorenzo Leland, clerk of the Northern Division of the Supreme Court of Illinois from 1848 to 1867, and brother Cairo D. Trimble, who was also clerk of the same Court 1872-1878, should have been recorded, also the name of brother Charles J. Yockey, sheriff of La Salle county, 1894 to 1898. The names of these brethren were unintentionally omitted, and not discovered until after the press work had been well along.

Since going to press I have learned that brother P. V. N. Smith, who was raised in 1852, was a partner of Benjamin Phelps (an old settler of Ottawa and brother-in-law of Col. D. F. Hitt) in the mercantile business, and was killed while hunting by the accidental discharge of his gun.

ACKNOWLEDGEMENTS.

I desire to express my acknowledgements to M. W. Bro. John Corson Smith, past Grand Master of Masons of Illinois, for plates of dispensation and charter of Western Star Lodge, No. 107, at Kaskaskia, Ill., and also plate of M. W. Brother Shadrach Bond, the first Territorial Governor of Illinois, and the first Grand Master of the first Grand Lodge of Masons in Illinois, 1822.

To our esteemed friend and brother Gil. W. Barnard for plate of the Illinois Masonic Orphans' Home, Chicago.

To the late R. W. Brother J. H. C. Dill and R. W. Brother Isaac Cutter, Grand Secretary, Grand Lodge of Illinois, for plate of R. W. Brother Abram Jonas, the first Grand Master of the present Grand Lodge of Masons of Illinois, 1840.

To R. W. Brother H. B. Grant, Grand Secretary of the Grand Lodge of Kentucky, for information pertaining to Ottawa Lodge, No. 114, working under the jurisdiction of the Grand Lodge of Kentucky, 1839.

To Miss Belle Wallace, daughter of Gen. W. H. L. Wallace, for notice of Lodge meeting, December 28, 1847, which she found preserved in her father's scrap book, also for the plates of her father, Gen. W. H. L. Wallace, and grandfather, Col. T. Lyle Dickey.

To Brother A. G. Uhles, Secretary of Alexandria-Washington Lodge, No. 22, A. F. & A. M., Alexandria, Va., and Brother Edward Grimm, Secretary of Miners' Lodge, No. 273, A. F. & A. M., Galena, Ill., for information concerning the Masonic affiliation of Col. Daniel Fletcher Hitt.

To the Ottawa *Free Trader* for "tidings" of some of the

pioneer members of Occidental Lodge, gleaned from the old files of long ago.

To Bro. Charles E. Pettit, Secretary of Occidental Lodge, and member of the firm of Sapp, Pettit & Sapp, printers of this work, do I tender special acknowledgements for the invaluable assistance he has rendered in proof-reading and publishing of this work.

THE END.

I have lingered over my task long enough. The benediction must be uttered and the best of friends part, severing the most intimate and beloved relations.

In compiling "The White Apron," or History of Occidental Lodge, I have endeavored to spread throughout the volume a fund of useful information, to the brethren, not elsewhere obtainable, as well as to impart the benefits of information I have derived from the works of such authors and distinguished men and Masons as Lawrie, Oliver, Mackey, Pike, Fort, Lyon, Findell, Mitchell, Gould, and other eminent Masonic scholars and historians.

And we hope that we shall not be disappointed in that, when you have read "The White Apron," you will feel that you had been honored in becoming a member of Occidental Lodge, and kneeling at the same altar in offering up your devotions to Deity at which knelt such men as Swift, Caton, Wallace, Dickey, Reddick, Walker, Osman, Nash, Gray, Avery, Bushnell, Cook and Hollister, long, long ago—men who were pioneers in developing the West; men of untarnished fame in both civil and military life; commanding officers and generals on the battlefields of our country; and municipal, state and national officials in civil and political life; lawyers, ministers, judges and congressmen, bankers and financiers, who honored themselves and thought it not beneath their dignity to meet upon the *level* in Occidental Lodge; the artisan, mechanic and laborer, squaring their actions by the rule of virtue and walking uprightly in their several stations before God and man.

I now have the pleasure of presenting you with "The White Apron." I trust that it is unspotted and that it is as much, of not more, than you expected of me. It is for you to decide whether my efforts in bringing up from the ruins of our temple, the history of Occidental Lodge, is a success.

If your judgment is against me, I shall not imitate the Archbishop of Granada, who expostulated with his critic, by observing, "Say no more, my child, you are yet too raw to make proper distinctions. Know that I never composed a better homily than that which you disapprove, for my genius, thank heaven, hath as yet lost nothing of its vigor. Henceforth, I will make a better choice of a confidant. Adieu, Mr. Gil Blas, I wish you all manner of prosperity, with a little more taste."

I entertain, however, a sanguine hope that "The White Apron" will be prized by you and looked upon as the evergreen or acacia that revealed and brought to light the history of Occidental Lodge.

Should my anticipations be correct, your approval will be a cheerful reflection in the declining days of my life, the prime of which was spent in the service of the fraternity, without the hope of fee or reward.

With an abiding faith in God, hope in immortality and charity to all mankind, I am,

Fraternally thine,

W. L. MILLIGAN.

w

APPENDIX.

We closed the history of Occidental Lodge, No. 40, A. F. & A. M., October 10, 1906, it being the sixtieth anniversary as a chartered Lodge, but owing to the encouragement in the publication of "The White Apron," received from R. W. Bro. Richard D. Mills and the officers and brethren of Occidental Lodge, during the year 1907, we feel justified in publishing this appendix to Occidental Lodge, reciting its record from October 10, 1906, to October 10, 1907, a period which has been one of the most prosperous in its history; and we old members, who once bore the "burden and heat of the day," look with much pride and satisfaction upon the achievements of the younger members, and the progress they are making in exemplifying the symbolism of our time honored fraternity.

OFFICERS, 1907.

Richard D. Mills..................Worshipful Master.
Harry W. Mitchell.....................Senior Warden.
Walter E. Speckman..................Junior Warden.
Samuel B. Bradford ....Treasurer.
Charles E. Pettit........................Secretary.
William H. Barnard.......................Chaplain.
William Scales........................Senior Deacon.
Tom W. Smurr.......................Junior Deacon.
Silas E. Kain........................Senior Steward.
John S. Rhoads.....................Junior Steward.
Joseph A. Wilson...........................Tyler.

RAISED.

Clarence Paul Provins.................. Dec.   1, 1906.
Everitt Anthony Sherwood............. Dec.   24, 1906.
Orvil James Beers.................... Jan.   28, 1907.

Francis Ellsworth Brumagim........... Feb.   25, 1907
William Abraham Mills............... March 11, 1907.
Linwood Blake Steward............... March 25, 1907.
Edwin Sherman Leland............... April   8, 1907.
James Francis Peattie................. April   8, 1907.
Arthur Joseph Bertiaux............... April   8, 1907.
John E. Edmunds.................... May   13, 1907.
Wilbur Grimes....................... Sept.   23, 1907.
Edward Lyle Yocum................. Sept.   30, 1907.
Charles Frederick Junod............. Oct.   7, 1907.

AFFILIATED.

Burton Lewis Stevenson.............. Jan.   21, 1907.
William Hugh Parker................ March 18, 1907.

DEMITTED.

Arthur W. Ladd..................... Jan.   21, 1907.
Augustus Ives, Jr. .... Jan.   21, 1907.
James H. Monteith................... Feb.   18, 1907.
James N. Downs..................... June   3, 1907.
Travers H. Barrett.................. June   17, 1907.
William H. Gruhlkey................ Oct.   7, 1907.

DIED.

Charles Blanchard................... Oct.   31, 1906.

R. W. Bro. Samuel Baldwin Bradford was appointed
District Deputy Grand Master by Grand Master Alexander
H. Bell October, 1907. Bro. Bradford is also honored with
a commission as Grand Lecturer, issued in 1906.

IN MEMORIAM.

CHARLES BLANCHARD.

Since closing the history of Occidental Lodge, No. 40, A. F. & A. M., October 10, 1906, we were called to mourn the death of one of its most distinguished members, when, on October 31, 1906, death claimed brother Charles Blanchard.

Brother Blanchard was born in Peacham, Vermont, August 31, 1829. Being ambitious for intellectual training and acquirements, he worked earnestly and persistently in his youth to gain a sufficient sum to defray the expenses of a tuition in a more advanced institution than the meager educational privileges his father was able to provide. He finally became a student of Peacham Seminary, and, when his education was completed, he came West, arriving in Peru, Illinois, in 1848. He taught school at Granville and Hennepin, Ill., and, during his leisure hours, applied himself to the study of law, in which he passed a successful examination before Judge Treat at Springfield, Ill., November 7, 1851. He moved to Ottawa in 1861. Was elected State's Attorney November, 1864, and served as such until December, 1872, from which office he retired as he entered it, with the good-will of the people. Through recognition of his ability as a lawyer, he was appointed, August 1, 1884, one of the judges of the Ninth Judicial Circuit by Governor Hamilton, to fill the vacancy caused by the resignation of Judge Goodspeed. At the ensuing election, in June, 1885, he was chosen by his constituents for the full term of six years, and in 1891, 1897 and 1903 was again elected and served until his death.

He was a man of strong mentality and possessed a thorough knowledge of the law, as indicated by his decisions. He was a man of well-rounded character, finely balanced mind and of splendid intellectual attainments.

Brother Blanchard affiliated with St. John's Lodge, No. 13, Peru, Ill., by demit from Social Lodge, No. 70, Hennepin, Ill., June, 5, 1856. Demitted from St. John's Lodge, July 18, 1867, and affiliated with Occidental Lodge, No. 40, August 17, 1874, and we believe that in all his long career as a citizen, man of family, and servant of the people, in positions of public trust, that he so deported himself that when the end came he could—

> "The darkened universe defy
> To quench our immortality
> Or shake our trust in God."

ERRATA.

Page 27.—"Lodges entering into *foundation*" should read, "Lodges entering into formation," etc.

Page 47.—Orville *C.* Moore should be Orville *L.* Moore.

Page 66.—St. Bernard Commandery, No. *36*, should read No. *35*.

Page 119.—*"Me,"* last word of first line in seventh verse should be *"Men."*

Page 181.—In recapitulation, "six hundred and *thirty-three*" should read "six hundred and *twenty-six*."

Page 151.—In second line, "*1804*" should be "*1864*.'

Page 200.—"Mrs. Miller died August 20, *1891*," should read "Mrs. Miller died August 20, *1901*."

Page 215.—Second line of verse: *"Where is the grave of that good man and true?"* should read, *"Where may the grave of that good man be?"*

Page 333.—First word 4th line should read *state* instead of *states*.

Page 333.—Second word in 12th line in second verse should read *vouch* instead of *touch*.

INDEX.

ILLUSTRATIONS AND PORTRAITS.

Lightning Source UK Ltd.
Milton Keynes UK
UKHW010012120119
335297UK00010B/960/P